Globalization and the Nation-State

D0550138

Globalization
and the
Nation-State

Robert J. Holton

First published in Great Britain 1998 by
MACMILLAN PRESS LTD
Houndmills, Basingstoke, Hampshire RG21 6XS and London
Companies and representatives throughout the world

A catalogue record for this book is available from the British Library.

ISBN 0–333–65783–7 hardcover
ISBN 0–333–65784–5 paperback

First published in the United States of America 1998 by
ST. MARTIN'S PRESS, INC.,
Scholarly and Reference Division,
175 Fifth Avenue, New York, N.Y. 10010

ISBN 0–312–21409–X

Library of Congress Cataloging-in-Publication Data
Holton, R. J.
Globalization and the nation-state / Robert J. Holton.
p.   cm.
Includes bibliographical references and index.
ISBN 0–312–21409–X
1. International economic relations.   2. International trade.
3. National state.   4. International economic relations—Social
aspects.   5. Cultural relations.   I. Title.
HF1359.H648   1998
306—dc21   97–52670
                                                                CIP

This book is printed on paper suitable for recycling and made from fully managed and
sustained forest sources.

10   9   8   7   6   5   4   3   2   1
07   06   05   04   03   02   01   00   99   98

Printed in Hong Kong

For Sandra

Contents

Acknowledgements

This study has drawn on a wide range of intellectual, material, and personal supports. The stimulating interdisciplinary milieu of the Research School of Social Sciences (RSSS) at the Australian National University was especially important in helping me to draw together the many threads that have gone into the making of this work of synthesis. Particular thanks are due to John Braithwaite and Geoffrey Brennan for many special intellectual conversations and much else. Other colleagues at the ANU who have influenced this study include Frank Jones, Peter Drahos, Deborah Mitchell, Jim Jupp, David Vines, and Paul Bourke. At Flinders University, I would like to thank Constance Lever-Tracy, Zlatko Skrbis, Ingrid Muenstermann, and Nicholas Procter for many insights, while I am indebted to the students taking the topic 'Migration, Global Capital and the Nation-State' for their steadfast resistance to my attempts to portray positive as well as negative normative aspects of globalization.

Papers drawing on particular aspects of this work have been delivered at the University of Kent at Canterbury, where I held a visiting fellowship in 1994, Essex University, York University in Canada, the Instituto Piaget, Viseu in Portugal, University College Dublin, the University of New South Wales, and Eastern Kentucky University. I am grateful to all those who participated in the ensuing discussions, especially to Edward Goldsmith and Ray Pahl, both of whom challenged, albeit in different ways, my framework of assumptions. I should also like to thank Steve Edwards for his critique of earlier versions of the manuscript.

I am grateful to Sage Publications Ltd for permission to reprint Figure 8.1, 'The Global Field', taken from R. Robertson (1992) *Globalization, Social Theory and Global Culture* (London: Sage).

I am also grateful to Polity Press for permission to use adapted versions of Figures 1.2 and 1.7 from A. McGrew, 'Global politics in a transitional era', in A. McGrew and P. Lewis (eds) *Conceptualising World Politics* (Oxford: Polity Press).

Material assistance in supporting the research on which this work is based has come from the Outside Studies programme of Flinders University, and the Reshaping Australian Institutions Program of

RSSS at the Australian National University, which generously funded a 6-month secondment in 1995. Technical assistance in scanning complex diagrams was provided by Karen Agerman. Flinders also assisted in funding multilingual research assistance, expertly provided by George Holton.

Flora Holton has cheerfully assisted me during some of the more difficult periods of writing this book, through her availability to take strike against my particular brand of spin bowling. Sandra Holton, meanwhile, has been my constant global companion in all these endeavours, our paths criss-crossing on an axis between Adelaide, Australia and Street, Somerset in the UK. Her keen historian's wits have cast a healthy scepticism in the direction of many early attempts to verbalize the arguments of this book. Her own work on women and transnational social movements has been a particular inspiration. This book is dedicated to her.

Without the mutual personal support of Sandra, Flora and George Holton, in sustaining the joys and handling the challenges of global migration and persistent periods of separation due to global travel, this volume would never have been completed.

1

Introduction

Globalization has, over the past decade, become a major feature of commentaries on contemporary social life. Wherever we look, global issues, institutions, and events seem increasingly to dominate discussion on the direction of social change and representations of the world in which we live. This global focus extends almost everywhere in business, sport, politics, fashion, the environment, music, law, and cultural identity. The constant references to global developments in newspaper headlines, journalistic commentaries, and academic writing constitute varieties of globe-talk. The rhetoric, hype, and babble of voices that are to be found engaging in globe-talk may well testify to a certain modishness or fashion for global things. Yet they are also symptoms of a widespread perception that we live in a period of rapid but uncertain social change. There is a sense that the fate of all parts of the globe is somehow bound together more intensely than before through ties of interdependence and the interpenetration of economic, political, and cultural relationships across existing borders and boundaries.

If we listen carefully to globe-talk, the message that comes through is that our lives are profoundly influenced in every aspect by global institutions and processes of change. The global economy, characterized by massive transnational flows of capital and labour, and dominated by multinational companies, looms large in this process. So too do global patterns of communication, in which new electronic technology, including satellites and the Internet, transmit messages and co-ordinate cashless financial transactions instantaneously across borders, obliterating any limits to communication set by distance or political boundaries. Geography has, in this sense, been pronounced dead. Within what has come to be called the 'global village', global products and services, produced by global companies, are purchased by consumers in virtually every country and region. These processes, along with the massive 20th-century international migration of people across territorial boundaries, has contributed to the idea of a global culture, in which identity is

1

increasingly determined by transnational developments rather than within the nation-state. These developments are sometimes seen as heralds of a new multicultural or cosmopolitan world. Globe-talk also extends to the world of politics. Predictions of the demise of the nation-state in the face of globalization occur, alongside an awareness of the growth of transnational political institutions such as the United Nations (UN) and transnational political norms such as human rights. New images of world order speak of the emergence of the global citizen and a global civil society, stimulated once again by the corrosive effect of migration and global communications on nationalism and parochialism. Underlying all these manifestations of globalization is the key idea of one single world or human society, in which all regional, national, and local elements are tied together in one interdependent whole.

Globe-talk is not only a discourse about powerful new forces transforming the lives and fate of the entire world's population, but also a matter about which individuals and nations find it necessary to take an evaluative stance. People and institutions are typically either for or against globalization. We are thus dealing not simply with a profound process of change, but also with issues that vitally affect moral and political concerns about human welfare, the good life, and the good society. Globalization has been evaluated according to a range of values such as social justice and freedom, individual autonomy and the sovereignty of nations to determine their destiny, freedom of personal movement, and human rights to decency and personal security. Developments such as the rise of multinational companies or attempts at transnational political regulation have been scrutinized for their effects on patterns of inequality or national self-determination. Put another way, we want to know *both* how and why globalization may be changing our lives *and* to determine whether these changes are good or bad, as a basis for more informed social action and political engagement.

For some, globalization is seen negatively, and at times almost demonically, as the dominance of Western economic and cultural interests over the rest of the world. This dominance means the perpetuation of inequality between rich and poor countries and regions. It is described variously in terms of the operation of the capitalist world-system or, more polemically, as 'the New World Disorder'. The problem here is not only the perpetuation of gross inequalities, but also what has been referred to as the Coca-Colonization of the world, whereby Third World populations are incorporated into the global economy as passive consumers of standardized products and nothing more. In other words, economic globalization rests on foundations of cultural imperialism.

For others, globalization is evaluated more positively. One strong current of opinion sees globalization in a triumphalist light, as the penetration of capitalism into every corner of the world, bringing with it the possibility for all of the world's population to participate in the fruits of the international division of labour and market economy. The arrival of McDonald's hamburgers in Moscow a few years ago symbolized an important moment in this type of thinking. In a somewhat different vein, other features of globalization associated with transnational developments such as the UN, or social movements such as Amnesty International and Greenpeace International, have become new vehicles for political and religious desires for the creation of one world free from conflict and a planet liberated from exploitation and environmental degradation. Alternatively, globalization is simply something to be enjoyed, as in the growing audience for world music or in the growth of global sporting contests co-ordinated by communications entrepreneurs such as Rupert Murdoch and Kerry Packer.

The burgeoning of commentary upon and analysis of globalization challenges (directly or indirectly) many of the ways in which we think about human society, especially the practice of defining society in terms of the activities that go on within individual nation-states. This has typically been the procedure of 20th-century social science, in which the objects of analysis have, until recently, typically been entities such as 'British society' or 'German society', considered as largely autonomous and self-constituting. The emergence of discourses about globalization, in contrast, represents a shift towards thinking of those aspects of social life that permeate national borders and connect the functioning of nation-states and localities with each other.

The rhetoric of globalization suggests that we are in the presence of powerful and perhaps unstoppable social changes, yet the precise nature of this fateful phenomenon remains rather vague and unresolved. This is reflected in the difficulty in answering the following set of questions.

Is globalization an unstoppable force that will destroy or maginalize the nation-state? And, as such, is it really only another name for the corporate economic power of multinational enterprises? Or do we need to question the assumption that globalization is a singular process based on a unitary master-trend? Should we consider the alternative possibility that globalization is an umbrella term for a number of processes, political and cultural as well as economic, involving different aspects of social change and leading in a variety of directions? How far, for example, are a global polity and a global culture emerging alongside economic globalization? Can inequalities of power associated with economic globalization or social conflicts engendered by nationalism be overcome by global political regulation, or is the dream of a single unified and harmonious world order still a remote Utopia? Is a global culture emerging, and, to the extent that it is, will national and local identities be replaced by cosmopolitanism? Or does globalization have limits; if so, what are they? What scope remains for nations, communities, or individuals to resist global influences or to redesign social institutions in an autonomous manner free from the coercion of global forces?

How far back into world history do we need to go to trace the development of globalization? Is globalization synonymous with the history and contemporary power of the West? Or does it derive from a range of regions and civilizations, remaining accessible to the non-Western world? Does globalization inevitably mean homogenization, and if so, is this equivalent to Americanization? Or does globalization encourage diversity, as nations, communities, and individuals choose selectively from a global repertoire of resources, technologies, ideas, and cultural practices? Is globalization a constraint on human action and choice, a source of opportunity and resource for creative deployment, or a complex mixture of all these things?

This book is thus, in large measure, a study of globalization, its meaning and scope, its history and dynamics, and its impact on economic, political, and cultural life. However, it is also equally a book about the nation-state and ethnicity. How do the many themes associated with these three terms fit together? The answer to this question begins when we start to scrutinize the assumptions of globe-talk.

Some problems with globe-talk

Globe-talk is not only widespread, but also has a compelling quality to it. So many different aspects of life in so many different parts of the world seem to be connected with processes that transcend territorial boundaries that the centrality and coherence of globalization take on an obvious taken-for-granted character. This appearance, however compelling, is nonetheless deceptive. There are certainly a number of transnational trends of major importance, but they do not by any means constitute the only significant trends in contemporary life.

The first major problem with globe-talk is its failure to consider other key developments in social life that point in rather different directions. If we look more closely, it is not hard to find major trends that appear to challenge the argument that social life is daily becoming increasingly more global. Foremost of these is the resurgence of both nationalism and ethnicity in many parts of the globe. Whether in the Balkans, central Africa, or the territories of the former Soviet Union, social groups are challenging larger structures and identities in the name of narrower loyalties. This has led to renewed episodes of genocide and 'ethnic cleansing', in defiance of international political conventions on human rights. These processes strike at the heart of attempts to build a global political community based on the peaceful resolution of conflicts.

Commentators such as Benjamin Barber (1991, 1995), have placed great emphasis on the limits set to globalization by counter-trends. He points to the coexistence of trends towards globalization on the one hand, and quite contrary trends towards tribalism and divisive cultural fundamentalism on the other. The dichotomy at work here is symbolized in the clash between what he calls McWorld and Jihad. Whereas the former stands for the global networks of capitalism and electronic communication, an amalgam so to speak of McDonald's and Apple MacIntosh, the latter stands for a retribalization process or 'Lebanonization' of nation-states, in which cultures stand opposed to each other, 'driven by parochial hatreds'.

The challenge to globe-talk here is that globalization represents only one of two major trends in the contemporary world, trends that point in very different directions. The formulation of Jihad versus McWorld is nonetheless problematic for two reasons. First, these powerful rhetorical labels tend to stereotype the two worlds referred to: the former seeming dynamic if soulless, the latter moralistic but overaggressive. Second, the dichotomy may encourage a simplistic approach in which McWorld is characterized by purely Western symbols, while the Arabic term Jihad, or 'Just War', is chosen as a seemingly non-Western counter-principle. The suggestion is that globalization is a purely Western phenomenon at odds with the non-Western world. Barber, however, disputes this, seeing McWorld as truly global, with resonances in Asia and Africa as well as Europe and the USA. Meanwhile, the forces of tribalization are as evident among Basques, Quebecois, and the Northern Irish as among Kurds, Tamils, and the Zulus of Inkatha. In this way, Barber wishes to move beyond crude stereotypes towards a more nuanced account of globalized rather than regionalized polarization.

Where Barber sets limits to globalization by emphasizing polarization, others challenge theories of globalization by referring to a proliferation or explosion of difference in modern life. Instead of the integration of all parts of the globe to a common pattern, what we find instead is the emergence of a complex plurality of different and often divergent economic, political, and cultural trends. These may be expressed at a national level, within the revival of ethnicity, and through major politicocultural movements such as the resurgence of Islam. However, it may equally be found in the proliferation of lifestyles and identities built around individual, local, or small group modes of social action. Examples include the gender politics of difference based on the assertion of individual rights of sexual preference and women's rights of self-determination, or, alternatively, the proliferation of local forms of community involvement and politics.

One of the most controversial issues in globe-talk is that of the nation-state. With the development of so many transnational organizations and processes, it has sometimes been assumed that the nation-state is about to be swamped by forces beyond its control. This argument should certainly not be taken lightly in a world in which capital and technology in the hands of multinational companies is highly mobile. This clearly limits the resources available to nation-states, especially outside the Western world, to act autonomously in determining their own fate. Yet the nation-state, whether in the Western world or elsewhere, has proved much more resilient in matters of economic and social self-determination than some predicted. Transnational entities must still reckon with national governments in securing their aims, this being true not simply of powerful Western nations, but also of certain developing nations such as South Korea, Malaysia, Brazil, Saudi Arabia, and Indonesia. Furthermore, when nation-states seek wider arrangements with others across territorial boundaries, they have looked as much to regionalism, as in the European Union (EU) and the more recent North American Free Trade Association (NAFTA), as to global arrangements.

Globalization, it seems, has not yet overrun the nation-state. Indeed, as we shall see in Chapters 4 and 5, individual governments, interest groups, and individuals have in many ways helped to create or harness global processes and networks to their own advantage. One important example is that of the UN, created by nation-states to mediate international conflict and promote peace and stability in relations between nations. Another somewhat different example is that of the modern Olympic Games, created as a global contest, reflected in the Olympic symbol of five interlocking circles representing the five continents, but co-ordinated through the sporting associations and governments of nation-states under whose banners individual athletes compete. The point here is not simply that nations have remained resilient in the face of globalization, but also that the 'national' and the 'global' are in many ways complementary rather than necessarily conflicting social forces.

The thrust of the discussion so far is that globalization, however important, is not the only major trend evident in contemporary society. Alongside globalization may be found the continuing development of the nation-state and a revival in ethnicity. These three trends should not, however, be regarded as self-contained but may be seen as being closely related to one another. The fusion of national concerns with ethnicity to produce what has been called 'ethnonationalism' (Connor 1973, 1977, 1994) may be seen, in part at least, as a reaction against homogenizing tendencies and inequalities of power at work in globalization. From this perspective, it is arguable that the late 20th-century resurgence of ethnicity is less an eruption of age-old primordial ethnic sentiments than a symptom of the failure of globalization to provide binding forms of cultural identity grounded in the history and experience of the peoples, especially the post-colonial peoples of the world. Here, then, is an example of conflict rather than complementarity between globalization and ethnonationalism. Alternatively, the relationship between globalization and certain forms of nationalism may be one of complementarity rather than conflict. One example of this, just mentioned, is the way in which nation-states have helped to create and/or participate in global political and sporting structures.

The foregoing discussion indicates why this book links together the theme of globalization with those of the nation-state and ethnicity. The justification for this is, first of all, that globalization is not a limitless and all-encompassing social trend but one that is both mediated through and limited by developments affecting the nation-state and ethnicity. Equally, however, the development of globalization sets limits to the sovereignty of nations and the capacity of ethnic groups to retribalize the world. This is true both where nations choose to cede elements of their sovereignty to global regulatory bodies in areas such as the conduct of war, human rights, or trade, and in situations where global influences are unwelcome and resisted. This, then, is the second justification for the structure of this study.

The assumption that globalization is the overriding trend in contemporary life is not the only difficulty with globe-talk. Another problem is the tendency to regard globalization as a very recent phenomenon, the product of the past 200 years or so, connected with developments such as industrialization, the advent of world markets, technological change in transport and communications, and the organizational and military power of Western nations over the remainder of the globe.

This identification of globalization with quite recent developments has some merit. Two hundred years ago, the world was far more fragmented, economically, culturally, and in terms of communications, than it is today. Notwithstanding the expansion of the international economy and Western power since the 16th century, significant areas of the globe remained embedded in hunter-gathering and subsistence agriculture with, at best, only rudimentary local trading activities. No standardized world time existed, while the reliance on sail and animal power for both long-distance transport and communication created what the Australian historian Geoffrey Blainey (1966) calls a 'tyranny of distance' separating many regions from each other. Geographical separation encouraged cultural parochialism and in some cases separatism, Japan sealing itself off from the rest of the world during the 18th and early 19th centuries.

Contrast this with the current organization of time and space. World-time based on the dominant Western calendar is ubiquitous, leaving Chinese, Orthodox, and Islamic calendars to perform limited cultural and religious functions. Meanwhile, the 'tyranny of distance' has been obliterated by a communications revolution commencing with the telegraph, telephone, radio, and television, and continuing electronically via the computer and satellite broadcasting systems, the digitalization of information transfer by means of the fax machine, and the advent of the Internet. These, together with air transport, have clearly shrunk the world, such that information can be transmitted instantaneously and people can move from one side of the world to the other in no more than 24 hours. The effect is what the geographer David Harvey calls 'the compression of time and space' (Harvey 1989).

These recent changes are clearly of fundamental importance. Yet, for all this, processes of change leading towards globalization, what Robertson (1992) calls 'mini-globalizations', are evident much further back in time. Developments such as cross-regional trade, imperial conquest leading to cross-regional transfers of resources, technology, and culture, the surging movement of religious conviction and enthusiasm across existing political and cultural boundaries, and, last but not least, population movement, whether through enslavement or the search for new land, have all been long-term features of world history for several millennia (McNeill 1986). Such developments were very far from being purely Western developments, for they involved China and the Islamic world as well as the classical civilizations of the Mediterranean and early modern Europe. Archaeologists of the ancient world are often surprised by the far-flung origins of artefacts located at individual sites of excavation.

While this understanding of the past is well known to historians, it has been fully appreciated neither in popular globe-talk nor by social scientists concerned simply with ahistorical accounts of the present. This neglect is partly a product of the 'failure' of many of the early episodes of mini-globalization to generate the self-sustainable expansion required to create one single interdependent world. Both the far-flung Roman Empire and the subsequent Islamic expansion of the Middle Ages eventually faltered. Similarly, the economic and technological dynamism of Sung China between the 10th and 14th centuries, which gave the world advances in movable-type printing and the use of gunpowder as an explosive, proved unable to sustain itself over the longer term (Elvin 1973).

Such episodes may be seen as 'failures', but they clearly indicate that the world before the Industrial Revolution of the 18th and 19th centuries was very far from static and far from being dominated by self-contained rural communities and horizons of localism. Accordingly, the mini-globalizations of the world before industrialization may be said to have 'succeeded' in influencing the present via the transmission of technology, models of imperial and trading organization, cross-cultural practices, and ideals of a single harmonious world linked with the great religious systems, such as Christianity and Islam. These developments will be discussed in more detail in the next chapter.

Meanwhile, an important point of historical interpretation needs further attention. The problem is that of regarding the history of globalization in evolutionary terms that assume an underlying logic to history, founded on the steady and inevitable accumulation of ever-widening interrelationships between different components of the global system. The familiar difficulties with social evolutionism (for a further discussion, see Nisbet 1980; Holton 1985) are that social change is invested with a sense of historical necessity, coherence, and continuity that derives from the concerns of the present. Applied to the world history of globalization, this approach would see the mini-globalizations of the past *only* as forerunners or early phases in the lead up to the current development of a single world. This is problematic insofar as contemporary globalization is seen as necessarily emerging out of earlier developments as the only possible present and the only conceivable future. It is also problematic because it rules out an awareness of historical discontinuities and of the contingencies that generate alternative pathways of development, including alternative futures.

This study therefore rejects the social evolutionist approach, which would see globalization as the culmination of previous mini-globalizations. In so doing, it draws attention to alternative interpretations of history, suggested in part by Barber's symbol of Jihad standing for tribalization and the primordial claims of ethnicity. Ethnicity and the fusion of ethnicity with the nation-state also have a history that must be taken into account alongside, and in relation to, that of globalization.

This, then, is a book about globalization, but the framework of the study has two features that distinguish it from many other current accounts of global development. First, it looks at both the *scope* and *limits* of globalization, setting transnational developments against the continuing robustness of the nation-state and the resurgence of ethnicity. Second, it treats globalization as a *historical* rather than a purely contemporary phenomenon. This historical focus is necessary to understand what is new about contemporary globalization. It is also important to any analysis of the relationship of globalization to ethnicity and nationalism, especially in determining whether Jihad and McWorld must necessarily be locked in mortal combat or whether their seeming incompatibility may be resolved.

Definitions, concepts and representations

The discussion so far has proceeded without any clarification of what the key terms 'global' and 'globalization' mean. Within the babble of globe-talk, and in much academic literature too, words such as 'global', 'international', 'transnational', and 'multinational' or simply 'worldwide' often appear as synonymous and interchangeable, but in other cases they may be used to make fine-grained distinctions. For example, the term 'international' is sometimes used to refer to relationships between nation-states, whereas terms such as 'transnational' are, in contrast, often meant to suggest processes that somehow stand above or beyond national determination and control. Corporations operating on a worldwide scale are referred to as 'transnational' in UN circles, in part to draw attention to their presumed power over nations. In much academic literature, the term 'multinational' is used instead, implying perhaps that such enterprises operate in many countries and can switch activities between them. Such variations in terminology abound, yet in the absence of any widely agreed conceptualization, it is dangerous to read too much into them.

While there is a certain semantic arbitrariness in the way in which concepts are constructed, it is clear that concepts gain meaning only in terms of that with which they are contrasted. The 'global', for example, is usually contrasted with the 'national', more precisely with the assumption that social life is organized and structured within the boundaries of nation-states. The rather minimal working definition of 'globalization', provided by Holm and Sorensen (1995, p. 1) reflects this, seeing globalization as 'the intensification of economic, political, social and cultural relations across borders'. This definition invites historical exploration of the dynamics of social change, by which the permeability of the political borders of the nation-state has become intensified. This definition is also useful in stressing that globalization is not simply an economic phenomenon.

One significant feature of this definition is that it refers to intensified cross-border relations while leaving open the nature of the entity within which such relationships occur. Holm and Sorensen are particularly interested in whether globalization in the context of the end of the Cold War is generating a new kind of global or world order. This question may be seen as part of a broader set of questions. Does globalization operate, for example, as some kind of coherent system or set of structures? Or is globalization disorderly, chaotic, and lacking in enduring patterns? If globalization is regarded as systematic in form, what is the logic that underlies such a system? Or are there several underlying types of logic rather than a singular master process? And within these various scenarios, what place, if any, remains for the nation-state?

For Immanuel Wallerstein (1974, 1979, 1984), pioneer of world-system theory, globalization represents the triumph of a capitalist world economy tied together by a global division of labour. This capitalist world system is driven by the logic of capital accumulation. Nations and regions occupy specific places in a hierarchical organization of power and space, subdivided between the core economies of the Western world, the poorest exploited peripheral sections of the developing world, and a semi-periphery in between. Alternatively, the world may be seen in politically centred rather than economically centred terms. Many theorists of international relations, for example, think of world society not in terms of a transnational economic division of labour but in terms of relationships between powerful, politically organized interests. These include national governments and also a range of international, as distinct from transnational bodies, which governments and powerful non-governmental organisations (NGOs) such as multinational businesses construct to further their interests. If there is a global system, it is, in this view, not constructed above and outside the reach of nation-states but largely through the need of nation-states to co-operate with each other to resolve common problems. Such a system is sometimes referred to as the interstate system.

World-system theorists and theorists of the interstate system differ in the emphasis they place on economic and political elements in the constitution of global or international relations. They do, however, share an appreciation that the world is an unequal place. Wallerstein's core–periphery model draws more explicit attention to economically generated inequalities that flow from the processes of capital accumulation. International relations theorists look at inequalities more in terms of the political power of individual nations and the interest groups within them, whether such power approaches hegemonic control, as with the USA in the 1950s, or alternatively, whether alliances of nation-states and interests dominate particular areas, or 'regimes', of interstate policy-making.

Emerging from the widespread sense of global inequality and the associated sense that those living in different places have sharply contrasting life opportunities is a sense that there may be one planet earth but that there is more than one human world living on it. This is reflected in the widely used vocabulary of First, Second and Third Worlds, and the more recent addition of a Fourth World.

The idea of Three Worlds appears to have undergone significant changes in meaning since it emerged, apparently for the first time in an article by Alfred Sauvy called 'Trois Mondes, Une Planete' that appeared in 1952 (see the commentary in Worsley 1990, p. 83). Written in the Cold War period, this not only drew attention to the Superpowers' drive to dominate the entire globe, that is, to the conflict between the First or Western and Second or Communist World, but also reflected the desire of many for a Third Way between the two. In this sense, the term Third World originated in the West without the connotations of radical politics and underdevelopment that subsequently attached to it.

It was, for example, only after the mid-1950s, with the rapid expansion of colonial revolution, decolonization, and the establishment of the Non-aligned Movement in 1955, that the term gained a wider currency. This involved extension from a description of the non-Western world by Westerners into a form of self-ascribed identification for many post-colonial nations as well. As Worsley (1990, p. 84) points out, this form of self-ascription had a largely political character in the late 1950s and early 1960s in the epoch of the radical post-colonial nationalism of Nkrumah and Nasser.

Later still, however, the pan-nationalist *élan* of these years became tarnished with the centralization of much post-colonial power in oppressive regimes, together with new wars between ex-colonial states. Within this context, argues Worsley, the preoccupations of the Non-aligned Movement and nationalist leaderships turned away from issues of decolonization towards those of economic underdevelopment. From the 1970s onwards, then, the concept of the Third World (whether used as a form of self-identification or as a Western term for the non-Western, non-Soviet world) has become synonymous with economic underdevelopment and deprivation.

The continuing use of the term 'Third World' is nonetheless problematic for two general reasons. First, there is the tendency to place all underdeveloped or non-Western nations in the same category, thereby minimizing important differences between them. Economically, for example, the Organisation of Petroleum Exporting Countries (OPEC) oil-producing countries are clearly in a far more advantageous position than are countries such as Bangladesh or most of sub-Saharan Africa, whose economic resources and market power are far less marked. Similar contrasts are evident between industrializing nations such as Taiwan, Singapore, or Malaysia, and the primary product dependency of large parts of Africa and Latin America. In addition, the success of parts of the Third World rebounds on the assumption that all parts of the Third World are somehow less developed than any part of the First World, such as South-East Europe. This is no longer tenable as 'Third World' successes overtake those of the least developed Europeans.

There is a second problem in the practice of identifying the Third World with all nations outside the first Two Worlds, a problem that is more directly related to the issue of globalization. This concerns the identification of various worlds with sets of nation-states. This national focus may be misleading in two ways. First, it fails to consider the possibility that integration into and position within global economic arrangements may occur at a subnational level rather than for nation-states as a whole. A major example of this concerns what have been called world or global cities (Friedman 1986; Sassen 1991). For Sassen, the recent shift in global economic activities to services and finance brings about a renewed importance for key cities as strategic centres for global economic power, leaving surrounding areas to become increasingly peripheral. This applies not only to global cities such as Paris and Frankfurt within the First World nations of France and Germany, but also to global cities such as São Paulo and Mexico City within the Third World nations of Brazil and Mexico (Sassen 1994).

A second problem with the nation-state focus is that it fails to address issues concerning political and cultural diversity within nation-states. Two groups are of particular importance here. The first is indigenous or aboriginal peoples marginalized in places such as the USA or Australia by colonial conquest and the processes of nation-state-building. The second is those peoples or nations who are politically and culturally distinct but who do not possess a state apparatus with sovereign control of a given territory. Examples here include the Palestinians, Kurds, and Catalans. It is to groups of these kinds that the designation Fourth World has been adopted. Orignally used in the early 1970s to refer to indigenous peoples (Manuel 1974), its meaning later became extended more generally to all those who consider themselves oppressed or unrecognized nations or national minorities within nation-states (Griggs 1992). A third, less precise, usage regards the Fourth World as the poorest or most oppressed groups and individuals, that is, as a residual category for all those excluded from the benefits and citizenship rights of the system of nation-states.

It may be concluded from this brief survey of the idea of Four Worlds within one planet that assumptions of a unitary homogenous globe are very dubious. To speak of Four Worlds is symptomatic of the divergent location of different parts of the world within structures of economic and political power, and is equally evidence of the divergent life chances and different types of cultural identity that emerge within this context. Beyond this, none of the Four differentiated Worlds is unitary in character or necessarily stable in terms of its internal composition. Conflicts within each of the Worlds are significant, as is the possibility of movement from one category to another. For the moment, however, more systematic enquiry into the question of whether a global or world-system exists will be left open for further analysis in later chapters.

It is helpful, meanwhile, in pursuing a more adequate working definition of globalization, to try to add some sense of greater complexity and an awareness of the existence of different worlds within the cross-national, multidimensional approach of Holm and Sorensen. One of the difficulties here is how simultaneously to draw attention to the development of the world as a single society, while doing justice to evidence of differentiation in the conditions of existence and forms of identity that the world's inhabitants express. Is globalization simply to do with the former, or is it intrinsically bound up with both processes?

Albrow (1990) takes up the former option, defining globalization as 'all those processes by which the peoples of the world are incorporated into a single world society', a society in which 'humanity' becomes for the first time a 'collective actor'. This latter role is closely connected with 'globalism', defined as 'those values which take the real world of 5 billion people as the object of concern, the whole earth as the physical environment, everyone living as world citizens, consumers, and producers, with a common interest in collective action to solve global problems' (p. 8).

This emphasis on collective human action gives greater and more plausible substance to the idea of a world society. Attempts at collective global problem-solving are certainly recognizable in the activities of the UN and its various agencies, within attempts to construct universal norms around the idea of human rights, and in the increase in social movements such as Amnesty International, Médecins sans Frontières, and Greenpeace International, which operate across political boundaries. Yet much of this work remains ineffective in the face of the revival of nationalism, the resurgence of aggressive forms of ethnicity, and national and local resistance to collective action proposed by the UN or other international agencies.

An alternative approach to globalization, which starts out from a position quite similar to that of Albrow, is suggested by Robertson. He uses 'globalization' to refer 'both to the compression of the world, and the intensification of consciousness of the world as a whole' (Albrow 1990, p. 8). This offers a useful working definition for a number of reasons.

First, it is somewhat broader than Albrow's definition, including both the economic institutions and communications technologies that have helped to create a single interdependent world as well as understandings of the world as a single place. Such understandings are not, however, restricted to the idea of humanity as a collective actor, seeking collective solutions to common problems. Robertson, like Albrow, wants to draw attention to political and cultural ideas such as human rights, global environmental responsibility and cosmopolitanism, which, in their various ways, project a sense of a single humanity. Coming to the study of globalization from the sociology of religion, Robertson emphasizes the meaningful and interpretative aspects of social life, including the world images in which globalization is represented. Globalization involves the ways in which we understand, experience, and act within the world and not simply the large transnational structures that form the subject matter of political economy or international relations. This approach is dramatized in his argument that we may now speak of globalization as an inescapable part of the 'human condition'. This is inescapable in the sense that globalization forms a reference point for those who reject it as much as for those who celebrate it.

This leads Robertson beyond the idea of globalization as a large-scale, world-centred process that is distinct from and antagonistic to smaller-scale processes that occur within the nation or locality. His move in this direction is prompted by evidence that the 'global' and the 'local', interact, often to the point of drawing from each other, rather than being locked in mortal conflict in which, according to the most demonic versions of globalization theory, local difference and particularity will be obliterated by global homogenization.

This argument draws first on the concepts of 'glocalization' or 'local globalization'. These were developed, initially in Japanese business circles in the 1980s (Ohmae 1990; Robertson 1995), to refer to the process whereby global corporations tailored products and marketing to particular local circumstances to meet variations in consumer demand. Debates of this kind within Japan had a wider significance in that they reflected on what remained particular to Japanese national traditions and contemporary activities, even during the process of increasing integration into the global economy (Miyoshi and Harootunian 1989). Robertson goes even further in seeing glocalization, or the interpenetration of the global and the local, as a defining feature of global society, evident not merely in business, but also in many other aspects of social life. For example, the 19th-century extension of nationalism was very much an international process, in the sense that particular nationalisms drew on other nationalist movements for support and inspiration, such that a transnational sense of what nation-building entailed developed. The point is not that each nationalist movement or nation looked the same but that highly particularistic national movements depended on a broader stock of ideas and models as well on a distinctive sense of identity bound up with a particular history.

Where, then, does this sense of interpenetration leave the definition of globalization? Robertson's answer is that a crucial distinction needs to be made between globalization and what he calls the global 'field'. Put in the simplest terms, the global 'field' is the singular social world within which social interaction and social change of various kinds take place. Globalization is the process by which a single global field has come into being, but it is not the only component part of the global field. Other components include particular localities, a term which, for Robertson, includes nations and other communities, as well as individuals. This way of thinking about globalization offers a number of advantages at the outset of a study such as this. One is that it allows us to avoid the presumption that globalization is an all-encompassing and unstoppable trend. Another is that we can leave open questions of the extent to which globalization operates as a system and the nature of the limits to globalization as one trend among several within the global field. Meanwhile, the associated concept of glocalization offers ways of connecting large-scale (macro) and small-scale (micro) aspects of the social world, connections that have often been obscured by the association of globalization solely with macro-processes, such as the world market, the multinational enterprise, or UN Declarations and Conventions, in contrast to the particular micro-worlds in which individuals households and communities are assumed to live. Glocalization, in short, offers ways out of the global/local, macro/micro dichotomies that plague many analyses of globalization.

We have rehearsed a range of issues about the substance of globalization in this section, in order to foreshadow a number of questions to be pursued later in this book. The aim at the outset has thus been to provide some initial conceptual clarification of the meaning of globalization, opening up questions for further scrutiny. Questions of definition and conceptualization cannot be fully addressed, however, without confronting the problem of representation.

When trying to interpret and decode any linguistic discourse, two interrelated problems arise. First, there is the issue of how far distinctions between concepts refer to distinctions between different kinds of observable social events, processes, and phenomena, distinctions that can be subjected to empirical analysis. Second, there is the problem of how far distinctions arise from variations in the purposes of observers. To ignore the second issue is to ignore the ways in which terms such as 'global' and 'globalization' are used not merely for intellectual analysis, but also for moral evaluation and exhortation as well as for corporate public relations and the selling of commodities.

Two contemporary examples may be used to demonstrate the way in which particular interests represent the 'global' and the way in which notions of the 'global' are given meaning in relation to contrasts with the 'local'. Both cases also shed more light on the importance of glocalization.

The first example is that of corporations that describe themselves as 'global' in order to draw attention to the cross-national scope and commercial strength of their operations. Localism, here, implies commercial weakness and vulnerability. The problem in selling this message, however, is that potential customers or investors are generally located in particular localities with their own specific market conditions. This requires some way of depicting global corporations in a manner that is responsive to individuals based in particular localities. Financial service providers have, for example, placed great emphasis on their capacity to link together the 'global' and the 'local'. Citibank claims a history of 'breaking down barriers' and 'building cross-border relationships', representing itself as 'a partner with global outreach and local expertise' (1995 advertisement). In a similar vein, the Zurich Insurance Group trades under the slogan 'Global Strength: Local Knowledge'. In these examples, the 'global' has a strong positive resonance connected with the extensive power of multinational companies. Global power by itself is, however, represented as insufficient, requiring further augmentation by 'local' relationships or sources of knowledge to be effective in the market. Whether this kind of rhetoric means a genuine blending of transnational and local interests of mutual benefit to each is implied but remains a matter of some contention (see Chapter 3).

Another contrasting representation of global–local relations may be found in the exhortation to 'Think Globally: Act Locally'. The origins of this slogan are not entirely certain, although its popularity among non-governmental movements, including Oxfam, environmental and women's movements, is clear. Whereas the corporate representation of global–local linkages has a significant top-down element, this second 'social movement' focus is projected in a grass-roots, 'bottom-up' manner. Instead of relying on transnational organization for strength, it is the myriad of local actors who are enjoined to think about the global consequences of their actions before acting locally. Such consequences include the impact made by local actions on the environmental sustainability of planet earth as well as the political solidarities that emerge from widespread local actions in support of a global goal, as in women's rights campaigns.

These two examples of the language of global–local linkage indicate that they are dealing with a vocabulary embedded in commercial and political rhetoric as much as with social scientific concepts. Scholarship too is not without its own rhetoric. For better or worse, the language of globalization carries with it an overlay of symbolic meanings and imagery that pertains to commercial persuasion, moral qualities, and political objectives. Such morally, politically, or commercially loaded representations should not be neglected, because they tell us much about how social actors understand and evaluate globalization. To ignore the issue of the empirical reliability of representations is, however, to say that the 'global' is simply whatever people say it is. To leave the matter there reduces analysis to the deconstruction of rhetoric, foreclosing on the opportunity to ask how far understandings of globalization are sustained by research findings established through the critical scrutiny of data. This study is thus not simply about accounts of globalization, their logical rigour, and conceptual coherence; it is also about their plausibility when judged against evidence.

The research upon which this book relies is drawn from a wide-ranging set of intellectual sources and disciplines. While it is true that much academic work remains focused on the nation-state as the core unit of social analysis, the study of aspects of globalization has recently begun to take off. This is evident in sociology (Featherstone 1990; Giddens 1990; Sklair 1991; Robertson 1992; Featherstone *et al.* 1995; Waters 1995), international relations and political science (Rosenau 1980; Keohane 1984; Holm and Sorensen 1995), history (Abu Lughod 1989; McNeill 1986; Mazlish and Buultjens 1993), political economy (Carnoy *et al.* 1993; Lever-Tracy *et al.* 1996), management and business (Bartlett and Ghoshal 1992; Dunning 1993), anthropology (Hannerz 1992; Friedman 1994), and political theory (Held 1991; McGrew and Lewis 1992), as well as in more explicitly interdisciplinary activities such as world-system theory (Wallerstein 1974, 1979, 1984, 1991; Chase-Dunn 1989; Frank 1990), migration and diaspora studies (Castles and Miller 1993; Gilroy 1993), and urban studies (Friedmann 1986; Sassen 1991, 1994). These major contributions are backed up by a proliferation of new journals dealing with global themes, such as *Transnational Corporations, The International Journal of Global Legal Studies*, and *Diaspora*.

Other work, while lying outside and sometimes sceptical of or hostile to a globalization framework, is also highly relevant to the argument of this book. Of particular importance is the literature on the resilience of the nation-state (Mann 1993), on nationalism (Anderson 1983; Hobsbawm 1990; Billig 1995), and on the relationship between the nation and ethnicity (Smith 1986, 1990; Connor 1994). This work is spread across the same range of disciplinary and interdisciplinary endeavours as that dealing with globalization itself.

The analyses developed in this study are therefore profoundly inter-disciplinary in scope and are designed for a broad, cross-disciplinary audience. However, they also necessarily derive from the personal experience and particular viewpoints of the author.

Social science must rest upon some kind of transcontextual appeal to truth and analytical rigour in order to have any credibility as scientific knowledge rather than opinion. Yet the numerous critiques of positivism over the past 100 or so years caution us to the realization that social knowledge can never be approached or understood in isolation from the social context, presuppositions, and interests of the author. I have thus written this book in the English language, as a white, middle-class, transcontinental academic migrant, albeit from one English-speaking liberal-capitalist nation, namely Britain, to another, namely Australia. The decision to write about globalization, and the interpretations offered in this study, has been very much influenced by the process of migration, which often acts as a solvent of pre-existing views and an eye-opener to new experiences. In my own case, migration has done something to unsettle a Eurocentric Northern Hemispheric vision of global order.

Migration is, of course, profoundly mediated by class, gender, and ethnicity, and my own experience is therefore neither more nor less typical or significant than that of others caught up in this quintessentially global process. Even though I have remained within the orbit of the liberal-capitalist English-speaking world, migration has given me a greater awareness of the Asia-Pacific as an emergent region than would otherwise have been the case. The experience of dual nationality and citizenship within the context of Australian multiculturalism is also significant, in that it has led me to consider more directly the desirability of interculturalism as a way of life and the political challenges to the cultural integrity of nation-states that are entailed.

This personal background does not render the analytical propositions advanced here any more or less true, or give then greater or lesser persuasiveness, but it may help to explain a good deal of what is present and what is absent in the analysis. Yet the scope and limitations of what has been said here are equally rooted in a body of scholarship and the way in which I have interpreted that scholarship according to norms of logical rigour and empirical plausibility. This book is thus written on the presumption that the search for truth matters, while realizing that my interests and discursive reference points are – like anyone else's – partial, selective, and culture bound.

2

Understanding Globalization: History and Representation in the Emergence of the World as a Single Place

The advent of explicit theories of globalization is a comparatively recent development that dates from the 1960s. Concepts such as 'globalization' and 'global village' are contemporary additions to the vocabulary. This does not, however, mean that globalization itself is a very recent development. Nor does it mean that attempts to understand matters that we now label 'global', have only emerged in the past few decades. So where should a survey of understandings of globalization begin?

A conventional way of looking at this question within recent social science discourse is to identify earlier social scientists who somehow anticipated the significance of processes now seen as central to globalization. Attention within sociology, for example, focuses on 19th- and early 20th-century forebears. A classic example is that of Karl Marx and Friedrich Engels, whose familiar conception of the expansiveness of the capitalist mode of production throughout the globe and through all sectors of society is worth recalling:

> The need of a constantly expanding market for its products chases the bourgeoisie over the surface of the globe. It must nestle everywhere, settle everywhere, establish connections everywhere.

> The bourgeoisie has through its exploitation of the world-market given a cosmopolitan character to production and consumption in every country... In place of the old local and national seclusion and self-sufficiency, we have inter-

course in every direction, universal inter-dependence of nations. And as in material, so also in intellectual production.... National one-sidedness and narrow-
mindedness become more and more impossible, and from the numerous national
and local literatures, there arises a world literature. (Marx and Engels 1962 [1848]
pp. 37–8)

This remarkably prescient text, with its emphasis on global economic
interdependence, and the erosion of national and local autonomy in
culture as in the economy, foreshadows many late 20th-century themes
in the contemporary literature on globalization.

Marx and Engels were not the only 19th-century social observers to
perceive and anticipate the importance of global themes. They were, like
many others, children of the 18th-century Enlightenment. This movement of thought had, in a general sense, set much of the intellectual
agenda for the 19th century by elevating the claims of reason as a
universally valid foundation for knowledge. This in turn offered the
promise of constructing universally valid social institutions that many
believed capable of emancipating all corners of the world from igno-
rance and exploitation. The late 18th-century philosopher Immanuel
Kant had articulated one element in this ideal by exploring the conditions for the emergence of cosmopolitan citizenship untrammelled by
the particularistic claims of national identity.

As Robertson (1992, pp. 15–21) points out, Marx's immediate 19th-
century forebears, Saint-Simon and Comte, had both advanced views
of social science as an element in the unification of humanity. For
Saint-Simon, science and industrialization reflected the same logic of
advancing internationalism and interconnection between nations. The
legacy of Saint-Simonian and Comtist internationalism of this kind is
symbolized on the Brazilian flag, which depicts the globe as a single
place united by the twin ideals of Order and Progress.

Nonetheless, as the 19th century proceeded, these early ventures in the
social scientific understanding of what we have called globalization
became eclipsed by the rise of nationalism, the nation-state, and
primarily nation-centred ways of thought. The presumption was that
human society was subdivided into bounded sets of peoples, be these
nations or races. Assumptions of a racial hierarchy between peoples
qualified any universal sense that all peoples had the potential to become
a nation. Nonetheless, for those perceived as nations, each was seen as
possessing a discrete national character. This was formed from a
complex variety of political, military, demographic, religious, and
linguistic elements. The idealized representations of national history and
character that emerged drew extensively on Romantic conceptions of the

essence of a people in ways that generally stressed boundaries rather than bridges between nations. Undoubtedly, the emerging world of nations was by no means obsessed with national particularism, being implicated in the growth of world markets, improved communications, and intensified processes of imperial conquest by the leading European nations. Nationalism, in some variants, may embrace a form of internationalism. One example is the liberal–democratic presumption that democracy, free trade, and peace require and enhance international co-operation between nations. Some types of socialism also lent themselves to ideals of international solidarity between the working-class movements of different nations. Having said this, it remains the case that more parochial and self-interested variants of nationalism prevailed. This applied both in the world of political action, and in understandings of how human society operated. This state of affairs is symbolized by the failure of Socialist Internationalism to combat nationalist political mobilization and thus prevent the outbreak of the First World War in 1914.

A national focus has thus been built into the analytical framework of social enquiry and social science over the past 150 years. The 19th-century legacy of thinking of society in terms of individual national societies is still very much with us. Yet precursors of global thinking, such as St Simon or Marx, introduced themes that have since been elaborated, refined, and subjected to critical scrutiny in recent scholarly debates. Much of this book will be concerned with social scientific thought of this kind.

Social scientific understandings of globalization are not, however, without their problems. One of these is the problem of exclusion. By this is meant the practice of separating off social science from the remainder of human thought while at the same time privileging the viewpoint of social scientists over others. This procedure often rests upon the unspoken assumption that social scientists are neutral commentators rather than participants in history. Their commentaries are thus somehow both distinct from and superior to the experience of historical actors. Hence, on the one side, we have theorists of globalization, who turn out to be mostly Western and historically located at some point in the past 250 years, while on the other, we have participants in the historical process struggling to make sense of, and respond to, the opportunities and constraints that theorists associate with the globalization process. This not only tends to exclude the thought of the non-Western world from consideration, but also fails to explain how and why the distinction between the West and the rest emerged in the first place.

There are two intellectual strategies, which, if taken together, offer ways around such problems of exclusion. The first involves integrating the understandings of historical actors into the analysis of globalization alongside more conventional social scientific accounts. In this way, theories of globalization can be more than the commentaries of current theorists on the work of previous generations of theorists. The second involves problematizing the distinction between the Western and non-Western worlds, rather than taking it for granted as a self-evident dividing line between those who have something to say about globalization and those who do not.

Understanding globalization: in search of the history of global structures and networks

So where to begin the understanding of globalization? If we associate globalization with developments such as the emergence of world markets for commodities, and technological improvements to communication, attention might, in the first instance, shift back several centuries. Wallerstein (1974), for example, cites the 16th century as a crucial watershed in the development of a capitalist world-economy. This is symbolized by the arrival of Christopher Columbus in the Americas in AD 1492. In the next three centuries, Western Europe developed not only the Industrial Revolution based on wage-labour, but also the plantation economies of the Caribbean and southern states of America using slavery, the West African region from which slaves were obtained, and the serf-based landed estates of Eastern Europe. All these are connected through the international exchange of commodities, be they Barbadian sugar, Polish grain, West African slaves, or Manchester textiles.

In contrast with Marx, it is not the presence of 'free' wage-labour relations that is crucial for capitalism but rather the integration of production within an international division of labour geared to capital accumulation. In this sense, Wallerstein regards slavery or serfdom as perfectly compatible with the operation of the capitalist world-system. This conceptual revision of orthodox Marxism enables him to draw attention to many facets of the global expansiveness of capitalism over a 400-year period that have been played down by analysts who focus mainly on indigenous change within the core region of Western Europe (as in the critique of Wallerstein by Brenner 1977).

Wallerstein's emphasis on the 16th-century origins of the capitalist world-system is not by any means conclusive. Even if we define globalization in narrow terms as economic globalization, alternative analyses identify earlier world economic systems or interconnections. These are not literally global in a geographical sense, that is, covering virtually every corner of the Earth, but 'global' or 'world' phenomena in a more restricted sense, namely that they apply to long-distance intercontinental and cross-cultural networks and linkages. Janet Abu-Lughod (1989), for example, discerns the existence of a world-economy based on long-distance trade between Europe and Asia, organized through a chain of trading cities from Bruges and Venice, via Cairo and Baghdad, to Samarkand and Canton, as early as the 13th century. At this time, Chinese fleets of a size much larger than anything seen again before the 18th century sailed regularly to South-East Asia, India, East Africa, and the Middle East. Philip Curtin (1984) also picks up the theme of cross-regional and cross-cultural long-distance trade. He argues that this process may be traced back several thousand years to the period 2500–1500 BC. In breaking with the emphasis on AD 1500 as the turning point in global economic history, this longer-run focus includes types of economic activity generally excluded by Wallerstein, notably the long-distance trade in luxuries. The reasons for this exclusion are, as Frank (1990, p. 188) points out, rather arbitrary and seem to depend on a fixation with establishing a clear-cut divide between 'modern' systems and those which went before, a divide that serves, in turn, to dramatize the supposed historical novelty of the post-AD 1500 modern capitalist world-system.

Many analyses, as we have seen, reject Wallerstein's periodization by projecting the understanding of globalization as a primarily economic phenomenon further and further back in time. In so doing, it should be emphasized that none of the authors cited sees the expansion of the world-economy as a smooth cumulative process of steadily expanding development. Rather, the pattern is one of expansion, crisis, and sometimes contraction and collapse. Abu-Lughod's 13th-century world-system, for example, stretching from North-West Europe to China, subsequently collapsed under the impact of factors such as the Black Death – arguably the first global epidemic – and the Mongol invasions of China and India. Abu-Lughod goes on to develop the argument that the 'fall of the East' preceded the 'rise of the West' (Abu-Lughod 1989). This did not mean the end of any kind of Eastern dynamic within world-systems. However, the axis of Central Asia, Anatolia, northern India, and the Levant-Egypt, was never again to play a central world role. Over subsequent centuries, the arena of change moved outward from the Mediterranean and points East to the Atlantic and North-West Europe, while the Western invasion and colonization of much of Asia established new mechanisms of global interconnection. The underlying mechanisms of change are thus discontinuity as well as persistence in the loci and forms of world-system development. In this sense, there is no evolutionary necessity for a fully fledged global economy to emerge directly from earlier historical episodes of global economic interconnection. Put another way, the 'rise of the West' was not predicated in any necessary way upon the previous 'rise of the East'.

If we widen the historical focus beyond economic forms of globalization, there are even more persuasive arguments for projecting the origins of globalization even further back in time. Andre Gundar Frank (1990), for example, speaks of 5000 years of 'world system history', taking the analysis back to 2500 BC and before. This argument, synthesized from many specialist texts, emphasizes the significance of systematic interconnections between the European and Asian worlds. These include trade but also involve cross-cultural contact through conquest and through the diffusion of cultural ideas and practices. In this way, increasingly global interconnections between the Hellenized Mediterranean, India, Africa, China, and the later Islamic world were developed.

This type of analysis draws in part on traditions of scholarship that treat the development of civilization as the major theme in human history. Because the concept of civilization has become such a controversial one, further comment on its usefulness is required.

The term itself first arose during the 18th-century Enlightenment as a description of the progressive application of reason in human affairs. 'Civilization' applied both to social and political life as well as to individual 'civilized' behaviour. By the 19th century, as Delanty (1995, pp. 93–4) points out, 'civilization' began to be used in the plural, whereby individual nations, regions, or races were classified as civilized or uncivilized. This classification had a moral and political as well as a descriptive function, in that it became a device for assertions of white European superiority over Asian or Oriental and African society. Europe was part of the process of civilization, whereas other societies lying beyond merely possessed culture.

This approach to civilization led to the construction of a view of history in which the rise of the European or Western history proceeded through a series of phases quite independently of the non-Western world. Eric Wolf has described this view of Western history in genealogical terms as one in which 'Greece begat Rome, Rome begat Christian Europe, Christian Europe begat the Renaissance, the Renaissance the Enlightenment, the Enlightenment political democracy and the Industrial Revolution. Industry, crossed with democracy, in turn yielded the United States, embodying the rights to life, liberty, and the pursuit of happiness' (Wolf 1982, p. 5).

The exclusively Eurocentric constructions of world history, of the kind Wolf describes, have repelled many scholars from having anything to do with notions of civilization. Many critics of the term see it simply as an ideological celebration of Western culture, that is, as a focus that excludes the greater part of humankind from the making of history. Norbert Elias put the objection well, as noted by Stephen Mennell, namely that 'the notion of civilisation represents the self-satisfaction of Europeans in a colonialist age' (Mennell 1990, p. 369). The question also arises of whether there is really one unitary history of humankind – the history of civilization – or a diversity of different histories lacking any common unifying thread.

Notwithstanding these major difficulties, it should be emphasized that a lively historical and archaeological scholarship has continued to utilize the notion of civilization and civilizations. Even Eurocentric accounts of the present day have sought understandings of how Western civilization has evolved, a search that involves extensive historical research on Indo-European legacies in the making of the West and especially on the impact of the ancient Middle Eastern and Mediterranean worlds. Aspects of non-Western art also became incorporated into Western modernism (Paz 1992, pp. 5–6). This Eurocentric exercise has encouraged a sense of there being civilizations, in the plural, in both the past and the present. This pluralism has been further extended in recent years with the post-colonial challenge to Eurocentrism, in the name of a more inclusive approach that brings in areas hitherto excluded or regarded merely as historical forebears of the West.

Within this broader civilizational framework, exemplified in the work of Toynbee (1934–61), the development of human history is conventionally linked with a set of dynamic centres such as ancient Sumer (Mesopotamia), the Indus valley, ancient Egypt, the ancient Mediterranean worlds of Greece and Rome, and, moving forward in time, the Chinese Empires between AD 500 and 1500, and medieval Islam. Each is considered as possessing a significant innovative capacity and a sufficient degree of autonomy to warrant description as a civilization. At the same time, these criteria do not necessarily rule out some elements of diffusion of influence from one to another.

Behind this intercivilizational approach to globalization lies an analytical point that has often been forgotten. As Curtin puts it, 'no human group could invent by itself more than a small part of its cultural and technical heritage' (1984, p. 1). This insight has been obscured by the tendency for individual societies and nations to indigenize that which was originally imported or introduced from outside. How many Italians, for example, realize that pasta originates from China, and how many English-language speakers appreciate that the alphabet came originally from Phoenicia centred on what is now the Lebanon. This argument suggests that human history from way back has a far greater syncretic character than is typically realized. What are taken-for-granted features of everyday life often have very diffuse origins derived or borrowed from many different sources. Curtin illustrates this with the example of the English language book. English, as a language, is of Indo-European origin. It developed in Western Europe in the hands of Germanic immigrants and became combined with elements from Latin that had come northward with the Roman Empire. The alphabet, as we have already noted, came from Phoenicea, while page numbers are arabic, in the sense that Europeans learned them from Arabs, who in turn learned them from Indians, who had earlier invented positional notation. Curtin also points out that until the recent electronic revolution transformed printing, a book would have been produced with movable type, a system that has Chinese origins.

Where, then, does the analysis of civilizations intersect with the study of globalization? The answer to this question involves us returning first to the issue of whether there is a unifying connecting thread in human history, and second to whether such a thread links together the history of different regions or civilizations into a single interconnected global history. Such a global history, it must be emphasized, need *not* take the form of a single unitary process (or metanarrative), such as the triumph of reason or Western civilization. Nor should it be taken to imply an inexorable process of homogenization to a single pattern. Nor finally need it entail any sense of evolutionary or teleological purpose, whether globalization is seen as a force for progress/good or domination/evil. In contradistinction to all of these, the minimum that is required for us to be able to speak of a single global connecting thread is that tangible interconnections exist between distinct regions, leading to interchange and interdependency.

The challenge of finding convincing evidence of interconnection is, however, an enormous one. First, there is the difficulty of bringing together data from different regions of the globe spread across long tracts of time. This is magnified by the fragmentation of academic specialisms by discipline (history, archaeology, anthropology) and area of study (China, Islam, the Mediterranean). Beyond this, there lies the evaluative difficulty that the interconnections specified must be more than trivial ones. Charles Tilly (1984) has warned against the construction of overblown world-historical and world-systemic studies that treat *any* kind of interconnection as significant. If any such connection (for example a visit by a European traveller to another continent, or the discovery of an artefact made in one region in another far away) is taken as significant, then, Tilly says, 'we will most likely discover... the world has always formed a single system' (1984, p. 62).

Tilly's own antidote to the challenge of trivial interconnection is to specify a minimum criterion for interconnectedness. This is 'that the actions of powerholders in one region of a network rapidly (say within a year),... visibly... affect the welfare of at least a significant minority (say a tenth) of the population in another region of the network' (1984). The problems with this definition are twofold. First, it is linked with the identifiable actions of powerholders; second, it is very much attuned to rapid instances of change characteristic of the contemporary world. What this excludes is examples of interconnection that are embedded more deeply in social life and which take longer to diffuse. Examples of such latter activities might include the diffusion of business practices such as the trading of new products or the use of new commercial practices. These are less clearly linked to central powerholders such as emperors, politicians, and generals, and may impact less rapidly than an invasion or a piece of legislation, nonetheless constituting over the longer term an interconnection.

While Tilly's definition of a significant interconnection is not entirely satisfactory, his general warning against the exaggeration of connections is well taken. What, then, does the evidence suggest about global interconnection prior to the modern period, and how far back in time can an interconnecting thread be traced?

Curtin's account of the syncretic character of innovation in human history goes some way toward suggestions of an interconnecting thread. Yet it remains compatible with the notion that individual nations or regions learn or borrow selectively from the more widely available stock of resources. The Chinese, for example, may have invented printing, yet they did not take up the printing of mass circulation publications in the same way as occurred in Western Europe from the Renaissance onwards. Alternatively, when the idea of windmill technology diffused from Islamic sources to the West via Mediterranean Islamdom, 'what passed was the basic idea and not the complex practice of building windmills in its particulars' (Hodgson 1974, vol. 2,

p. 363). Whereas the arms of the windmill spread horizontally among the Muslims, they became repositioned vertically in the Occident.

A recent attempt to develop stronger notions of a global connecting thread has been attempted in accounts of what is seen as a 'Central Civilisation' (Wilkinson 1987). Wilkinson's argument centres on the bold proposition that 'Today there is on the Earth only one civilization, a single global civilization' (p. 30). This originated in West Asia in Egypt and Sumer around 1500 BC. This core subsequently expanded to cover the entire globe, first through the Europe–Asia links and later through the incorporation of Africa and the Americas. In his commentary on this scenario, Frank (1990, p. 230) argues that this world-system had included 'most of the Asian-African-European' landmass by 600 BC and had incorporated much of the New World by AD 1500.

For Wilkinson, the Central Civilization has been neither dominated by one form of economic system (be it capitalist, feudal, or peasant-based) nor been fully political centred or statist. It has never been capitalist, owing to the robust persistence of a succession of state forms, impermanent over long periods of time but grounded nonetheless on a variety of different modes of force, rent-seeking, and coercive taxation. It has, on the other hand, never been fully statist because of the incapacity of particular states to survive over significant periods of time without reliance on private sources of economic power and resources. Thus 'the Central economy is at all times a mixed political economy, embodying trade and war, coercion and bargaining... the balance shifts with time, scale, region, and commodity' (Wilkinson 1987, p. 51). In a wider sense, Wilkinson's choice of the term 'Central' to characterize the development of this singular Civilization is deliberately designed to avoid any necessary reference to a particular sociogeographical locus of globalization. Given the complex and changing multilateral interconnections of the Central Civilization across history, it would be 'too parochial to label the civilization by the nomenclatures of any of... the states that have successively dominated, or the regions that have successively centred it' (Wilkinson 1993, p. 227).

This recent work by Wilkinson and Frank builds, in part, on the earlier studies of Marshall Hodgson (1974) on Islam. Hodgson argued for the existence of an Afro-Eurasian Oikoumene. He conceived this as 'the interdependent and more or less parallel development of four major complexes of civilised traditions', namely the Chinese, Indic, European, and Nile-to-Oxus. The specific linkages between them related to commerce, art, religion, and science. William McNeill, who had earlier thought of individual civilizations as being largely distinct (1964), has more recently come to support Hodgson's intercivilizational approach (McNeill 1990). Nonetheless, he gives pride of place in the dynamic of the Eurasian Oikoumene to different regions over time, Hellenic civilization holding the key role between 500 BC and AD 200, the Indic region that from AD 200 to AD 600, the Muslim world that from AD 600 to AD 1000, and the Chinese that from AD 1000 to AD 1500. Such discourses of civilization have broken with a Eurocentric or Western approach in two ways. First, they have identified the centrality of non-Western sources of dynamism in areas such as trade, technology, and science. Frank calls this a 'humanocentric' approach (1990, p. 157). For Mazrui (1990), it means recognizing that, for much of human history, the Chinese, Indian, and Islamic worlds have been net exporters of innovations to others. This has been obscured by the rise of the West to become the leading exporter of innovation in the 19th and 20th centuries.

Second, the civilizational discourses draw attention to the arbitrariness of associating geographic continents (or regions within them) with exclusive and autonomous centres of global development. In this sense, 'Europe', 'Asia', and 'Africa' are not to be regarded as continents with separate independent histories reflecting the distinctive nature or character of the continent. The peoples of the geographic continents do not have separate natures – some dynamic, others passive or conservative. The attribution of distinctive characters to the continents, or to the Western and non-Western worlds, is, on the contrary, an invention of the human imagination, very often based on a highly selective or arbitrary interpretation of the evidence. This alerts us, once again, to the problem of representation discussed in Chapter 1. Within the present context, it may be said that historical understanding of globalization has been distorted by the representation of 'Europe', or 'the West', as the dynamic force behind the development of a single world. This distortion has two main effects. First, the historical contribution of non-European regions to the history of globalization is marginalized. This leads to the ironic presumption that the non-Western world can only participate in the global by assimilating to 'Western' practices, many of which actually originated outside the West.

Second, the very idea of the West is an elastic concept used to appropriate any development regarded as dynamic and desirable rather than being a social scientific term with an objective meaning. Two thousand years ago, the intellectually and commercially dynamic Hellenic world spanned Mediterranean Europe, Asia, and North Africa. This world thought of itself as Occidental more than European, but Occidental referred to the Eastern Mediterranean, that is, the Hellenic Occident, rather than to current notions of Europe as a continent distinct from Asia. As Delanty points out, 'For the peoples of Antiquity the divide between north and south was a more significant one than that of east versus west' (1995, p. 21). It was only far later in European history that representations of the classical past were reconstructed around the myth of a pure Western Europeanized legacy stretching from ancient Greece and Rome to the present (see, for example, the discussion in Bernal 1987).

On this basis, Christianity too originated in the Middle East rather than Europe and may in this sense be regarded as an Oriental religion that was subsequently Westernized and Europeanized. This indigenization of an Oriental import was so successful that Christianity was subsequently represented as the bulwark of Western civilization against Islam within the medieval crusades of the 11th and 12th centuries (Delanty 1995). Once again, a non-Western development is appropriated by powerful elements within the emerging West, as part of its own distinctive way of life.

A final latter-day example of this kind of appropriation of new elements into representations of the West concerns the rise of the Japanese economy to a dominant position in the global economy. This has led to its transformation from an Asian power, perceived at the turn of the 20th century to be inferior to European civilization, into a member of the Western camp, symbolized by membership of the G7 group of the world's most powerful economies. This assimilation has been made in spite of major contrasts in social structure and culture between Japan on the one hand, and Europe and North America on the other (see, for example, Dore 1973). For the Japanese themselves, integration into the Western camp is seen as selective, that is, as economic and technological but not cultural Westernization. This is reflected in the slogan 'Western Technique, Japanese Spirit' (Mazrui 1990, p. 4).

Notwithstanding these complexities, the idea of the West continues to function as the most influential representation of dominant forms of global power. These include the institutions of private capital and entrepreneurship, and the institutions of the nation-state and the interstate system regarded in an – often idealized – sense as open and democratic. This projection of the West is further highlighted by the drawing of sharp contrasts with 'others', who can be represented as both different and challenging. Islamic 'fundamentalism', in which economy and politics are subordinate to a religious world-view, continues to be cast in this role.

From the discussion so far, it is clear that the search for an understanding of globalization requires attention to structures and networks that extend far back in time and range widely in space. This historical and culturally inclusive way of approaching globalization is not easy to operate because it demands attention to complex processes of historical change across a wide spatial canvas. Beyond this, there are further challenges involved in understanding globalization when we switch our attention from the historical origins of structures and networks to look more explicitly at issues of cultural representation. What is at stake here is how people come to conceive of the world as a single place.

Understanding globalization: seeing the world as a single place

Roland Robertson (1992), who comes to globalization from the sociology of religion and modernization theory rather than political economy, includes images of globalization or world order, whether from religion, science, or political ideology, within his conceptualization of globalization. In this sense, globalization is not only about structures, institutions, and networks, but also about the ways in which we think of social life and our place within it. Robertson goes on to argue that the idea of the world as a single community (be it in reality or in potential) goes back a very long time, reflected in notions such as the Kingdom of God on Earth (Robertson 1992, p. 81).

For the more recent period, he provides a very useful 'temporal-historical' sketch of the globalization process, beginning in early 15th-century Europe. Moving forward in time from that point, he lists as relevant developments such as the Heliocentric (that is, sun-centred) theory of the universe, ideas about a common humanity linked with humanism and individualism, citizenship, and, most recently of all, ideas of world citizenship and environmentalism. These are not only manifestations of globalization, but also, in a sense, causal elements within its emergence. How important such causal elements are is a controversial matter that remains to be established.

What all these developments have in common, according to Robertson, is that they contain within them ways of seeing the world as a single place occupied by a single humanity, sharing converging conceptions of rights and identities. This is not to deny that major counter-trends are also evident in this period of history, including the intensification of slavery and the development of racism, both of which challenge notions of a common humanity. Nonetheless, what

Robertson seems to have in mind is less the reality of one world than the emergence of globalization as an 'imagined community'. This term, first applied by Benedict Anderson (1983) to the world-view of nationalism, seems equally applicable to globalization. Both involve images of a community composed of people most of whom will never meet face to face but who nonetheless possess a shared sense of common bonds intensified by changes to communications. What the printing press did for the diffusion of nationalism as an imagined community, satellite communication and the Internet may now be doing for contemporary globalism.

So when did human beings first begin to think of the world as a single place? Is the 15th-century European Renaissance the watershed, or should we go even further back in time?

It is unclear whether the Renaissance really is such a watershed, since so many features of world-views current at that time derive from the thought of ancient Greece, as developed and mediated by the medieval Islamic world. Certainly, Heliocentric views of the cosmos, with which Robertson commences his sketch, were well known to the ancient Greeks (Kopal 1973, pp. 2–3). Nonetheless, Heliocentrism was never the dominant world-view, being subordinated to the systems of Ptolemy and Aristotle, both of whom took the Earth as the centre of the universe. The alternative Aristotelian-Ptolemaic view of the Earth as a planet differentiated between distinct continents, and connected to the cosmos through spheres, continued to be influential right up to the renewed Heliocentric challenges of Copernicus, Keeper, and Galileo during the 16th and 17th centuries.

Even so, the Ptolemaic view did not inhibit thinking of the world as a single place, either in Europe or in the Arab world. In terms of the representation of space in cartography, for example, David Harvey (1989) argues that the rediscovery of the Ptolemaic map in 15th-century Florence represented a fundamental breakthrough in the construction of geographic knowledge of the world as a single global entity. The revival of Ptolemy's 2nd-century AD geographical mapping in terms of co-ordinates of latitude and longitude created the possibility of both a cartographic and a spherical representation of global space. The subsequent development of cartographic representations of the globe by map-makers such as the Dutchman Mercator nonetheless had a strongly Eurocentric bias. This is reflected in Mercator's projection, which gives undue prominence to the northern hemisphere. Meanwhile terrestrial globes soon became features of every European court as symbols of statecraft, and in the universities as accoutrements of learning. In more recent times, globes depicting the world became domesticated, serving as fashionable items of interior bourgeois furnishing, so much so that the significance of their way of representing the world as a single place has become taken for granted. For Harvey, however, such intellectual changes cannot be regarded as free-standing causes of change but rather as responses to the demands of expanding capitalist commerce. This reminds us that an exclusive reliance on intellectual history may be misleading. Before disposing of the autonomy of changes in ideas altogether, it is necessary to ask whether or not there are more satisfactory ways of reformulating the significance of changes in representations of the world. The pursuit of particular doctrines within intellectual history is an important exercise, but it does have its limitations. One is the emphasis on scientific doctrines and the tendency to neglect broader world-views, which may be amalgams of metaphysics and mythology as much as what is regarded as science. Rather than picking out precursors of globalization within intellectual history, an alternative anthropological way of addressing the question may yield more insight. This starts out from the basic point that all human societies have, from prehistoric times, developed cosmologies that situate the life of tribes, or communities, nations, empires, and individuals, within a broader, sometimes mythical realm composed (variously) of gods, monsters, natural phenomena such as rivers and mountains, animals, and, of course, other humans. Such cosmologies, in the loosest and most general sense, may have a sense of unity, be it the unity of God's creation, the natural world, or the history of the social group. Yet this unity would scarcely qualify as an intimation of globalization, that is, of the world as a single place, because it lacks any of the substance of interconnection between human groups that is a basic feature of globalization.

Accordingly, it is not so much the sense of the world as a single place that matters as a sense of the interconnections that exist within that space. The long-run history of emergent understandings of globalization is therefore contained, as pointed out by the anthropologist Jonathan Friedman (1994), within the ways in which people think about the relationship between themselves and others.

For Friedman, spatial classification of the external world within some overarching sense of a finite and closed universe is a feature common, in his view, to Amazonian Indians, to African chiefdoms, and to feudal Europe (1994, pp. 44–5). Typically, the world is pictured as a set of concentric circles, the tribal or kinship group lying at the centre, around which are placed concentric circles representing increasingly non-local and often non-human segments of the world. These images are, in a sense, projections of the world as a single place, but the sense of interconnection between the inhabitants of the various circles is very weak. We therefore need some more tangible indicators of an emergent sense of globalization.

Friedman tackles this problem by exploring the social conditions under which such concentric cosmologies broke down to be replaced by clearer senses of the world as a single place based on interrelationships and interdependency. He locates two major contributions to the process. One is the process of expansion and conquest by powerful interests, which creates civilizational centres and a sense of differentiation between centre and periphery. The other, interrelated mechanism, is the set of processes whereby closed kin-centred worlds are eroded by developments such as cross-regional trade as well as conquest. Two major types of social structure that eventuate are centralized bureaucratic empires and commercial capitalist world-systems. It is these structures, according to Friedman, which generate cosmologies with a clearer sense of interdependency between the different elements that comprise the world as a single place.

Movement beyond the model of concentric circles is analysed by Friedman in terms of two alternative world-views. In the first, the wider world is pictured hierarchically, positioning other peoples and regions in terms of their correct place in a hierarchy defined in terms of a varying criterion. This shift from a spatial to a hierarchical approach is seen to characterize both centralized bureaucratic empires and commercial capitalist states. The case of the Chinese empires represents the most static model, China being represented as the universal centre of an unchanging universe, surrounded by various types of civilized and uncivilized barbarians (Friedman 1994, pp. 63–4). A more dynamic and pluralistic example is that of early Arab cosmologies. These typically identify six zones beyond the Arab centre, each with certain attributes but none surpassing the Arabs. Thus the Chinese appear as the people of technology and artisanry, and the Persians the people of ethics and politics, while the Blacks are treated as a 'lower' zone, characterized merely by sheer numbers. All this contrasts with the Arabs, who possess the 'higher' gift of poetry (Yapp 1992; Friedman 1995, p. 61).

Similar hierarchical and often racist classifications appear in the commercial capitalist civilizations of ancient Greece and early modern Europe. Once again, hierarchies develop that differentiate the centre from the barbarians, savages, or, in the later period, infidels and Orientals that lie outside. In all cases, the shift from an enclosed concentric cosmology to a hierarchical classification reflects both the greater intensification of contact and interaction between different parts of the globe, and the pressing into service of representations of 'the other' that legitimate conquest, domination, and racist superiority.

For Friedman, however, the intensification of interconnection associated with commercial capitalist expansion encourages further changes in the way in which the world is conceived of as a single place. There is thus a further shift from concentric hierarchy to evolutionism. The point about evolutionism, as he defines it, is that spatial classifications become subsumed into temporal classifications. That is, other groups, once seen as living out there in a space other than our own, become recast as groups whose otherness reflects their location within modes of human endeavour characteristic of our past. 'We' therefore stand for what is advanced and progressive, while 'they' represent an earlier, less developed stage of social life. Evolutionism does, however, offer the promise of advancement provided the institutions and techniques of advanced society are taken up by the less advanced.

This proposition of a further shift to evolutionism is sustained through a comparison of changes to world-views in two major phases in the history of what he calls commercial capitalist civilizations. These are, first, the commercial, imperial, and intellectual expansion of the Athenian and later Hellenic world of ancient Greece in the period between roughly 800 and 200 BC, and second, the Western European expansion associated with the period between roughly 1500 and 1750AD embracing the Renaissance and the Enlightenment. The argument is that both exhibit a similar shift away from both concentric anthropocentric and hierarchical representations of the world to more evolutionary approaches. These are connected with a secularization of thought and the detachment of understandings of the world from both theology and nature.

Developments of this kind are evident, albeit fleetingly, in 6th-century BC Greece, among writers such as Democritus and Hippocrates, and again in the period from the 1st-century BC Roman Republic to the 1st century AD. For Friedman, 'the classical Mediterranean world reveals a succession of mentalities strikingly similar to that of Western Europe in the era of expansion' (1994, p. 60), culminating in the 18th and 19th centuries.

So what does all this mean for the understanding of globalization? Three points may be made here.

First, Friedman's work, building on a range of specialist studies of the ancient Mediterranean, Arab, and Chinese worlds, alerts us to the long and complex historical emergence of views of the world as a single place. This process may usefully be traced further back than 15th-century Heliocentrism. Second, the analysis is both comparative and non-inclusive in extending the analytical framework well beyond the spatial and temporal setting of the expansion of the Western world since the 16th century. Third, it seeks to integrate together the long-run inclusive analysis of structures and institutions attempted by writers such as Frank with the analysis of world-views and representations of globalism, the importance of which has been advanced by Robertson.

If representations of the world as a single place are to be integrated into the historical analysis of globalization, it is clear that some kind of distinction should be made between representations that somehow encourage globalization and those that do not. Put another way, the existence of many different views of the world as a single place is not, in and of itself, a causal influence on the further development of globalization. Many of the concentric representations discussed above, notably those of the Chinese, do not lend themselves to engagement with the external world. This does not mean that long-range interregional relationships with other parts of Europe and Asia did not take place in areas such as trade and technology transfer. What it does mean is that, in such cases, emergent globalism did not find its way into dominant representations of the world.

Conversely, the particular character of certain world-views may have exerted considerable influence on the direction taken in trends towards globalization. As Friedman points out, debate raged within 16th- and 17th-century Europe over the full humanity or otherwise of the newly found South American Indian populations. Were they to be regarded as barely human and thus fit for slavery, as claimed by the so-called 'civilizationists', or as no less human than Europeans and therefore entitled to the same rights? In the former case, representations of the globe as a single place see the population of that place as rigidly stratified and use this as a basis for a potentially globalized exploitation of labour through the commercialization of slavery. In the latter case, images of the world as a single place draw on notions of the unity of humanity as the basis for ideas that are today labelled as human rights, ideas that have fuelled both the transnational 19th-century antislavery movement and more recent moves to institutionalize a worldwide set of human rights.

This example indicates that the way in which images of the world as a single place are articulated may matter a very great deal to the kind of global interdependencies that are created. This particular argument is at variance with the excessively materialist approach of Marxist-influenced writers such as David Harvey and Immanuel Wallerstein, who explain systems of ideas or cultural representation in terms of the functional requirements of modes of production and the capitalist world-system respectively. The more general underpinning of this challenge to materialism is familiar in sociological theory, namely that the character of cultural representation cannot simply be read off from the nature of economic life.

The example of differing approaches to the understanding of South American Indian populations also reflects a major theme throughout this study, that of the ambivalence of globalization in relation to any single set of evaluative standpoints. That is, globalization as an idea is neither the monopoly of the economically powerful and imperially rapacious nor solely and exclusively a positive Utopia based on the inviolability of human rights and human community. Ideas of a single world may be hierarchically ordered and used to justify the most brutal social arrangements, but they may equally be strongly egalitarian.

The foregoing discussion gives some anthropological and historical depth to a major insight of Robertson's concerning contemporary images of world order. While all images of the human world now conceive of it as a single place, the nature of such representations varies considerably according to the connections that exist between the component parts. In other words, the world is singular yet somehow differentiated and subdivided. Some images of the world take a 'strong' form, as in ideals of a single, integrated world community or the idea of single world government incorporating all parts of the globe in a single polity. Others posit weaker interconnections and levels of integration, major boundaries between nations and localities persisting in spite of the development of global interconnection.

This argument is pursued schematically in Table 2.1 in terms of two types of distinction. On the vertical axis, images of world order vary according to the extent to which they represent principles of community (or *Gemeinschaft*) compared with a voluntary association of consenting parties (or *Gesellschaft*), a distinction introduced into sociology by Ferdinand Toennies (1955 [1887]). On the horizontal axis, types of world order vary according to whether they exhibit strong centralized bonds or weaker decentralized linkages.

This generates four major types of world-image. Along the community dimension, the strong version of global community without boundaries is contrasted with a world subdivided into local communities between which only limited connections exist. While the former includes religious Utopias such as 'The Kingdom of God on Earth', the latter is reflected in antiglobal, green, communitarian thinking about ecology. On the voluntary association dimension, the strong project of world federalism builds persistent local differences into a world polity in which rational agreements to co-operate are more important. Examples of this orientation are more easy to find on a regional than strictly world scale, as in ideals of a federal Europe. This strong associational pattern, meanwhile, contrasts with a world of weaker types of associational linkage, in which nation-states co-operate globally but only out of self-interest. This arrangement is the one which many would identify with the contemporary interstate system and the apparatus of international bodies such as the UN or World Bank, as they currently exist, as distinct from the Utopian projections sometimes placed on them.

Table 2.1   Images of world order developed by Robertson (1992, pp. 78–83)

Principle of social organization	Type of interconnection	
	Stronger bonds	_Weaker linkages_
Gemeinschaft (community)	_One single worldwide community_. Belief in communal _unity_. Connection with religious or Utopian dreams of an earthly paradise	World consists of _bounded communities_, such as nations or localities
Gesellschaft (voluntary association)	_World government_, in federal rather than communitarian form. Constituent parts of the world order agree to _co-operate_ together	World composed of _bounded nation-states_, who sometimes agree to co-operate together out of national _interest_ rather than commitment to world government

This schema is clearly exactly that – an abstract way of distinguishing between the logic of contrasting ways of picturing world order rather than a set of stark contrasts to be applied mechanistically to each example under consideration. Robertson stresses the need for flexibility in the way in which his schema is used, for several reasons. First, the generalized images may have subvariants depending on the degree of equality or symmetry of status that exists within the global arena. What has been here termed the 'weak' or decentralized version of the global *Gesellschaft*, for example, may be conceived of in terms of contrasting patterns of participation available to nation-states within transnational organizations. The contrasts between Western G7 nations, who also occupy key positions in the UN and the World Bank, compared with the developing nations, who generally occupy less central positions, indicates inequality between nations in terms of levels of access to organized global power and influence. Alternatively, more accessible forms of integration may be possible in areas where the symbolic equality of autonomous nations within the world order is more central, as in images of a family of nations of equal social and cultural worth. Some such image often underlies images of global cultural activities such as the Olympic Games.

Second, and more provocatively, Robertson argues that images of the globe as a single place implicate both those who evaluate globalism positively and those who are explicitly antiglobal. Examples of the latter include movements that appeal to particularistic claims rooted variously in locality, religion, or ethnicity. Robertson's point is that these claims are today globally orientated rather than being the primordial manifestations of ancient historical allegiance. Robertson maintains that antiglobal movements are globally orientated even where no direct or explicit concern with world order is evident, as among some fundamentalist American Christian groups. Such movements are regarded, by those which they oppose, as being held in 'subliminal thrall' (1992, p. 80).

Robertson's work on images of world order is of major significance to the analysis of representations of the world as a single place. In the first place, it is a useful reminder that images of globalization are not restricted to Utopian desires for one world or political movements for world government. Nor do such images necessarily imply homogeneity or equality between the various parts of the globe. Second, Robertson's emphasis on images of the globe and global order assists in opening up excessively economic or political accounts of globalization to wider issues of cultural representation and evaluation. Put another way, globalization is as much about ideals and values as economic development, about ideals of what the world should be as well as what it currently is or is thought to be. Such normative issues recur as we move forward in time to consider the historical sociology of globalization and its relations with Western modernity.

Globalization as Western modernity

The historical perspectives on globalization sketched in the first part of this chapter are important for a number of reasons. One of the most important of these is that they provide a broader transhistorical context to globalization than is conventionally found in recent social enquiry. There have been many calls for sociology to become more historical, and this has produced some outstanding work of breadth and vision (for example, Mann 1986). However this may be, many of the versions of history that have emerged in the literature on globalization are still too often flawed by the adoption of short-run time horizons and by the adoption of what might be called the Great Divide approach to social analysis.

This approach, already foreshadowed in Chapter 1, sees human history in terms of a single great divide between the modern, Western, industrial world and that which went before. The assumption is that the contours of the contemporary world only began to emerge comparatively recently. There are two versions of the timing of this. One places the date around 500 years ago, focusing on the consolidation and expansion of Western capitalism from the 16th century onwards. The second focuses on a supposed divide occurring about 200–250 years ago, around the time of the so-called Industrial Revolution. Whichever of these watersheds is chosen, it is typical to regard prior social changes as, at best, early forerunners of the present, as pre-modern attempts to understand the social world. This foreshortened sense of time horizons inevitably gives pride of place to the Western world in the making of contemporary social life and the development of globalization.

The work of Anthony Giddens represents a major contemporary reaffirmation of this 'great divide' approach. He argues that modern society is fundamentally different from what went before, and that the history of civilization is of far less significance than the recent history of capitalism. Thus 'The history of human "civilisation" stretches back some 7000 years – so far as we know… Capitalism is at most some 400 or 500 years old, yet it has introduced social and material transformations of quite staggering proportions compared with the range of societal variations that existed previously' (Giddens 1981, p. 164).

In a later work, the dynamism of the contemporary world is linked more broadly with modernity, that is, a social process that subsumes capitalism in a broader set of features. Globalization is seen as having been made possible by modernization (Giddens 1990, pp. 55–78). Four major aspects of modernization are identified as being important: capitalism, industrialism, the surveillance capacities of the nation-state, and nationally based military power. These trends are then identified with the recent history of the Western world in such a way that globalization is interpreted, up until the present, as a primarily Western phenomenon. It is therefore only in the future that globalization will involve significant inputs from 'non-Western settings' (Giddens 1990, p. 175).

The strength of this approach is that it correctly emphasizes the leading role of the 'West' in many *recent* phases of globalization. Capitalism has clearly created a single worldwide division of labour and market for capital and commodities, while industrialization has formed the technological and organizational base for the 19th- and 20th-century consolidation of these trends. Modern communications advances, such as satellite delivery systems and computer technologies based on the silicon chip, are, for example, unthinkable without a strong industrial base.

Similarly, the rise of powerful and autonomous nation-states has, over time, encouraged the development of transnational political organizations designed to regulate relationships and conflicts between nation-states. The UN, to take one prominent example, was founded by a set of nation-states, and it is nation-states that form the basis of formal representation within the UN and its many agencies. While economic globalization has so far been more successful than political globalization, there is no denying the centrality of interstate mechanisms to the consolidation of global institutions in the past 50 years.

Finally, there is the issue of Western military force in global affairs. In one sense, the military superiority of this kind of power may be seen as resting upon industrial capacity. Similarly, the huge fiscal demands of war machines depend in the long term on the continuing capacity of capitalist economies to generate increased economic growth and higher productivity. These underwrite the sustainability of high levels of government expenditure on research and development, armaments, and service personnel. In another sense, however, military power has been an important causal mechanism in its own right in securing suitable resources and overcoming obstacles that threatened to inhibit Western globalization. This is reflected in the colonization process, which, from the 16th century onwards, opened up the New World and later acted as an arm of political and economic imperialism in South and East Asia. Military capacity, as Michael Mann (1986) shows, is an autonomous feature of power rather than a simple instrument of economic or political interest. Also, it is superior Western military power rather than any historical advantage in technological capacity that explains a good deal of Western Europe's success in sustaining worldwide expansion. The military capacity to act globally is thus interwoven with other aspects of Western modernity, as both cause and consequence of many key aspects of globalization.

A further underlying strength of the Great Divide framework is that it focuses on the shift from episodic to self-sustained global economic development that characterized 18th-century Europe. It is arguable that previous attempts at globalization within the ancient empires achieved much but never succeeded in generating self-sustainable economic growth to support geographical expansiveness. This is taken to be a fundamental reason for the collapse of the (Western) Roman Empire, an aspect of the 'Central Civilization' that had absorbed so much from the previous Hellenic expansion. Economic historians argue that what 18th- and 19th-century Europe was able to do was transform the relationship between economic productivity and population growth, allowing economic development to outstrip the growth in population. This released human society from the periodic crises identified by Thomas Malthus, whereby increases in output would always be threatened by even greater increases in population unless fundamental restraints could be introduced into procreative behaviour.

The Eurocentrism of this Great Divide argument is, of course, very clear. It is the West rather than the global system as a whole that solves the Malthusian subsistence crisis. Furthermore, it is said to be only by adopting Western economic and social institutions that other nations and regions can advance. Parts of this line of interpretation have much merit. The West (meaning Western Europe and its extensions overseas) has indeed been the dynamic force behind many recent decisive phases of globalization, notably between 1750 and 1950. During this period, globalization has indeed been largely synonymous with Western modernization.

The Eurocentrism of the Great Divide argument does not, in and of itself, negate the proposition that the West has been the major historical force behind globalization in recent centuries. Before this view can be confidently accepted, however, it is necessary to ask what, if anything, is excluded by this focus. Three major problems may be identified.

The first is that the Great Divide argument downplays or forgets the significance of global developments prior to the Western epoch of hegemony. These include the development of an expanding global division of labour built on the experience of millennia of cross-regional and cross-cultural trade, and the diffusion of key technologies and organizational forms within the central civilization, including printing, property law, conceptions of the individual as a free-standing entity, and laws and conventions regulating trade with foreigners. The second is that many of these developments have non-Western origins. Indeed, Western Europe remained on the periphery of the Central Civilization until the 12th and 13th centuries (Hodgson, 1974 [1958–59], vol. 2, p. 329). This has been obscured by the decisive economic and military victories of the West over other key components of the Central Civilization, including Islam, India, and China.

The third point, one which has been continuously stressed in this study, is the elasticity of what constitutes the West. This looks like a term with a precise geopolitical and geocultural reference, but its usage over the course of history suggests otherwise. Indeed, it would be true to say that 'the West', in contemporary parlance, is very much more a term for the club of the economically and politically successful.

Towards a speculative history of globalization since 1750

Giddens' work is an important example of the Great Divide argument that engages explicitly with the relationship between globalization and Western modernity. It may nonetheless be criticized not only for its excessive Eurocentrism, but also for an excessively 'top-down' approach. By this I mean that it focuses on large institutions such as capitalism and the system of nation-states, giving little attention to cultural change or to social movements influencing states from 'below'.

A useful corrective to Giddens may be found in Robertson's historical sketch of the recent development of globalization since 1750 (Robertson 1992, pp. 58–9). Looking at the period from the mid-18th century to the end of the First World War, Robertson identifies two phases: the first, from 1750 to the 1870s, is regarded as one of 'incipient globalization'; the second, from the 1870s to the 1920s, is seen as the crucial phase of 'take-off' into the establishment of a global society. These two phases are identified with a mix of political, economic, cultural, and technological developments.

The phase of incipient globalization, based primarily on Europe, may be associated with the following checklist derived from Robertson's work and a range of other sources:

● The development of more formalized international relations between increasingly consolidated nation-states. Nation-states consolidated their rights of self-determination in written

declarations and constitutions (Weissbrodt 1988, p. 6), while
international relations between states were increasingly embodied in
bilateral and multilateral treaties.

• An increase in the number of legal conventions and agencies
concerned with the regulation of international relations, including
war and communication (for example, the 1864 Geneva Convention
for the Amelioration of the Condition of the Wounded and Sick in
Armies in the Field, and the 1868 St Petersburg Declaration to
prevent the use of incendiary substances in war).

• The establishment of the International Committee of the Red Cross
in 1863 as the one of the first global NGOs.

• The growth of social movements stressing internationalism
alongside nationalist movements.

• The beginning of the era of international exhibitions.

• Progress towards the achievement of a more concrete sense of a
single humanity, through moves against slavery, condemned in the
1814 Paris Peace Treaty between Britain and France, and
articulated at the 1840 World Anti-Slavery Convention.

Robertson's next phase of take-off into global society comprises the
following:

• The development of world-time, replacing a myriad of local times.
Twenty-four nations meeting in 1884 established Greenwich as the
zero meridian and divided the world into 24 time zones (Kern 1983,
p. 12).

• The consolidation of four interlinked trends in Western modernity:
 – national societies, reflected in the spread of the nation-state as the
 typical political form
 – autonomous individuals, reflected in the growth of institutions of
 citizenship and consumer markets
 – a single international society
 – a singular conception of humankind, which includes all rather
 than perpetuating the hierarchies of racial exclusion.

• A sharp increase in the number and speed of global forms of
communication (for example, the telegraph, telephone – invented in
1876 – and radio), together with invention of the key global
transportation innovation: the aeroplane.

• The first international novels, symbolized by Jules Verne's *Around
the World in Eighty Days*, published in 1873 (Verne, 1873).

• The inclusion of a number of non-European societies, including

Japan, into 'international society'.
• The development of international competitions, for example the modern Olympic Games, begun in 1896, and the Nobel prizes, which commenced in 1901.
• The First World War.

In this way, Robertson combines Giddens' 'top-down' focus with a 'bottom-up' approach including developments within civil society, involving cultural change and the agency of social movements. If this sketch has a weakness, it is the curious neglect of economic aspects of globalization in favour of the political and cultural. The take-off phase, in particular, should be supplemented by developments such as:

• the institutionalization of the Gold Standard as the framework for global monetary exchange;
• the massive expansion of capital export from Western countries;
• the origins of multinational companies.

Robertson continues his historical sketch onwards from 1920, noting, among other trends, the gradual re-emergence of the non-Western world in the ongoing development of globalization. In the next phase, between the 1920s and the 1960s, labelled 'The Struggle for Hegemony' (Robertson 1992, pp. 58–9), the following key processes and events took place:

• Disputes and wars about which nations had hegemony over globalization, including the relative decline of Britain and the rise to post-war dominance of the USA.
• The establishment of League of Nations in 1919, and the renewal of global political organization through the UN in 1945; a rapid increase in UN membership with colonial independence, bringing non-Western voices to the fore.
• Increased reference to the interests of humanity as a whole in the light of Hiroshima and the Holocaust.
• Cold War conflict over conflicting conceptions of modernity and global order.
• Crystallization of a sense of the Third World and of non-aligned countries poised between the superpowers.

In the final stanza of this speculative history, dubbed 'the uncertainty phase', the following trends are identified:

- The end of the Cold War and bipolarity, in favour of a shift toward a more fluid but uncertain international system.
- An acclerated expansion of global communications, notably through electronic technology, allowing virtually instantaneous transfers of information around the globe.
- Civil rights becoming a global issue, reflected in expanding reference to human rights.
- Concern for humanity as a whole, enhanced by concern for the environment being seen as an intrinsically global issue, as symbolized by the Rio Earth Summit in 1992.
- The number of global institutions and movements rapidly increases. The establishment of key global social movements such as Amnesty International (1961) and Friends of the Earth (1969) dates from this time.
- An increased transcontinental migration of people, and an expanded challenge to monocultural nation-states in the name of multiculturalism and polyethnicity.
- The explosion of difference around gender, sexuality, ethnicity, and race eroding any universalistic conception of the individual.
- The uncertain impact of Islam, which may be interpreted either as a deglobalising trend towards localism or regionalism, or as a reglobalising movement challenging the credentials of Western approaches to globalization.

Such trends are once again only a sketch, but they do begin to reintegrate non-Western elements into the picture. These later phases in Robertson's global history show the same attention to influences from both above and below as we saw in the earlier periods. Their major limitation is again the curious submerging of economic aspects of globalization. This list should thus be supplemented by the following:

- The key role of the Bretton Woods institutions, notably the International Monetary Fund (IMF) and the World Bank, in re-stabilizing the post-war economy on economically liberal market-oriented principles.
- The rapid expansion of foreign direct investment from core Western countries, much of it concentrated in the triad comprising North America, Europe, and East Asia.
- The increasing consolidation of the power of multinational companies and the development of cross-national strategic business alliances.

Concluding remarks

Recent changes in the globalization of social life are undoubtedly important, and there can be no denying that globalization processes have intensified over the past 100 years. A longer-run historical perspective is nonetheless important in drawing attention to significant continuities in interconnection and interchange between the different regions of the world, going back several millennia. While the pace and intensity of such interconnections have changed, their importance for world history is far from trivial. Repeating Philip Curtin's point that no human group has developed from within its own resources more than a small proportion of its current repertoire of practices and stock of ideas, this longer-term framework enables us to identify the slow and uncertain prehistory of current global developments. These include technology transfer, linguistic development, the establishment of long-distance trading networks, and the spread of religious movements.

From this historical perspective, globalization may be regarded as a long-run process of diffusion across borders and boundaries, moving outward from multiple sources and centres. This historical and diffusionist viewpoint also enables us to see globalization as something much more than the recent triumph of the West, even allowing for the key role of Western sources of global change in recent centuries.

The other major theme developed in this chapter is that of the multifaceted nature of globalization processes. Robertson's work in particular is helpful in emphasizing the political and especially cultural dimensions of globalization. This focus embraces how religious conviction and the cultural imagination enter into the way in which globalization is understood and the standpoints that individuals and groups take towards it. Put another way, globalization is as much about 'thinking globally', or about aspirations for a single harmonious world order, as about the visible and powerful organizations of global economic power and international relations.

This multifaceted or multidimensional view is intrinsic to the way in which this study is constructed. It is reflected in the following chapters, where economic, political, and cultural aspects of globalization are discussed singly and in relation to each other. We begin with a discussion of economic globalization.

3

The Global Economy: Organizations, Networks and Regulatory Arrangements

'Man buys the world.'

This headline appeared in *Business Week* magazine on the occasion of the acquisition by the international entrepreneur Rupert Murdoch of the full assets of Hong Kong-based Star TV (*Guardian* 24 July 1995). Murdoch, whose business career started when he inherited the Murdoch family newspaper empire in Australia, is, at the time of writing, head of News Corporation, a media-centred global conglomerate spanning television, cable vision, and print media as well as satellite broadcasting and information technology industries across four continents. Familiar names such as *The Times* newspaper of London, Twentieth Century Fox Films and Television, HarperCollins, the world's largest English language publisher, as well as Star TV, broadcasting to 54 Asian countries, are all part of this empire. Deals have recently been signed or are pending with the Globo organization, the largest TV network in Brazil, for a Latin-American satellite service, and with the *Chinese Peoples Daily*, to enter the Communist party newspaper into the world of global information technology. Meanwhile, Murdoch renounced Australian nationality for American citizenship in order to pursue media acquisition in the USA, thereby surmounting legal restrictions on foreign media ownership.

The Murdoch anecdote illustrates some of the ways in which concentrations of economic power and control over information transcend political boundaries for both businesses and individuals. This globalization process is, as we have seen, not new. Yet it has intensified in recent decades with the rapid expansion of the ratio of transnational to

50

purely domestic activity and with technological changes that facilitate communications and virtually instantaneous transfers of information and finance. This intensification of economic globalization raises many important issues, not least of which is the spectre of the concentration of economic power in a few hands, beyond the jurisdiction of democratically elected governments. This has led many observers to question whether the nation-state has any kind of long-term future in a world of intensified globalization. Taken literally, the Murdoch-inspired headline is, of course, exaggerated. The scale of global economic activity is such that no one person could take over a single industry, let alone the entire world. This much is obvious. In any case, it is private *corporate* power, represented by multinational or transnational entities such as General Motors, Sony, Exxon Petroleum, or the Bank of Tokyo-Mitsubishi, the world's largest bank (*Economist* 25 January 1997), as much as the activity of particular entrepreneurs that lies at the heart of concerns about the demise of the nation-state. These giants of globalization operate on a scale that exceeds the gross national product of most of the nations of the world. Their control over access to capital investment and new technology gives them considerable leverage over even the most powerful governments anxious to attract employment-generating and taxation-generating investment.

Meanwhile, the fate of most individuals also appears dwarfed by such concentrations of economic power. Rupert Murdoch, who shifted his citizenship and domicile from Australia to the USA in the 1980s, represents one of a very few individuals who can exploit the opportunities of globalization by, in effect, purchasing a new nationality. For the majority of individuals, processes of international movement are more circumscribed, both by shifting patterns of international investment and demand for labour in the first place, and by restrictions on population movement imposed by nation-states in the second. Even so, transnational immigration is on the increase (Castles and Miller 1993), reflecting an intensification in the global movements of labour alongside the mobility of capital.

While such trends are clear enough in broad outline, there are a number of misconceptions or exaggerations current in much of the commentary on economic globalization. First, as we have already discussed, there is the idea that the global economy is entirely new. Second is the emphasis on mobility, change, and transformation, at the expense of any understanding of the ways in which economic globalization is institutionalized and regulated. Third, there is the fashionable but superficial view that the nation-state has been both overtaken and marginalized by globalization. This chapter is designed to highlight the weaknesses of such approaches. It proceeds by first identifying some of the main contours of economic globalization, with particular reference to the operations of multinational enterprises and a range of economic networks. Attention then shifts to a wider consideration of the range of institutions seeking to regulate aspects of the global economy.

Some contours of economic globalization

One major conceptual distinction worth making at the outset is that between what will be called an international economy and a transnational economy. An international economy may be thought of in terms of exchanges between national economies carried out by economic actors and institutions based within particular nations. Typically, raw materials, goods, or services produced in one country are sold in another. The expansion of world trade between national economies is a key indicator of this process. Economic globalization of this kind is not new. Much of the expansion of the international economy in the 19th and early 20th centuries took this form and was further associated with processes of international migration. International flows of capital, often in the form of loans from the major Western nations, were also significant, although their relative importance was nowhere near as great as it has subsequently become. As late as the 1950s, 'the major international flow was world trade, concentrated in raw materials, other primary products, and resource-based manufacturing' (Sassen 1994, p. 11). This system, encompassing both manufacturing and primary production, involved both the developed capitalist world and developing countries.

A transnational economy, in contrast, while incorporating international trade of this kind, has additional features. These include the development of transnational processes and institutions. The recent integration of the world's financial markets through information technology, for example, allows virtually instantaneous transactions across political boundaries on a vast and unprecedented scale. By 1989, trading in foreign exchange alone averaged $650 billion per day, that is, 40 times the value of world trade (Frieden 1991). By the late 1990s, daily volumes exceeded $1000 billion. Meanwhile, capital investment and marketing are increasingly being conducted on a global scale in a range of interconnected and shifting locations according to transnational calculations of optimal profitability. This typically involves one or more of the following: foreign direct investment (FDI) in production outside the country of origin, the articulation of specialized production or service provision from a wide range of national sources in an integrated global production or service delivery strategy; and the development of strategic business alliances across political and industry boundaries. One effect of this is constant shift in the location of employment as existing economic activities shift their location and new activities start up in previously undeveloped sites.

This kind of transnational economy has been the characteristic mode of economic globalization since the 1960s. This change is reflected by the fact that the rate of growth of transnational financial flows such as FDI has been increasing more rapidly than the rate of growth of exports (Sassen 1994, p. 10). More than this, trade statistics no longer adequately measure or encapsulate the multilateral economic linkages that constitute the global economy. Ohmae (1996) claims that such data fail to count 'revenues from services, licenses, or intellectual property, or from goods manufactured by US firms in third countries but sold in Japan, or from goods both manufactured and sold in Japan by US firms' (p. 17). An example would be computer chips produced by US multinational enterprises (MNEs) in Malaysia and then shipped to Japan for sale.

Within the new transnational economy, individual nations are increasingly dependent not only on trade, but also on flows of capital from outside. These are seen as necessary to achieve economic growth, gain access to new technology, and maximize employment. The increased demand for foreign investment has also been associated with processes of deregulation of capital transfers and with opportunities created by the privatization of former public monopolies in sectors such as power supply and telecommunications.

This development of a transnational economy has also seen a relative shift in global economic activity to the developed world, linking the three core areas of the USA, Western Europe, and Japan. These regions and countries have large markets, generate huge sums of capital available for investment, and drive much of the technological innovation process, especially that which involves information technology. They are also home to the world's largest banks. According to UN data for the second half of the 1980s, around 80 per cent of all FDI inflows were concentrated in the developed countries (UNCTAD 1993, p. 16). While the more recent opening up of the Chinese economy in the 1990s is shifting the FDI inflow pattern back towards the developing countries, it is consolidating the East–West axis of the global economy by widening Asian representation from Japan alone to a broader East Asian group, including China, Taiwan, South Korea, and Hong Kong, and South-East Asian economies such as Malaysia, Singapore, and Indonesia. The most tangible institutional form within which this new pattern has emerged is the MNE. Since 1950, international trade has grown considerably, yet the value of production by multinational companies now exceeds that of world trade itself (Dunning 1993, p. 107). This reflects the fact that production of goods and services outside their original boundaries accounts for a large proportion of the total sales of MNEs. This proportion varies from around 35–40 per cent for companies originally based in nations with large home markets (for example, the USA), to upwards of 80–90 per cent for MNEs such as the Swiss-based Nestlé or Dutch-based Philips, where home markets are much smaller. Most FDI and a good deal of technology transfer between nations is carried out by MNEs.

The multinational enterprise: the global organization of production and consumption

The history of the MNE is instructive in clarifying the dynamics of the recent development of economic globalization. Trading organizations operating across political boundaries go back a long way in human history. However, the origins of MNEs go back to the period from 1870 to 1900 when enterprises began to set up foreign branches and become involved in FDI (Corley 1989). Many contemporary multinationals, such as Ford, IBM, and General Motors, began their own multinational operations in the period from 1900 to 1930 (Dassbach 1989). The number of MNEs expanded more rapidly still after 1950. Multinationals originating in the USA and Western Europe were first in the field but have in the past 15 years been challenged by the rise of the Japanese. More recently, countries once labelled as part of the Third World, such as Brazil or Malaysia, have developed multinational corporations though very few of these are listed in the Fortune 500 digest of the largest global businesses.

The image of the typical multinational is often associated with corporate giants in industry or raw material extraction and processing. Symbols of multinational activity that often first come to mind are the automobile companies such as Ford, General Motors, and Toyota, or the oil companies Exxon, Mobil, and Royal Dutch Shell. The impression is one of a large hierarchical corporation that has dominated production and marketing in a particular sector of the industry. This image is of some value, but it has the danger of underestimating the changing face of multinational enterprise in several senses.

In the first place, it should be emphasized that MNEs are not restricted to manufacturing and raw materials but extend to the rapidly growing service sector. This includes banks and insurance companies, accounting, advertising and consultancy bodies, and the hotel and leisure industries. At the time of writing, Citicorp, American Express, McKinsey and Arthur Andersen, Coopers and Lybrand and KPMG, and the Hilton and the Sheraton Hotel chains all comprise significant parts of the multinational presence with the service sector (Campbell and Verbeke 1994).

While some analysts have interpreted the growth of the service sector and of service-based multinationals as an indicator of the development of a global postindustrial economy, this argument exaggerates the distinction between the production of goods and services. Producers of goods need accountants and information technology consultants, just as hotels need tourists and business clients, and banks need a prospering manufacturing sector able to take on loans. In other words, the service sector is not an autonomous engine of economic growth but part and parcel of the broader economy. For Sassen (1991, 1994), producer services are a major and growing element in the growth of services within the global economy.

An even more fundamental aspect of the changing face of MNEs within the global economy is the growth of information industries. These typically link together production and service provision in a network of interconnected activities. Castells (1993) argues that the productivity growth largely responsible for driving forward the global economy has depended increasingly on the application of science and technology to economic life. Microelectronics, informatics, and telecommunications not only stimulate the global economy through productivity growth, but also change the basis upon which business is conducted, further minimising the constraints of geographic distance upon exchange. Even more fundamental than the shift from industry to services, then, is the development of what Porat has called the 'information economy'.

This information technology has not only created new MNEs, such as Microsoft, Sun Microsystems, and Apple, but has also enhanced the capacity of other multinationals to operate across geographical and political boundaries. For Sassen, this proliferation of activity across borders does not lead to a decentralization of multinational control over its activity but to a new kind of centralized control. The spatial location of multinational power, she believes, is now centred on global cities. Places such as New York, Tokyo, London, and Frankfurt now contain the head-quarters of many MNE corporations together with the business networks within which financial, banking, business consulting, advertising, and other types of service are concentrated. Such cities have, of course, a long history as economic centres. What has happened recently is a relative decline of older, urban centres of global economic power associated with manufacturing areas, such as Detroit or the Ruhr, and a growing importance of producer service centres, linked as much with each other as with their respective national hinterlands. Added to such cities, of course, are new information-based regions such as Silicon Valley in the San Francisco area and a similar area to the north around Seattle.

Why then has this wide range of MNEs developed? The answers to this question depend, in part, on the advantages that accrue (or are perceived to accrue) to businesses who take up transnational investment and business partnerships, as against the exporting of domestic production. Dunning (1993, p. 109), in his major study of the globalization of business, identifies four general reasons for MNE activity: *market-seeking, resource-seeking, efficiency-seeking,* and *strategic asset-seeking.* He argues against any general theory of MNE activity, such as the search for cheap labour or market access, and in favour of a pragmatic approach in which one or more reasons may be relevant. MNE strategy depends on the type of industry activity involved, complementarity with existing activities, and the competitive position of the firm *vis-à-vis* other enterprises. For example, mining multinationals may be more likely to engage in resource-seeking, while firms facing high-cost technological investments in a competitive environment may seek to command strategic assets, such as new technology, in partnership with major business partners. Access to cheap labour may be important to certain manufacturing industries involved in the assembly of prefabricated parts, including automobiles or electronics, as well as in processes requiring limited skill, such as garment and shoe manufacture. Many Nike shoes for the US market, for example, are made in low-wage South-East Asian countries. Cheap labour is, on the other hand, far less relevant where greater levels of skill and education are needed, as in high-technology businesses and many aspects of financial services and consulting.

The shift from an international to a transnational form of global economy also involves qualitative changes in the strategic orientation of businesses. Instead of seeing foreign activities as simple subsidiaries or as a series of bilateral linkages to the home base, a transnational orientation encourages genuinely global strategic activity. What this means, in the case of global production, is that MNEs may choose to subdivide the production process across of a range of locations, according to pattens of cost and final market advantage, and that locational preferences may change over time as conditions change. A contemporary example is the new Ford Escort car, coded CW 170 and scheduled for 1999, jointly designed by Ford Europe and Mazda Japan, to be built in Britain, Germany, the USA, Japan, Argentina, Mexico, and Brazil, and marketed on an even wider global basis (Tuckey 1997).

The relationship of MNE activity to technological change is also a highly significant issue. On the one hand, changes in information technology in telecommunications and data-processing have tended to lower the costs of transnational activities such as the intra-firm coordination of cross-border activities. On the other hand, global competition between major worldwide corporations has intensified the struggle to remain a viable player in the market.

Contrary to perceptions of their monolithic strength, MNEs are not so powerful in relation to each other that their market position and economic viability are guaranteed. Bartlett and Ghoshal (1992), in a major study of nine MNEs, argue that 'The world's largest companies are in flux. New pressures have transformed the global competitive game... While a few players have prospered by turning the environmental turmoil to their advantage, many more are merely surviving – struggling to adjust to complex, often contradictory demands. Some large, well-established world-wide companies have been forced to take large losses or even to abandon businesses' (pp. ix, 3). Two major examples of competitive challenge and corporate crisis may be cited. The first is the case of US giant General Electric being forced to sell off its consumer electronics business under Japanese competition. The second is the abandonment by ITT, a symbol of multinational power, of its planned entry into the US switching market, followed by the sale of its European telecommunications business.

One major response by MNEs to increased inter-firm competition and the increased costs of technological change is the strategic business alliance (Dunning 1993). There are many examples of these, from the collaboration between General Motors and Toyota or Ford and Nissan in automobiles (Sasaki 1993), to the alliances between IBM and Siemens or AT&T and NEC in the semiconductor branch of information technology (Lei 1993). The massive research and development costs involved in new product innovation in these sectors have been the main driving force behind such alliances.

A good example of this is the development of the compact disc player. In technical terms, this involved linking a digital audio play-back system with an optical disc and laser pick-up (this section is based on the discussion in Shibata 1993). The research, development, and production costs involved were too great for any single MNE to entertain. Instead, the new product was developed in collaboration between Sony in Japan, who were mainly responsible for developing the digital audio-recording side, and the Dutch MNE Philips, who were responsible for the optical video disc side. In addition, both had already developed linkages with music software supply, Philips through the Polygram label, Sony through links with and the subsequent purchase of CBS records.

Changes in the organization of production and in technology are vital aspects of the global economy, yet their importance can be exaggerated in relation to parallel changes in marketing and consumption. It is sometimes assumed that MNEs are so powerful that consumers have no choice but to buy their products, or that technology is a virtually unstoppable force driven by the world economy (Holm and Sorensen 1995, p. 4), pulling all other interests, including consumers, in its wake. How far these assumptions are accurate is, however, debatable.

We have already noted that the relationship between MNEs and the market is often characterized by high levels of inter-firm competition. The dominance of key firms over markets at one point in time may not be perpetuated into the medium and long term. How then do MNEs typically orientate themselves to markets?

A transnational orientation in this area is where marketing is viewed, from the viewpoint of the firm, on a global basis. Several alternative orientations to global marketing are possible. One is that of standardization, whereby the same product with the same characteristics under the same brand name is sold in a range of different markets. This has several advantages, including economies of scale in production and the enhancement of brand loyalty through the achievement of reliability in the character of the product wherever it is purchased. Up until recently, the McDonald fast-food operation marketed hamburgers in basically this manner. The use of standardized ingredients meant that a Big Mac would look and taste the same in Los Angeles, Moscow, Sydney, or Madrid. A similar approach characterized the thinking of Coca-Cola. Kline (1995) cites the comments made in 1992 by Coca-Cola's senior Vice President and director for global marketing:

There is global media now… and there is a global teenager. The same kid you see at the Ginza in Tokyo is in Piccadilly Square, in London, in Pushkin Square, at Notre Dame. (p. 109)

Widespread perceptions that this was a general model for global marketing led to the theory that globalization means homogenization (Levitt 1983). It also led to the spectre of the McDonaldization of the world (Ritzer 1993) and to parallel concerns that globalization means Americanization (this specific issue will be picked up again in Chapter 7). Standardization remains a major element of much global marketing. Universal advertising themes delivering standardized products remain, for example, a major element in the global youth market. As Kline (1995) points out, Coca-Cola, Levi-Strauss, McDonald's, and Disney 'have become the source of endless campaigns designed to enfranchise youth in the globalizing democracy of the market' (p. 110). A typical example of this is the recent global slogan 'Be Young, Have Fun, Drink Pepsi'. At the same time, many MNEs have come to realize that consumers are not entirely standard, and that tastes and demands vary across nations, cultures, regions, and localities. This realization has often arisen in part as a result of consumer resistance to standardized products and marketing campaigns (Bartlett and Ghoshal 1992). For example, the original Barbie doll, developed as an American television toy and then marketed globally, sold less well in Europe, especially Britain. The existence of transnational variations of this kind led the toy manufacturer Mattel to develop product and marketing changes, including a UNICEF Barbie doll (Kline 1995, pp. 124–5). Such shifts may reflect consumer resistance to a particular product, but they are not in and of themselves evidence of effective resistance to consumerism itself. All that the MNE may need to do in such situations is modify the product.

Consumer resistance can, however, prove more intractable. This was the case in Japan in the 1950s and 60s. At this time, US manufacturers of breakfast cereals and other foodstuffs, such as Kellogg's and General Foods, found it hard to persuade the Japanese to abandon their traditional breakfast of rice, fish, and seaweed, as well as other dietary practices. Nonetheless, by the close of the 1970s, and largely under the impact of MNE advertising, the situation was changing, teenagers adopting fast- and frozen food preferences and rice gradually being replaced by bread. Even so, such developments have not led to the final abandonment of traditional diets in Japan and other parts of East and South-East Asia in favour of homogenized Western taste. Multinationals exporting processed food out of Australia, for example, have found the assumption that markets would accept ever-increasing volumes of 'Western food' to be unfounded. Rather, consumers want a choice from a range of Western *and* Asian products. Meanwhile, Asian foods have, over the past few decades, significantly penetrated Western markets, increasing the complexity and segmentation of markets already thought to be under multinational corporate domination.

Standardization continues to have many attractions for consumers, especially when associated with powerful brand images of consistency, reliability, and competitiveness in process and design. Yet it clearly has its limits too. Global producers have not succeded in creating standardized global consumers whose tastes and behaviour may be manipulated at will. Variations in consumer behaviour affecting the acceptability or otherwise of particular goods and services may depend on a range of cultural factors as well as differential incomes. An example of this is the requirement that McDonald's operations in Israel abandon the company's standardization routines in favour of a Kosher system that recognizes Jewish religious practices. Research indicates that the expectation of increased standardization in marketing has not taken place in any straightforward way. Cultural resistance and variations in consumer taste have led to significant elements of localization and regionalization (Boddewyn *et al.* 1986; Tai 1997). The emergence of niche and micro-marketing within the operations of MNEs is encapsulated in the term 'glocalization'.

This process has been enabled by an increasing use of information technology that permits constant feedback about variations in consumer behaviour to corporate producers. A highly significant example of this is the Benetton clothing company's use of information systems across the range of countries in which they sell goods to analyse weekly variations in retail sales patterns in different markets. Rather than insist on standardization in apparel market profiles according to style, colour, and volume per head, information technology allows market variations to be fed back into the production and design process in determining production mixes, the size of product runs, and distribution patterns. The overall effect is to create a greater global flexibility in matching supply to highly complex patterns of demand. Knowledge and information are thereby at an increasing premium.

The need for flexibility in production and marketing strategies is thus an increasingly significant characteristic of the highly competitive global environment in which MNEs now find themselves. Producers can no longer expect to remain indefinitely in the same industry or the same market sector. This reflects not simply uncertainties arising from the complexity of consumer behaviour in different cultures and across time, but also the increasing penetration of every market by other producers. Within this context, the development of flexible specialization has been seen by theorists of capitalist development as some kind of sea-change in the nature of economic life. For Piore and Sable (1984), the shift represents a move beyond the large-scale standardized production strategies associated with Henry Ford (labelled Fordism), to post-Fordist flexible specialization based on computer-assisted design, production, and marketing in shorter production runs, often met through subcontracted production carried out by small producers. Outsourcing of specialized services in areas such as information technology or human resources may also be seen as a further example of corporate decentralization. For Lash and Urry (1987), this shift in seen in terms similar to one from organized to disorganized capitalism. The latter term is meant not as a synonym for chaos but as a way of referring to the growth of decentralized or decentred patterns of economic activity. While organized capitalism was characteristically centred on the large-scale industrial giants of the leading Western nations in sectors such as iron, steel, and automobiles, disorganized capitalism is more economically and spatially mobile.

We have emphasized both the power of MNEs and some limits to this power. Such limits apply both to the capacity of MNEs to sustain a competitive advantage *vis-à-vis* each other and in relation to their relationship with consumers within the market. While significant asymmetries of power are evident between producers and consumers, standardized marketing strategies do not always work, sometimes failing. In this sense, economic globalization promoted by MNEs is not always an all-powerful juggernaut, nor is it necessarily a harbinger of the McDonaldization of the world.

It would be foolish to exaggerate the power of MNEs but equally shortsighted to underestimate it. Their centrality within the global economy is evident in the scale of their operations, measured both by the value of their operations and in terms of their geographical scope. It is also evident in their command over many new technologies. This should not simply be seen as power over innovatory wealth-generating assets. To do so would underestimate the integral part played by MNEs in a range of activities, including research and development, technology transfer through licensing, the setting of industry standards for goods and services, and control over many aspects of the development and delivery of information through advertising and through private ownership of the mass media. In so doing, multinational enterprise has become a major political and cultural force, as well as an economic one.

The wider institutionalization of the global economy

MNEs are crucial players in the global economy. The disproportionate emphasis usually given to their dominant role does, however, create the impression that the global economy is more tightly organized through free-standing corporations than is really the case. In the next section of this chapter, we shall explore a number of ways in which this picture is misleading.

Four general considerations may be listed at the outset, which, taken together, suggest a rather different account of the organizational shape of the global economy. First, as we have already indicated, MNEs have become increasingly involved in inter-firm collaborations or strategic business alliances. In the process, the principles of vertical hierarchy through which corporations are organized have become less important than the networks or chains through which inter-firm relationships take place. Second, other more informal types of global business network have arisen, dependent on personalized ties of family and ethnicity rather than formal corporate bureaucracy. Third, the global economy contains a significant anarchocapitalist sector connected in large measure with organized crime. Fourth, the global mobility of labour is largely dominated by informal micro-level decisions by individuals, families, and kinship groups. The net effect of these four characteristics is to suggest a model of the global economy based less on organization than on networks.

Organizations and networks

An important shift has recently taken place in some recent accounts of the global economy, from a primary concern with processes of economic development (for example, world-system theory), to a broader concern with questions concerning the organizational and normative shape of global economic life. In the latter perspective, the concern is less with the historical emergence and dynamics of global capitalism and more with more fine-grained accounts of how particular global markets and organizations actually function. One feature of this organizational perspective is a growing emphasis on the importance of personalized networks of co-operation, exchange, and trust in the successful constitution of global economic activity.

From this perspective, multinational enterprises remain central players in the global economy, although increasingly as part of co-operative 'alliances' or 'chains' that link firms together rather than as free-standing hierarchies operating separately in competition with each other. One striking example of this perspective is the idea of global commodity chains (Gereffi and Korzeniewicz 1994; Gereffi 1996). Such chains link together sets of firms such that no individual corporation has unilateral control over the chain. Co-operation between automobile companies whereby producers share technological and organizational competencies is one such example.

Recent research emphasizes the emergence, alongside this kind of producer-driven chain, of chains that are buyer driven, in the sense of being dominated by retail chains such as Wal-Mart or Target. This has occurred in sectors such as clothing, toys, shoes, and various electronic goods (Gereffi 1994). Buyers (or retail capitalists) drive production, which is often organized through complex subcontracting arrangements with producers.

Complex inter-firm chains may involve large producers, subcontractors, wholesalers, and retailers, as well as banking and other financial service providers. Some of the largest chains of this kind occur within Japanese business networks such as those centred on the Mitsubishi or Mitsui groups (Gerlach 1992). The net effect is to create great flexibility in flows of resources and information, which gives considerable advantage in competitive global markets.

Such commodity chains do not, of course, supplant the MNE as a key player in the global economy. In this sense, they contrast with a second type of global economic network, dependent on personalized ties of family and ethnicity, namely the global business diaspora. Ties of this kind have considerable significance where business conditions are uncertain and unpredictable, such that MNEs decide it is too risky to get involved. This may arise as a result of political instability, chronic social unrest and dislocation, or an absence of secure property rights. Problems of this kind have sometimes been overcome, as in parts of Latin America, by alliances with authoritarian social and political interests, including the military. This option has been far harder to achieve elsewhere, as in many parts of the former Soviet Union, where organized crime has stepped in. In other cases, such as contemporary China, invitations to invest on the part of an authoritarian government, which lacks the capacity to co-ordinate and deliver a stable set of administrative rules, has also in the past deterred many MNEs.

Lever-Tracy *et al.* (1996) point out that the spectacular growth of the Chinese economy in the past decade has undoubtedly depended on foreign investment, but that only one-fifth of this derives from American, Japanese, or European sources. A far greater role has been played by Chinese diaspora capitalists from Hong Kong and other parts of East and South-East Asia, including Taiwan, Singapore, Malaysia, Indonesia, and Thailand. These typically operate on a personalized basis through family and friendship networks rather than through the formal bureaucratic structures of MNEs. Personalized networks generate trust, which is at a premium where property rights are insecure and reliable formal legal arrangements for commerce largely non-existent. However, the scope for global economic networks involving diaspora groups of common ethnic ancestry operating across national boundaries is not simply a product of uncertainty. It also draws, according to Lever-Tracy *et al.* (1996, pp. 6–7), on developments in technology and consumer demand. Innovations in microelectronics, for example, have cheapened costs of production in manufacturing, lowering the costs of entry for new producers, while also undermining economies of scale. Similarly, consumer demand, as we have seen above, has become more diverse, leading to the expansion of specialized markets in which local knowledge and contacts may be as important as global corporate strength.

For Kotkin (1993), diaspora groups such as the Chinese, Jews, and Indians have come to represent *global tribes*, combining geographical dispersal with cultural networks and economic adaptiveness to new and changing conditions. These characteristics will allow them to outflank nation-states. Lever-Tracy *et al.* dispute this general proposition about diasporas. Yet they insist on the importance of global business networks under the conditions specified above as a major feature of the global economy, particularly relevant to the integration of East and South-East Asia into the global economy.

Another informal component of the global economy involves what might be termed anarchocapitalism, that is, activity expressly based on the evasion of formal visible structure of business organization and legal regulation. Based around illegal or clandestine activities such as drugs, armaments supply, and criminal extortion, this type of activity clearly depends on global networks of an informal kind able to evade legal and business regulation (Freemantle 1986; McDonald 1988). At the same time, it may have an interface with the formal legal side of economic activity through money-laundering and unofficial deals with nation-states (Mills 1986), including activities such as arms procurement.

The scale of global anarchocapitalism is not easy to quantify, but it cannot therefore be dismissed as marginal. Rather, its impact is concentrated in particular nations and cities. In the late 1980s, for example, it was calculated that cocaine exports represented 10–20 per cent of

Columbia's legal exports, 25–30 per cent of Peru's, and 50–100 per cent of Bolivia's (Lee 1989, p. 60). Meanwhile, a US Congress source estimated that the Medellin syndicates at that time themselves held $10 billion worth of fixed and liquid assets in North America, Europe, and Asia (Lee 1989, p. 61). For the late 1980s period, this scale of assets is dwarfed only by the world's largest 50 banks and top 30 insurance companies, and the biggest manufacturing and mining MNEs (see the discussion of UN data in Sklair 1991, pp. 48–9). Many of the world's smaller nations had a gross domestic product smaller than $10 billion (Sklair, p. 48). Global cities that play a significant part in the unofficial global economy include Miami, New York, and Hong Kong. It has been calculated that the US retail market for drugs towards the end of the 1980s alone totalled around $100 billion (Craig 1989, p. 27).

While not marginal, the limited scale and uneven incidence of anarchocapitalism suggests neither that it is the dominant mode of economic globalization nor that there is a clear trend toward greater rather than lesser levels of global economic anarchy. Anarchocapitalism is not, however, to be confused with disorganized capitalism (Lash and Urry 1987). This influential but somewhat confusing metaphor is not meant to suggest a shift into anarchic disorder and an absence of structure. Rather, it is concerned with moves away from nationally centred organizational forms, such as the regulation of national product markets by national companies or the regulation of national labour markets by national-level collective bargaining. Disorganized capitalism thus means greater autonomy of MNEs from national organizational arrangements and hence greater global flexibility.

For the most part, then, global capital does not operate in an anarchic manner, but neither is it wholly contained within free-standing centralized corporations, centred upon one particular nation-state. Formal organizational structures such as the MNE remain important, but equally significant are the more fluid global networks that link firms with each other. Such linkages are, moreover, increasingly constituted electronically as much as through direct physical contact.

Moving beyond networks of capital, it is important to emphasize that the global economy also depends, to a significant extent, on the mobility of labour. It is true that capital has been more mobile across national boundaries in seeking markets, raw materials, and suitable types of employees, than labour has been in seeking employment. It is nonetheless evident that international migrant workers play a considerable part in key sectors of the post-war global economy, in meeting local labour and skill shortages, and in stimulating economic growth. In the USA, for example, the foreign born constituted 7 per cent of the workforce in 1989 but accounted for over 20 per cent of the growth in the US workforce during the 1980s (cited in Castles and Miller 1993, p. 171). Global migrants have been disproportionately concentrated in sectors such as automobiles, building, and clothing production. They are thus not always clustered in sectors that are directly linked with the operation of multinational companies. Undoubtedly, many of the manufacturing workers in multinational car plants around the world are global migrants, such as Turkish 'guest workers' who work for Ford in Germany, or Italian- or Greek-Australians employed by Ford in Australia. Less visible perhaps is migration between developing countries, for example that between Asian countries such as Pakistan and the Philippines to the oil-rich Gulf states, and involving manual and service employment, with little direct MNE involvement.

As with diaspora capitalism, much labour migration does not operate spontaneously but takes place within networks. Chain migration, for example, within family, extended kinship, or close-knit, village-based groups plays an important role in maximizing information about opportunities elsewhere while minimizing the disruption costs to those who eventually emigrate. This cost-minimization consideration has even been built into the immigration intake regulations of countries such as Australia through family reunion schemes. These are built on the assumption that the family rather than the receiving government will bear the bulk of the financial and social costs associated with international migration. Chain migration of this kind assists economic migrants in seeking out employment within a global economy characterized by mobility of capital and consequent shifts in the location of employment. In addition, such networks may tie into the business of ethnic diaspora, by providing new injections of kin-based labour. Alternatively, migration may be more short term and contract bound in nature but again dependent on networks organized directly by potential employers or through intermediaries. Women are particularly vulnerable to physical and sexual exploitation in such arrangements where they become attached to private families, as in the domestic service sector within the Gulf states.

In all of this, the highly visible presence of nation-states in formulating immigration intake targets and policing illegal migration represents only the formal part of the more complex multicentred process of global labour migration. Economic networks, both legal and clandestine, are evident here, as with global capital movement. Processes of economic globalization cannot thus be understood simply by reference to the more formal organization side of corporate and governmental decision-making.

Institutional regulation of the global economy

It is commonplace to regard economic activity as fundamentally driven by economic interests, through relationships between economic institutions such as markets, businesses, and labour-supply networks, within which such resources as land, capital, entrepreneurship, technology, knowledge, skill, and labour power are deployed. Within this conventional approach, governments and cultures are typically seen as *responding* to economic and technological change rather than playing a significant role in driving or shaping processes of change.

While the 'economic primacy' model is widely held, it has itself been challenged by political science, economic sociology, and international relations. A major difficulty with it is the presumption that economies are somehow self-constituting and self-reliant, such that economic activity happens first, as it were, leaving states or governments to intervene subsequently should problems arise that markets appear unable to resolve. This presumption is not altogether unreasonable, since it is a characteristic of market economies to operate with a higher degree of differentiation between economy and society than, for example, the command economies of former State Socialist societies such as the USSR or of economies centred on local self-sufficiency (Granovetter 1985). This kind of differentiation does not, however, dispose of the objection that governments and cultures enter into the constitution, reproduction, and regulation of economic life (Polanyi 1957; Holton 1992).

In the case of public bodies, embracing government and non-governmental organizations, this may occur through securing stable and secure property rights for private interests and through the construction of frameworks of rules and procedures that minimize crisis or economic dislocation and maximize orderly expansion. They may also involve infrastructural investments, including human and physical capital commitments, that are neither profitable nor appropriate for private interests to undertake. Such public initiatives need not depend on direct state investment and planning but on strategies that are designed to provide incentives for private capital rather than standing in its place. Consequently, when we talk of the regulation of economic activity, this refers to a broad set of activities, including some that are often designated deregulation in political discourse. Free trade, for example, requires deregulation in matters such as the ending of tariff barriers, but forms of regulation are still evident in the sets of rules and rights that the various parties to regulatory arrangements establish to institutionalize stable regimes for trade in general and certain types of trade in particular, such as agricultural products or information technology. From this perspective, any account of the global economy must necessarily include the broader regulatory frameworks within which the activities of MNEs and other economic networks take place. Put another way, regulatory institutions are a constitutive part of the global economy rather than external constraints.

The construction of a global regulatory framework over the past 50 years began with the Bretton Woods system (Table 3.1). This involved the IMF, the World Bank, and the General Agreement on Tariffs and Trade (GATT). Another major body of particular significance for Western economies is the Organization for Economic Cooperation and Development (OECD). Beyond this, there are the UN organizations whose operations impact on economic activities, such as the International Labour Organization (ILO) and the Food and Agricultural Organization (FAO). Finally, and possibly even more significantly, regional forms of transnational governance have been significantly extended, notably through the establishment and expanded functions of the European Union (EU).

Table 3.1   The Bretton Woods system

Aim	Institution	Programme
Stable exchange rates and orderly adjustment of balance of payments problems	IMF	Financial support packages conditional on national economic adjustment (for example cuts in public spending)
Economic development	World Bank	Provision of loan capital for public projects, conditional on an approved public framework
Expansion of world trade	GATT	Negotiation of tariff reductions
Full employment	National governments	Demand management based on fiscal policy

Source: This schematization draws very heavily on the work of Vines (1996).

The Bretton Woods system has been of particular significance for the post-war regulation of global economic activity. In the period between 1929 and 1945, the world had been afflicted by the Great Depression, economic nationalism, Stalinism, Fascism, and then the Second World War. As the war came to a close, initiatives were begun again to restabilize both world politics, through the UN (successor to the ill-fated League of Nations), and the world-economy. The institutional framework that emerged from the Bretton Woods Conference of 1944 may be seen as an amalgam of international and national modes of regulation. Nonetheless, the various aims listed in Table 3.1 are clearly interdependent, in the sense that national measures to achieve full employment are not independent of the regulatory system surrounding balance of payments patterns, the availability of development capital, and the conduct of world trade. The impact of this system has clearly varied, according to the capacity of particular national interests to influence regulatory objectives as well as to operate without reliance on IMF or World Bank support. The more powerful economies, such as the USA, have had a disproportionate influence on the operation of global regulatory bodies, although others, like Japan, have spent less time influencing the regulatory framework on the basis of outcompeting economic rivals whatever the rules of the regulatory game may be. The capacity to opt out of the regulatory framework proved possible in the medium term for the command economies of the former USSR, but the collapse of Communism has led to growing involvement, notably of the IMF, in this domain. Meanwhile, those most vulnerable to the operation of a regulatory framework have been those emergent developing nations with little formal power within the deliberations of bodies such as the IMF and lacking economic stability and development capital. We shall pursue such inequalities in the functioning of the regulatory system below.

The original Bretton Woods system lasted, in a strict sense, until the 1970s. In the preceding 25 years, it undoubtedly contributed to the restabilization of the global economy in general and to the dominance of a market-orientated global capitalist economy in particular. Neither worldwide economic nationalism nor world depression returned, initial capital shortages were largely overcome, and world trade and global investment rapidly increased. This apparently 'golden age' of the post-war boom received its first shocks in the 1970s with the breakdown of the fixed exchange rate system – usually regarded as the 'collapse of Bretton Woods' – and the 'oil price crisis' of 1973. In one sense, however, this breakdown occurred, as Vines (1996) points out, because of the previous success of the Bretton Woods framework in underpinning global economic expansion. One of the fundamental mechanisms of breakdown was the globalization of international capital flows that far exceeded the value of World Bank development capital. Transnational capital markets were, in large measure, incompatible with the Bretton Woods emphasis on fixed exchange rates and the sparing use of devaluation to correct national balance of payments crises. The combination of fixed exchange rates and national monetary policy levers to fine-tune interest rates and prevent capital outflows proved ineffective in a world of mobile capital and increased economic flexibility. Greater levels of fluctuation in exchange rates are thus a concomitant of the globalization of capital.

The post-Bretton Woods regulatory framework still embraces matters such as exchange rate relationships and financial crisis resolution, development capital, and trade liberalization, but this now occurs in a looser structure. Meeting the aim of orderly expansion of the global economy has shifted away from bodies like the IMF and towards the G7 intergovernmental summit of the world's seven leading national economies. This body operates in an *ad hoc* way to try to secure the international co-ordination of fiscal and monetary policies. Animating this body and the broader operation of global economic regulation is a kind of trilateralism between the USA, the major European nations, and Japan.

Within this framework, a disproportional part is played by the more powerful nations in general, particularly the USA. From the outset, the wartime discussions that led to the formation of the IMF, World Bank, and GATT were essentially between the USA, as the new aspiring leader of the world's international economic order, and the UK, as the outgoing leader whose 19th-century dominance had already been significantly eroded after 1914. Such institutions were planned and subsequently located in the USA (Mitchell 1992). Managerial arrangements currently in place mean that the Fund has a European Director, while the USA appoints the Head of the Bank.

Underlying trilateralism, nevertheless, is the relative economic decline of the US in relation to Japan and also the enhanced European capacity to act as a regional bloc via European economic integration. The end of US hegemony means that the USA must now negotiate with others; it can no longer dominate global economic institutions. This trilateral institutionalization applies not only to GATT, but also to other areas, such as international standard-setting.

Trilateralism, however, also means that governments and other organizations based outside the dominant triad are placed in a far more vulnerable position in relation to the institutional regulation of the international economy. Decisions, as in the recent resolution of the Uruguay round of GATT, are essentially the product of trilateral negotiation by the big players. Another example in the area of pharmaceutical standards, cited by Braithwaite (1995, p. 123), is the abandonment of the World Health Organisation (WHO) as a standard-setting agency by the three big players and their establishment of a rival forum – the International Commission on Harmonisation (ICH). Within this G7-trilateral framework, the 'Bretton Woods' organizations persist, but with changing roles. Of increasing importance is the trade liberalization programme, extended with the transformation of GATT into the World Trade Organisation (WTO). The aim here is to extend the 44 per cent of world trade currently zero tariff rated while simultaneously addressing non-tariff barriers to international trade, such as national process standards, which regulate how goods are produced. Since the mid-1970s, meanwhile, the major thrust of both the IMF and the World Bank has been directed toward the developing nations.

Both the Bretton Woods and post-Bretton Woods regulatory frameworks have come under consistent criticism for their bias towards Western interests and towards liberal market-orientated economic policies. The conditionality of IMF and World Bank support for developing countries has been seen as both economically destabilising and quasi-colonialist in its overriding of national political priorities. The conditions attached to such support have varied between the IMF and World Bank, and also over time within the development of each institution (Mosley *et al.* 1991). In most cases of programme aid, conditionality has required changes in the recipient country's public policies. Areas affected have included levels of public spending, including public employment and social welfare provision, fiscal policy such as taxation levels, industry policy incorporating privatization measures, tariff policy, and pricing levels for local producer support schemes. Devaluation of currencies has also been regularly proposed. In addition, the IMF has required debtor governments to develop export revenue through an open-door policy of attracting foreign investment and the abandonment of protectionist and regulatory controls. These problems of conditionality have persisted into the 1970s and 80s, even though the IMF modified part of its operation to include 'low-conditionality' loans. The World Bank's new 'structural adjustment' programmes of the 1980s have meanwhile come in for particular criticism.

Brett (1985, pp. 221–6), among others, argues that conditionality has had especially onerous effects on the less developed countries. Meeting IMF conditions has provoked domestic political conflict and undermined social cohesion. Several instances from the mid-1980s may be cited as examples. In 1986, antigovernment demonstrations in Zambia against IMF conditions, notably cuts to food subsidies, led to riots and the deaths of 15 people. The following year, the President of Zambia accused the IMF of blackmail in the stringent conditions put on African countries seeking loans (Jackson 1990, p. 127). In 1989 around 300 people were killed in riots in Venezuela after the implementation of an IMF austerity programme, prompting similar complaints by the Venezuelan President against both the IMF and the Western governments who stood to gain most immediately from its market-orientated policies (Jackson 1990). Meeting IMF conditions also undermines the efforts of countries that wish to attempt redistributive social policies involving state intervention. Countries such as Tanzania and Jamaica argued in the early 1980s that IMF-induced wage and public spending cuts favoured the rich rather than the poor. In effect, IMF intervention ceases to be neutral economic assistance and has a direct political effect. While the IMF refused support to the Allende government in Chile, it generously supported its military successor in the economic crisis of 1983 (Anglade and Fortin 1990).

Leftwich (1993) notes that the World Bank has sometimes declined to lend on political grounds, as in Chile, Nicaragua, and Cuba. Yet he concedes that loans have been made to both democratic and authoritarian governments, both civil and military, implying that political considerations are not necessarily paramount. The World Bank has also explicitly widened the basis of conditionality beyond economic development aims in recent years, to include issues such as human rights.

Set against interpretations of IMF–World Bank activity as quasi-colonialist intervention is evidence that the power of regulatory institutions is not unilateral and that recipient countries cannot be regarded as passive victims. In their recent study of World Bank lending in the 1980s, for example, Mosley *et al.* (1991) claim that the initial terms of conditionality are often relaxed or not strictly enforced. In contrast with more draconian terms surrounding IMF standby finance, Bank conditionality is more loosely administered, and the time-frame for compliance is of necessity longer. In the early 1980s, for example, a number of countries, such as Kenya, Ecuador, and the Philippines, were highly remiss in complying with conditions yet had no difficulty in negotiating follow-up support (Morley *et al.* 1991, p. 67). The argument, then, is that 'structural adjustment' conditionality should be regarded as a bargaining process, even if it is one that takes place under unequal conditions.

Regulation and power within the global economy

How then is the relationship between regulation and power within the global economy to be understood? The first general point to be made is that this relationship is complex rather than being a simple case of unilateral US or Western domination. Bargaining between parties is evident within regulatory arrangements, suggesting a model of what might be called imperfect multilateralism rather than unilateral domination. Pieterse (1995) makes a similar point in distinguishing between imperialism and globalization. Yet for all this, regulation still tends to be in the interests of the powerful.

A second related consideration is that the agenda of regulation has not been wholly dominated by liberal capitalist objectives over the entire post-war period, even though economic liberalism is the single most important element in the framework. Additional concerns for social justice, environmental regulation, and human rights have, by the 1990s, become significant, although their impact is greater in certain regulatory bodies, such as the World Bank, than others.

These two propositions may be pursued through two examples, the first concerning the regulatory framework surrounding property rights, more especially intellectual property rights. The recent Trade-Related Intellectual Property Rights (TRIPS) agreement contained in the recent resolution of the Uruguay round of GATT is particularly instructive in this respect. This agreement, mandatory on all GATT signatories, requires governments to take a greater role in enforcing existing rights, mostly held as patents by MNEs, and allowing new rights (the following analysis being based on Drahos 1995). Many patents will be valid for longer than before, while certain new areas, such as plant variety protection, will now be subject to property rights, a matter of particular concern to underdeveloped and developing countries. The net effect is to increase the price of information, a major problem for most countries outside the USA who are net importers of information.

Not surprisingly, the USA was the major advocate of TRIPS. This emerged as a result of at least two developments. The first was the concern of MNEs such as Microsoft, Pfizer, and IBM, over the pirating of their products, thereby lowering profits through the evasion of property rights. The second pressure, largely exerted by politicians, was the fear that the USA was losing its competitiveness and power in the global system. The net effect was the successful deployment of US power simultaneously to skew market rules in favour of multinationals and to regain some political bargaining power for the USA as a nation-state.

This example is a telling one, not least because of the growing importance of intellectual property in the science- and knowledge-based industries in the global economy. Yet it is not the whole story. Even in the seemingly unambiguous case of the GATT, Braithwaite (1995, p. 121) argues that adherence to TRIPS among the agricultural producing nations of the Cairns group was dependent on the USA agreeing to sanction the liberalization of agricultural trade. The picture is thus not completely one of unilateral domination, nor was the TRIPS outcome entirely preordained. The disproportionate influence of the powerful is nonetheless clear.

A second example of regulation in the interests of the powerful concerns the regulation of the global monetary and trading environment. This seems to have been skewed towards the welfare of powerful economic interests rather than being aimed at achieving social justice or protection of the interests of the poor and defenceless. Multinational business, for example, is generally successful in pressing for trade to be regulated in such a way as to open up markets to penetration, but it has been far more difficult for underdeveloped countries to have regulatory arrangements put in place that protect them from the dumping of dangerous pharmaceuticals. The UN has established a Commission on Transnationals and stimulated much of the basic information on their operations, data it has not been in the interests or capacity of any single nation to provide. Nevertheless, attempts over the past two decades to institute a Code of Conduct for Transnationals or UN Guidelines on Global Business have failed (Sylvan 1995). Similarly, while the WTO supports free trade in commodities, which is of particular benefit to those able to export products and services, it has generally opposed the free movement of labour, which might be of far more benefit to many developing countries. All this is not, of course, to deny that there are powerful groups in developing countries (the most spectacular example being OPEC), as well as groups with little power, such as the poor, unskilled, and many elderly, in developed countries, some of whom are migrants from developing countries.

One major problem affecting most global regulatory bodies is the lack of effective representation for the interests of the countries of the developing world. One manifestation of this is the broad commitment of all such bodies to policies of market-led economic growth, referred to by some commentators as a kind of embedded liberalism within the global regulatory framework. While such growth-focused development policies are often said to be best for the long-term interests of developing nations, this rationale fails to come to grips with the point that such nations, in the aftermath of decolonization, 'want power and control as much as wealth' (Krasner 1985, p. 3). This aim is difficult to reconcile with the interventionist market-orientated policies of the Bretton Woods institutions. Political redress has, however, been difficult to realize in such institutions, inasmuch as these bodies are not based on a one-nation-one-vote basis but have constitutions skewed to overrepresentation of Western interests, which historically set them up and financed them. Accordingly, developing countries have looked elsewhere, mainly to the UN General Assembly and associated UN agencies, to promote change. One example of this was the foundation of the UN Conference on Trade and Development (UNCTAD) as a counter-weight to the market-orientated policies of GATT. At the first meeting of UNCTAD, the so-called Group of 77, representing 77 developing nations, was established to co-ordinate the Third World push for change in such areas as Third World debt relief for the poorest nations. This led, in turn, by the early 1970s, to a greater awareness of North–South conflicts over the direction of the global economy, and the development of a new global economic agenda around the idea of a New International Economic Order (NIEO).

By the late 1970s, critics of the economic institutions of the global system identified a number of areas of weakness. Many of these centred on the multiple problems of lack of economic development, increased indebtedness, and lack of social justice in the countries referred to as the Third World. Continuing poverty and increasing inequalities between rich and poor were cited as the main symptoms of the failure of global regulatory institutions to secure world· development. Another growing dimension of the problem was the Third World debt crisis. This involved the incapacity of Third World countries to service the debt burden of loans previously contracted with rich countries, many of them via private bank loans from giant multinational banks.

From a social justice perspective, the major problem was seen by many as the increasing inequality between the northern and southern hemispheres. This was dramatized in 1980 with the release of the so-called Brandt Report, *North-South: A Programme for Survival,* prepared by the Independent Commission on International Development Issues. Here the 'North' symbolizes the developed world of the USA, Europe and Japan (together with Australia and New Zealand, the 'two rich industrialized countries south of the equator'), while the 'South' (including China) symbolizes poverty, hunger, and underdevelopment (Brandt 1980, p. 31). On this definition, the 'North' (*c.* 1980) had a quarter of the world's population and four-fifths of its income, while the South contained three-quarters of the world's population living off only one-fifth of its income (Brandt 1980, p. 32).

The problems of global indebtedness, underdevelopment, and widening economic inequality represent major challenges to the Bretton Woods system of global economic institutional regulation. However, they do not mean that the North–South divide is absolute, nor that the Bretton Woods institutions remain unreconstructed and immune to productive reform. The starkness of the North–South divide, as pictured by the Brandt Commission, is telling in its dramatization of the size of the gap between rich and poor. Nonetheless, the fate of particular nations within the global economy is far from being separable into one of two contrasting outcomes. The differentiation of economic performance within the 'Southern group', referred to above, has become more rather than less noticeable in the 18 years since Brandt.

While global inequality remains firmly on the agenda as an unresolved issue for global economic regulators, it is arguable that the current problems facing the global economy are even wider than those identified by Brandt. They are also very different in the late 1990s from what they were 50 years earlier. The spectres haunting Bretton Woods were a revival of protectionism, exchange rate instability, and the return of serious economic depression. The potency of the fears was based very largely on looking back to the failures of the inter-war period, which caused, in the short term at least, a retreat from economic globalization.

By the late 1990s, in contrast, many of the salient issues and underlying conditions changed. Part of the change is clearly about distributive issues arising from inequality and the capacity of poor post-colonial countries to influence the political agenda of UN forums and agencies, but beyond that, the fears of deep-seated depression and imminent tariff wars have been replaced by other issues. In the trade area, for example, as Vines (1995) points out, the concern is with standards and rules rather than tariffs. These include matters of property rights and the need for more ethical behaviour of businesses, as well as technical production standards. The regulation of multinational companies, whether in the developed or the underdeveloped countries, is also now on the agenda, involving concerns about global flows of investment and information. A final overarching issue, foreshadowed in Brandt but again of worldwide significance, is the issue of global environmental protection. This involves conflicts between 'green' values and 'green' production standards on the one hand, and the liberal agenda of free trade and private property rights on the other.

One reason for scepticism about the general applicability of the uni-lateral, power-centred model of the global regulatory system is that multiple actors are now involved. These include not only national governments with a variety of interests, MNEs and transnational regu-latory bodies themselves, but also NGOs, such as Consumers Inter-national or Greenpeace International, and scientific bodies. This multi-actor system is very far from being a pluralist democracy composed of interests with roughly equal power. The governments of rich countries and large multinationals clearly have organizational and legal resources superior to those protesting issues such as global poll-ution or lax food standards. The politics of economic regulation is nonetheless subject to complex processes of contestation and negot-iation rather than unilateral dominance. Above all, no single interest is sufficiently powerful to dominate the regulatory agenda.

While it is hard to generalize across all areas of regulation, this picture of complex contestation within a multilateral system is supported by some suggestive evidence. Braithwaite (1993) cites the case of the regulation of the international pharmaceutical industry. At first sight, this would appear a most inauspicious example of multilater-alism given the poor post-war record of the industry in terms of corpo-rate crime and law violation, Braithwaite argues that significant regulatory inroads have been made into its activities. These have not emanated from any single source, be it transnational regulation, national controls, professional criticism, self-regulation, or consumer activism. Rather, they have emerged through combinations of these elements.

UN agencies connected with the WHO have, for example, had some success in achieving harmonization of good manufacturing and marketing practices across countries, in conjunction with regional regu-lation in the EU and Central America, and with the involvement of international and national NGOs in securing legislative reform and the monitoring of corporate practice. Meanwhile, corporate and profes-sional self-regulation in firms such as Ciba-Geigy is, according to Braithwaite, not insignificant in such areas as business ethics and more effective quality control and legislative compliance mechanisms. He also goes on to make the point that self-regulation is cheaper and often more effective than inappropriate forms of state control. The implica-tions of this case for the study of global economic regulation are that the process can act as 'a web of controls' flowing from the actions of a range of transnational, national and community-based actors rather than a unilateral system of capitalist dominance. Each element in the web, acting by itself, is weak but, when operating together, the effect is more powerful. We shall return to the web model in a later chapter dealing with the general shape of global politics.

Regulatory bodies within the global economy and the nation-state

One of the key issues in the functioning of global regulatory arrangements is the role of nation-states in general and in particular the influence of the powerful nation-states. The underlying question raised here is how far global regulation is simply an international or intergovernmental matter, and how far there exists a more genuinely transnational regulatory framework that is not simply a form of interstate co-operation. Three basic points are pertinent here.

The first is that nation-states have been major players in the foundation and continued funding of the regulatory bodies discussed above. As with the UN itself, participation in the IMF or WTO is through nationally based representation. Those nations which provide disproportionate funding of these organizations exert disproportionate influence on their objectives and functioning.

The second point is that the many such bodies function as something more than simple intergovernmental organizations. Formal moves beyond intergovernmentalism occur wherever significant regulatory power has been devolved from national governments to transnational regulatory bodies. Autonomy, be it formal or informal, is exercised through directorates, secretariats, and technical committees. Vines (1996) reports that the World Bank now employs 6000 staff and the IMF 2000. Beyond this are networks of consultants, advisers and lobbyists for NGOs. Autonomy involves not simply the negotiation, management, and policing of intergovernmentally sanctioned rules or programmes, but also sustained analysis of the global economy and of national economies, and the feedback of research into global intervention.

More striking evidence of transnational moves beyond intergovernmental economic regulation has emerged within the recent evolution of the EU. This finding arises as a result of two processes. First, as Schmitter (1996) points out, there has been a marked expansion in EU authority across a range of economic policy areas in the past three decades. Most policy decisions are now taken at the EU level in matters such as international commercial policy, policies on foreign exchange relations, agriculture, capital and labour flows, and movements of goods and services within the EU. There are significant areas, such as transport and communications, in which national authority remains significant, but the trend is towards the enhancement and expansion of the EU's role.

Second, the nature of EU authority, while derived from the formal adherence of nations to major rule-making and substantive decisions, contains significant and growing elements of legal, executive, and judicial authority as nations devolve executive and judicial functions to EU institutions. While intergovernmentalism remains crucial to the EU's work, it is also the case that 'the member states of the European Union are no longer the sole centres of power within their own borders' (Held 1995, p. 112).

The EU example, then, offers an even stronger example of transnational regulatory economic arrangements moving beyond intergovernmentalism than the global organizations discussed above. This in turn raises issues about both the future of the nation-state and the future shape of the global political economy. First, are the regulatory economic functions of the nation-state being progressively devolved to regional or global state-like structures? Second, does the combination of powerful private as well as public transnational regulatory bodies, of MNEs as well as the World Bank, IMF, and EU, mean the end of national economic sovereignty? These questions will be pursued in the next two chapters.

4

Is the Nation-State Finished?
The Challenge of
Globalization

It is sometimes said that the nation-state is fast becoming out-moded by economic globalization. The global economy is characterized by massive flows of money and capital across political boundaries. Integrated global finance markets shift billions of dollars around the world daily in a manner that influences national economies through its impact on foreign exchanges, interest rates, the stock market, employment levels, and government tax revenues. Meanwhile, powerful multinational enterprises are able to transfer investment across political boundaries, control the terms of technology transfer, and negotiate favourable tax and subsidy deals with governments. Global business strategies are themselves enhanced by radical changes in information technology and telecommunications. These flows of investment, technology, communications, and profit across national boundaries are often seen as the most striking symptom of global challenge to the nation-state.

This challenge is, however, a more extensive one. As we have seen in the previous chapter, economic globalization involves not only flows of finance, capital investment, technology, and labour, but also an expanding web of transnational regulatory institutions. Many of these may have started out as intergovernmental bodies or bodies sanctioned by governments, but over time, their autonomy from national governmental control has increased. This is reflected in the growth of the regulatory capacity of bodies such as the IMF, GATT/WTO, and, on a regional scale, EU. These are accompanied by an expanding set of declarations, conventions, and international legal instruments to which governments have become signatories, in the economic sphere and many other areas of public policy and law. Individual nation-states, in this sense, are confronted not only by transnational economic power, but also, and in large measure, by transnational regulatory institutions. Economic globalization is not, of course, an evenly spread process, while nation-states themselves vary in size, wealth, and power. To speak of the impact of globalization upon the nation-state, as if this were a unitary process that took the same form in every sector of the economy and for every nation-state, is therefore highly misleading.

The global cross-border mobility of certain kinds of economic processes is, for example, more easily perceived and policed by nation-states than other kinds. Physical movements of goods or peoples have proved less difficult for individual nations to regulate, monitor, and tax than has the electronic transfer of funds or information. Even so, levels of the illegal importation of drugs or of illegal immigration are considerable. The existence of variations in regulatory standards, and the ineffective policing of activity that crosses several jurisdictions, does, however, lend itself to global evasion of controls, through devices such as tax havens and the construction of corporate structures that are impenetrable to national scrutiny. In some cases too it is expedient for government agencies and powerful political figures to have access to clandestine channels of activity, operating outside conventional regulatory processes. The case of the Bank of Commerce and Credit International (BCCI) is particularly instructive in this respect.

BCCI, founded in 1972, had grown over the next two decades to an entity with $20 billion in assets and branches in 70 countries. Created by a Pakistani banker, its corporate structure involved a Luxemburg-based holding company with two main subsidiaries, one in the Cayman Islands, the other in Luxemburg (Kapstein 1994). Designed to evade scrutiny, these two jurisdictions offered banking secrecy and virtually non-existent regulation. No consolidated accounts of the holding company were ever prepared, and Luxemburg authorities found it impossible to exercise any control over a body 98 per cent of whose operations were in other jurisdictions. It has been said that BCCI was constituted to be effectively 'offshore' in every jurisdiction in which it operated. It was on this basis that the Bank provided a lucrative basis for deposits of both Western capital and Middle-Eastern petro-dollars as well as an even more lucrative money-laundering operation for international drugs and arms dealers. Clients included General Noriega of Panama. Expansion into the financial centres of London, Hong Kong, and New York, despite the concern of regulatory authorities, was facilitated by lawyers and lobbyists, including Bert Lance, briefly director of the Office of Management and Budget in the Jimmy Carter administration. Although finally closed by the combined efforts of regulators in 1991, BCCI had for 20 years capitalized on both the inability of nationally based regulators to co-operate effectively and the existence of lax regulatory standards in a number of jurisdictions. Financial transactions are especially hard to police, and regulatory standards lax; many jurisdictions may be found wanting. Yet the BCCI case is by no means typical of the relations between nations and transnational economic actors. One reason for this is that the global economy is a good deal less anarchic than this case study implies. This reflects the value of order and coherence in economic transactions for most parties, most of the time. Lax regulatory standards may arise when nations lack the willingness to regulate, a problem that in its extreme form involves corruption. However, regulatory problems also emerge where nations lack the capacity to regulate.

Variations in the capacities of nation-states to regulate cross-border transactions are an important variable when we come to consider variations in the impact of globalization on individual nations. As already indicated, the position of powerful players such as the USA, and other G7 nations such as Japan or Germany, contrasts markedly with the poorest nations such as Bangladesh and Mozambique. While the former group of nations has high levels of national capacity to regulate and exert considerable influence within transnational regulatory organizations such as the World Bank or WTO, the latter group possess very little bargaining strength or regulatory capacity beyond their formal juridical independence as nations. Between these two categories comes a third set of nations, such as Malaysia, Indonesia, and Brazil. Some members of this group are currently facing problems of global indebtedness and instability. Yet, judged over the longer term, they have achieved much economic success and recognition within regulatory bodies, especially those of a regional character. Contemporary China, meanwhile, is in a category of its own, still unrepresented in the major transnational regulatory institutions but wielding considerable power over the regulation of access to its rapidly expanding economy.

Another reason for divergence between nation-states in relation to the impact of globalization is that some nations are the home base of MNEs, although most are not. Those that are, differ from all other nations, in that much of the profit made elsewhere may be expected to be repatriated to the country of corporate origin. The link between most multinationals and a particular national jurisdiction is often obscured by talk of cross-border transactions and the mobility of capital (Hirst and Thompson 1996). Although shareholdings in many MNEs have become transnational, most MNEs have headquarters within a single nation, hold annual shareholders' meetings within that nation, and cultivate close relations with the government of the country in which they are domiciled. In a number of sectors, such as banking, telecommunications, and the media, they are often subject to national controls limiting foreign ownership. Balancing such restrictions are the power and influence exerted by MNEs within the nation of domicile. The strategy of most MNEs on most issues is to utilize this power and influence to obtain a favourable regulatory environment and the support of governments for their global activities rather than to evade regulation in a footloose manner. Governments, for their part, welcome the investment, financial returns, and international prestige that such relationships bring.

These are preliminary observations, but they do pose some awkward questions for those who predict the demise of the nation-state under the impact of globalization. MNEs do not typically operate outside national jurisdictions, whether at home or abroad. Rather, they depend on state structures to guarantee stable property rights or at least predictability in determining the rules of the game under which they operate (Krasner 1985). In addition, states may also provide infrastructural support and favourable fiscal treatment. Given that MNEs depend or rely on nation-states in this manner, it might well be supposed that the nation-state is alive and well rather than in decline. Theorists of the robustness of the nation-state point to its continuing role in many aspects of economic and social regulation and its involvement in the revival of nationalism, evident in many parts of the globe. This alternative view, as we shall see, has much to be said for it. Yet the destabilizing impact of globalization is not so easily dismissed. This applies particularly as it concerns conventional ideas and practices of national sovereignty.

The question of sovereignty is a controversial issue within political science and the study of international relations (for a recent review of the main issues, see Thompson 1995). One of the major difficulties with the argument that national sovereignty is under attack from globalization is the presumption that there was once a golden age when states possessed some kind of absolute control over their territory and the movement of resources, people, and cultural influences across their borders. This presumption is, however, very much a myth. National sovereignty, as it has evolved over the past 300 years or so, has always been more conditional than the myth implies. This is partly because the sovereignty of any one nation has usually depended on recognition by other nations within the interstate system, and partly because states have never been able, even if they wanted to, to achieve absolute control of transnational movements of people and resources across borders.

If national sovereignty has never been absolute and unconditional, some care is needed in assessing the argument that contemporary processes of globalization undermine national sovereignty. If absolute sovereignty never existed, what exactly about sovereignty is being undermined? This difficulty does not, however, dispose of the argument that globalization challenges national sovereignty. Two points may be made in reply.

The first is that limits to national sovereignty on the part of transnational processes and actors are certainly not restricted to the contemporary post-1945 world. In addition to limits set by the interstate system, it is important to note that economically derived restrictions on sovereignty also predate the post-war period. Globalization, as pointed out by world-system theorists among others, involves the development of transnational processes such as an international division of labour and the development of a world market over several hundred years. MNEs have been around for 100 years, while banking and trade have, for much longer, exhibited a transnational character, connected in part with diasporic groups such as Jews, Lombards, and the Chinese. In the past two centuries, private international bankers, for example, have periodically influenced the terms upon which nations responded to fiscal or military crisis by conditions placed on credit, whether in France in 1870–71 or Britain in 1931.

Recognition of these historical parallels with the present is perfectly compatible with arguments about continuing contemporary global challenges to national sovereignty. Such present-day arguments need not necessarily depend for their cogency on dubious assumptions about a golden age of sovereignty in the past. On the contrary, it is possible to speak of significant continuities over time in attempts by nations to regulate and control the mobile flow of economic resources across political boundaries, and in bargaining or conflict between nations and the more powerful economic actors over the regulation of this kind of activity.

This emphasis on continuity in the conditional nature of sovereignty should not, however, obscure the rapid intensification of cross-border transactions in the latter part of the 20th century. This process has impacted not only upon the pre-existing, mostly Western, nations of the pre-1939 world, but also on the vastly expanded number of newly independent post-colonial states established between 1945 and 1980. The global interdependence of national economies, polities, and cultures is not by any means a product of the post-1945 world (Thompson and

Krasner 1989). Yet the process of interdependence has undoubtedly accelerated in the past 50 years (Keohane 1995). This has impacted in turn not only on the sovereignty of historically well-established states, but also, and perhaps especially so, on newly established states in the developing world, typically equipped with fewer resources and less experience in dealing with powerful transnational actors.

It is in this historically qualified sense, to be more fully developed in this chapter, that contemporary globalization may be said to pose intensified challenges to the conditional forms of national sovereignty that nations, both old and new, have inherited from the past. In this chapter, we shall pursue this question of the impact of globalization on national sovereignty, identifying both the reasons for the robustness of the nation-state within the global economy and the changing and more conditional nature of national sovereignty.

A final introductory point is necessary to distinguish between two aspects of what is typically bundled together in the singular concept of the nation-state. This is obviously a hybrid word, linking the idea of 'nation' with the idea of 'state'. While the former refers to what might loosely be termed a 'people', that is, to a cultural entity often defined in terms of ethnicity, the latter refers to a set of institutions through which public authority is exercised within a particular territory.

Although the connection between the two has become conventionally regarded as a necessary one, this is largely a reflection of the formative experience of European nation-state building, founded on the normative concept of rights to national self-determination. This has helped, first in Europe and later in the colonial world, to legitimate the idea of 'one people – one nation'. This normative principle is not, however, reflected in the basis of many existing nation-states, which, for one reason or another, contain a mixture of peoples or ethnicities. (For further elaboration, see Chapter 6.) In such cases, the identity of the nation has often become a matter for dispute and sometimes national fragmentation. Even in such instances, however, the nation-state is more than a state apparatus.

The reason for raising the distinction between nation and state is to emphasize the twofold problem involved in assessing the future of the nation-state in an epoch of globalization. The first problem, that of the maintenance of state sovereignty in relation to cross-border economic activity and regulation, has already been sketched. The second problem, that of the national integrity of a people, brings into focus questions of cultural identity. These are influenced not only by the internal cultural composition of the nation, but also by global trends such as culturally diverse labour migration, the globalization of culture industries such as music and film, and the cultural impact of transnational regulatory bodies in areas such as human rights and citizenship. The underlying question here is whether nations, as culturally distinct entities, will be eroded by an emergent global culture, and if not, whether nationalism will be the major vehicle of resistance to global cultural trends.

Within the present chapter, we will focus solely on the first of these two questions, leaving questions of global cultural development for subsequent analysis.

Globalization and the sovereignty of the state

Absolute sovereignty may well be a historical myth, but it is still popularly said that the sovereignty of the nation-state is being undermined by globalization. This applies whether the threat is perceived to come from multinational enterprises or transnational regulatory bodies. Protests against the interference by outside groups in domestic affairs are widespread. Nonetheless, protest is rarely against outside interference in principle. Rather, different kinds of interest group are likely to protest against different aspects of global 'interference' while welcoming others. As Alston (1995, p. 7) points out in an analysis of Australian responses to globalization, business groups have supported the GATT/WTO type of global trading rules in support of free trade while often opposing global environmental treaties. Similarly, opponents of the penetration of MNEs into national affairs often welcome international human rights treaties and conventions. This suggests that widespread rhetoric about the negative consequences of globalization is often combined with a less obvious but equally significant acceptance of some global trends as helpful to the realization of nationally based socioeconomic objectives. But where does all this leave the question of sovereignty?

Contemporary ideals of national sovereignty derive in the main from 17th-century European discussions of political theory and international law. Writers such as Bodin and Hobbes developed theories of sovereignty that focused on the necessity of vesting power in a single centralized unified entity, generally a monarchy. In a very familiar argument, Hobbes saw this as necessary to constrain the war of self-interest between individuals. Without sovereign power, life would, in Hobbes' much cited phrase, be 'solitary, poor, nasty, brutish and short'. Equally, however, the prospect of a unitary Leviathan state raised the spectre of despotism, that is, the creation of a predatory oppressive regime, unchecked by institutional regulation. This creates what Martin Wight (1992, p. 35) calls the Hobbesian paradox, that is, the need for sovereign power to check anarchy but the equal need to protect society from autocratic despotism.

Hobbes, however, devoted more attention to the projection of sovereignty as the remedy for anarchy than to the problem of the predatory state and the question of the limitations appropriate to its power. This has in turn contributed to traditions of seeing sovereignty as an absolute or unconditional type of power.

Seventeenth-century discussions of sovereignty raise a further issue, namely the distinction between internal sovereignty within a given territory and external sovereignty evident in relations between states. While Hobbes was aware of both dimensions, he tended to concentrate on the former. This created a situation whereby national sovereign power might resolve internal war, only for war to break out in the international arena. Hobbes' main contribution here was to assume that national sovereigns would be able to protect their subjects. In one sense, international warfare, from the European Thirty Years War of 1618–30 to the present day, suggests a major flaw in this argument. The national populations of even the strongest states have not proved immune from the anarchy of war.

Clearly, the external aspects of national sovereignty, as they have developed in the interstate system since the 17th century, depend on some sense of commonly agreed rules governing political reciprocity between sovereign states. From the Peace of Westphalia in 1648 onwards, international law developed on the basis of the legal immunity of states from prosecution in the courts of another state for actions performed in pursuance of national sovereignty. States have conventionally been seen as the appropriate parties to international law, before which they have juridical equality. In Oppenheim's (1905) formulation, international law is and should remain 'law between states only and exclusively'.

While such principles are reaffirmed in the UN Charter (Art 2(1)), they have not gone unchallenged. Held (1991, 1995) has argued that there has occurred a shift away from exclusive emphasis on the claims of states, with the emergence of claims in the name of humanity and the world order pursued, in large measure, through the judicial processes of the International or European Courts of Justice and the European Court of Human Rights. Here, both states and individuals may and do take action against states in the name of broader transnational principles.

The earlier work of the League of Nations in relation to treaties with national minorities went some way towards challenging the exclusive monopoly of states within international law. However, the major watershed in undermining the exclusive juridical rights of nations to pursue their sovereign interests in foreign policy were the Nuremberg war trials after the Second World War. The judgement of the International Tribunal was that where state laws, such as those underlying much of the German war effort, were in conflict with international humanitarian rules, state laws should be disobeyed wherever scope existed for the exercise of moral choice (Cassese 1988). By affirming circumstances in which the rights and obligations of individuals take precedence over those of the nation-states of which they are members, the Tribunal took a step of major historical significance in the creation of a transnational legal and political system in which nation-states were no longer to have an exclusive *de jure* monopoly of sovereignty within international law.

Having said this, there remain significant limits in the extent to which international law, or the regional law of the EU has proved able to constrain the actions or usurp the ultimate autonomy of nation-states. Transnational legal bodies generally lack the ultimate capacity – military or otherwise – to force recalcitrant nations to participate in or accept the outcome of judicial process.

In the case of the UN, for example, as Held (1995) points out, members are automatically parties to the Statutes of the International Court of Justice (ICJ) but need not accept the Court's jurisdiction (Held 1995, p. 96). Suter (1996) calculates that only around a third of UN members accept its jurisdiction (Suter 1996, p. 247). Many authorities cite as a prominent example of non-recognition the case brought by the Nicaraguan Sandanista Government against the USA in 1984 for the mining of its harbours and the support given to insurgents. The US response was first to challenge the ICJ's competence in the matter and, when this failed, to refuse to accept the Court's ruling. In an earlier case in 1973, New Zealand and Australia took France to the Court over atmospheric nuclear testing in the Pacific (Templeton 1996, p. 52). While France refused to accept the Court's jurisdiction, it did thereafter cease atmospheric in favour of underground testing. This may reflect the greater importance of international public opinion over legal enforcement, whereby nations choose to regulate themselves rather than being coerced to change direction.

It is arguable that European attempts to establish systems of transnational law have proved more effective. One such attempt in the human rights area stems from the European Convention for the Protection of

Human Rights and Fundamental Freedoms, ratified in 1950 to come into force in 1953 (Weissbrodt 1988, p. 14). Under the convention, individuals as well as states may petition the European Commission of Human Rights. If the Commission believes that the Convention has been breached, cases may be referred to the European Court of Human Rights. States and individuals involved may also take cases to the Court. By 1986, all 20 members of the then Council of Europe recognized the court's jurisdiction, and over 100 cases had been dealt with. These challenged states over matters recognized in the Convention, such as guarantees of a fair public trial, or freedom from torture or degrading treatment.

The European Court of Justice has a wider remit. It is concerned in large measure with determination of the legality of the powers claimed and exercised by the central EU institutions, notably the Council of Ministers. Unlike most of the transnational political institutions centred on the UN, the EU has the right to make laws in certain areas, such as trade, which it may impose, if necessary, on members through regulations and directives. A recent example is the power to impose a worldwide ban of exports of British beef made in the light of the 'mad cow disease' controversy. Nations may, of course, appeal to the European Court of Justice, as the British government, at the time of writing, intends to do in this case.

The Court also takes appeals on the legality of individual member governments' actions towards its citizens in relation to foundation treaties of the EU, formerly the EEC and EC. Member states must comply with the Court's rulings on these matters. This has led, for example, to changes in British law regarding sexual discrimination and equal pay (Held 1991, p. 220). Although uncertainties over the future direction of transnational European institutions abound, it appears that recent shifts in regional European law have made greater inroads into national sovereignty than is evident in international law, enforced through the UN system. This may reflect the greater degree of enforceability possible in Europe, which may in turn reflect a greater normative commitment to compliance on the part of members of the EU.

We shall return to more specific issues of the exact extent of national sovereignty later in this and the next chapter. For the moment, the following more general observation may be made, that such shifts as have occurred in international law have not entirely or even substantially undermined the interstate system of national sovereignty. As Held points out, 'the development of the UN system did not fundamentally alter the logic and structure of the Westphalian order' (1991, pp. 97–8). In this sense, new norms of international law are at best emergent, and at worst still very much visions of a possible future, yet (if ever) to be implemented.

What have survived then, over the last 350 years, are conceptions of national sovereignty that allow states to exercise a near monopoly of juridical authority within a territory. While the juridical threat of international law has been, for the moment, mostly held at bay, what counts more is the extent of practical sovereignty that states can exercise over a range of economic, social, and political matters in relation to powerful global economic as well as political forces. This question of what might be termed the conditionality of sovereignty is, however, hard to pursue, while issues of sovereignty continue to be enveloped in the myth that national sovereignty is, and has always been, absolute.

It has been argued that nostalgic conceptions of absolute sovereignty are especially inappropriate in an epoch of intensifying globalization. As Keohane (1995) argues, the nature of sovereignty that applied in the 17th century was developed under conditions of relatively low interdependency between nation-states. These conditions no longer apply. The far higher levels of interdependency that apply in the late 20th century, with large flows of capital, labour, technology, and information across boundaries (Williams 1993), have emerged within changing rules of sovereignty that are increasingly more conditional, negotiable, and complex.

Sovereign statehood never existed in an absolute sense. Even so, it is an institution whose meaning and conditionality have continued to evolve and change, this having taken place unevenly in different regions of the world. What characterizes the late 20th century is, according to Keohane, not a shift to idealistic institutionalism in global politics, along the lines of the failed interwar League of Nations, but rather the development of a mixed system of 'multilateral cooperation and tough inter-state bargaining' (Keohane 1995, p. 176). This reflects the simultaneous expansion of global regulatory organizations and national assertiveness in the pursuit of interests. Within this framework, 'Sovereignty is less a territorially defined barrier than a bargaining resource for a politics characterized by complex transnational networks' (Keohane 1995, p. 177).

For sovereignty to survive in any form, it is necessary for states to remain institutions with capacities to act that are of potential benefit to particular sets of interests. These capacities may involve a range of areas ranging from economic rule-setting, industrial relations regulations, and fiscal policy, to capacities that involve legitimizing particular institutional arrangements. An example of this function is where states possess the capacity to speak for the national interest involving matters of national identity and the cultural integrity of the nation. These may be deployed to mediate controversial issues such as foreign take-overs of major companies or increases in culturally diverse immigration levels.

The types of interest involved may include domestic organizations such as businesses, labour organizations, consumers, and those with interests in the cultural integrity of the nation. Such groups may, singly or in alliances, pressure the state to secure freer or more protected trade, to ratify or reject international treaties and conventions, and to expand or contract flows of immigrants. Simultaneously, external interests such as MNEs, international regulatory bodies such as the IMF and GATT, and international non-governmental bodies such as Amnesty International or Greenpeace International may press for various changes to national policy-making, affecting issues such as controls over foreign investment, fiscal policy, or human rights practices.

How these pressures work out, and how consistent they are with conventional notions of democracy, is a complex matter. As Held (1991, p. 201) points out, most conceptions of liberal democracy have generally assumed state sovereignty 'subject only to compromises it must make and limits imposed upon it by actors, agencies, and forces operating within its territorial boundaries'. This assumption is, however, rendered highly problematic by globalization, inasmuch as transnational regulatory bodies are not governed by the majoritarian procedures of liberal democracy.

Relations between national and transnational interests may involve negotiation and the search for common or complimentary interests. However, they may equally mean conflict and sometimes coercion where interests differ. A major factor here is the underlying structure of interdependency, whereby the various external interests are dependent on elements of state support, while state institutions are dependent on various resources from without. The limits to models based on bargaining are twofold. First, there is the limit set by irreconcilable conflicts of interest. Second, there are limits set when asymmetries of power between particular external interests and the state are so great that domination replaces bargaining. While the fundamental 'asymmetries of power' model is widely canvassed in world-system theory, there is considerable evidence in favour of the alternative approach suggested here, which draws on Keohane's analysis of bargaining and on notions of the possibility of complimentarity of interests between MNEs and nation-states.

Global capitalism, MNEs and the nation-state

Notions of bargaining and the development of common interests between MNEs and the nation-state conflict with widely held beliefs that global capitalism is not merely corrosive of the nation-state, but also obstructive of national political autonomy over economic and social policy. An important version of this claim is that economic globalization undermines the capacity of nations to pursue or maintain welfare states, based on the redistribution of resources to those unable to secure a decent life from market transactions. The argument here depends not only on the actions taken by MNEs, but also, in a broader sense, on what is seen as the underlying logic of capital accumulation operating through markets within a framework of private property rights. Under these conditions, it is claimed that national forms of redistributive politics according to social need are undermined by market-driven capital accumulation imperatives. Welfare states and socialist polities tend to limit the power of capital and reduce profit. This renders them either liable to erosion through a revived politics of economic rationalism or to neglect through the flight of capital elsewhere. In both cases, investment and employment levels would suffer, and increases in social dislocation and uncertainty would ensue. These kinds of spectre, it is said, create great pressure on politicians acting in the present to limit welfare and other kinds of redistributive spending. The assumption is that increased globalization means increased competition, and increased competition requires cuts in welfare spending (Flora 1987; Pierson 1991; Scharpf 1991). This entire scenario may be regarded as a worst-case reading of the impact of economic globalization on the nation-state.

This argument certainly has some credibility. Economic globalization within an increasingly interdependent world undoubtedly rules out economic autarky, while the mobility of finance and capital exert limits on national decision-making (even for the most powerful nations) over matters such as interest rates and foreign exchanges. It is also the case, as Carnoy points out, that the past decade has seen the collapse of the 'most historically important counter-multinational alternative – international state socialism' (1993, p. 47). Whether this leaves nation-states with little alternative but to 'fall deeper into the waiting arms of technology-bearing, capital-laden multinational firms' (Carnoy 1993, p. 48) is, however, more debatable.

In the first place, it is by no means clear that economic globalization does require the end of the welfare state and redistributive reform, to be replaced by convergence around a market-orientated national politics, regulated in a manner that suits only MNEs. Cameron (1978), for example, found that exposure to foreign trade did not create negative effects on welfare state spending. In more extensive recent research on 14 industrial countries between 1966 and 1990, Garrett and Mitchell (1996) found that, for this group of nations at least, greater exposure to international trade and foreign capital penetration exerted no downward pressure on welfare state expenditure. The emphasis here on measuring income transfers, such as pensions, rather than education or health spending was designed to focus on those forms of spending seen as less directly relevant to meeting the challenges of economic competitiveness.

Garrett and Mitchell explain their findings in two ways. First, globalization increases levels of insecurity for large sections of the population, thereby heightening expectations of redistributive social support. Second, welfare spending does not necessarily lead to capital flight because countries with greater social stability offer a better environment for investors than more unstable milieux. In addition, the connection between globalization and welfare spending is greater in countries with strong labour movements and weaker right-wing parties. All this does not mean that the welfare state is not in crisis, but only that the reasons for the crisis are not primarily to do with globalization.

Second, it is not at all clear that nations in general lack bargaining power in dealings with MNEs and transnational global agencies. To say that nation-states cannot ignore multinational enterprise is not, however, to say that MNEs are typically beyond the scope of nationally based negotiations concerning the terms of their operations or beyond any kind of national regulatory control or influence. The underlying reason for this is that MNEs remain dependent on nation-states for certain types of resource in a range of circumstances. This is not to say that MNEs are dependent, in similar ways, on all the nation-states within which they operate. Nor is it to say that MNEs do not exercise considerable leverage in bargaining to the extent that certain asymmetries in power are evident. Rather, the argument is that a number of patterns of MNE dependency on the state are evident. These are often the outcome of negotiation and the development of common or compatible interests rather than unilateral domination.

A special case of the relationship between MNEs and the nation-state is that of the home base or jurisdiction in which most multinationals operate. Michael Porter (1990) has argued that the multinationals' home market is a major base for expansion and that national policies have a major bearing on the competitive advantages that accrue to home-based MNEs. He links this point with the observation that some *nations'* MNEs (for example, those of the Japanese) have recently been growing faster than those of other nations, irrespective of the industrial sector within which they are located.

The national policies that have been seen as relevant to home-based competitive success include the quality of the public education system, management training, protection, and the investment in infrastructural items such as telecommunications. These policies have been evident in Japan and Western Europe, and have contributed to productivity growth, profitability, and employment. Carnoy (1993, p. 89) argues that national governments receive a pay-off from such public investments in that local productivity growth has provided 'greater political space', presumably in the form of increased fiscal returns and hence the capacity to utilize public resources for other ends.

The argument here is a variant of the complimentary interests approach, but even here the scope for bargaining over the terms of national–MNE collaboration is considerable. For example, debates occur over what commitments is it appropriate for domestic MNEs to make to national research and development efforts and what kinds of local employment guarantee should be sought in return for government infrastructural support.

A further type of governmental support to MNEs, on which the post-war global capitalist economy has depended, involves the military and political support of the USA as a superpower. Gilpin (1975, p. 41) has argued that multinationals prospered because they were 'dependent on the power of, and consistent with the political interests of, the United States'. This power was instrumental in the restabilization of Europe and Japan, which were to become major sites for the operation of American MNEs as well as home bases for expanding European and Japanese multinationals.

One obvious problem with this general argument about the multinationals' home base is that MNEs are domiciled in only a relatively few nation-states, perhaps 25 in all. For those outside this club, including most of the poorer nations, the mechanisms relating to home-base activity do not apply. The more typical situation is where MNEs operate in countries other than those of their home base. These may vary between economically advanced Western nations, successfully developing nations outside the West, and the poorest underdeveloped nations dependent on a narrow range of economic activities. This latter arena is where the corrosive power of MNEs is believed to be most fateful for the nation-state and national control over economic affairs.

A range of mechanisms has been identified as important in limiting national sovereignty and national control over economic affairs. While some of these are corrosive of state powers *per se*, others are directed more at business competitors in the countries of origin. First and foremost is the point that MNEs make decisions on the basis of optimizing the private profitability of the corporation rather the economic health of particular nations. Such decisions include whether and where to locate investment, how to articulate flows of resources and semi-finished products within the global operations of the corporation, what intra-firm prices to charge, and where to generate profit within the organization. Such decisions apply especially to MNEs such as car manufacturers, with multiple investments in different countries linked together in a global production strategy that sources components from locations different from those where car bodies are manufactured and/or where car assembly is completed.

The decisions made in such circumstances affect individual nations in multiple, intersecting ways. Decisions about investment affect national growth rates, employment levels, and government taxation receipts. Once established, decisions about intra-firm flows of resources and profits affect a nation's balance of payments and levels of national income. The optimization of corporate interests within such a system takes precedence over harmonization with national interests. The dilemma for the nation is that economies may stagnate without MNE involvement, but the price for bringing them in may be too high in terms of loss of control over economic affairs or in relation to opposition from domestic economic and political interests. Economic globalization thereby reduces the influence that governments can exercise over the economic activities of their citizens, while not in any way guaranteeing social consensus among citizens on the desirability of global penetration into domestic economic affairs.

A second mechanism whereby MNE operations have disadvantages for the host economy is the unwillingness to share firm-specific intellectual property and technological and managerial skills with national competitors (Carnoy 1993, p. 62). The more fundamental types of research and development are generally not located outside the home base. The policies of the MNEs' home-based governments, especially the USA, often serve to compound this situation in areas such as intellectual property rights and controls of certain types of sophisticated technology transfer (for example, in aerospace and weapons systems). All of this threatens to create a dualistic system in which information-rich corporations dominate nations who lack intellectual property advantages. Such nations are either shut out entirely or must pay high royalties to MNEs for access to selected areas of information technology.

The two mechanisms of potential MNE dominance identified above represent serious challenges to national autonomy and hence national sovereignty over economic matters. But how far is it the case that MNEs dominate individual nations?

Theories of multinational dominance assume that such decisions are made, more or less, under the unilateral dominance of MNEs. Looking at this from the vantage point of a theory of pure coercion, the argument is that governments could act differently by organizing investment and economic planning on a national basis but are constrained to do so by the power of multinationals backed up by the ideology of economic liberalism and free trade, and, in cases such as Allende's Chile, by US-backed political destabilization.

In one sense, this argument about viable alternatives that have been closed off draws on an old socialist or communist dream of the possibility of operating planned command economies outside the global capitalist system. At the time of writing, Fidel Castro's Cuba is possibly the sole surviving governmental home of this kind of thinking. Contemporary experience, on the contrary, is that *some kind of engagement* with the global capitalist economy and global markets is unavoidable. Moreover, this is not just an unavoidable fate but a process that may bring benefits as well as disadvantages and a process that can be shaped, in a number of ways, by nation-states.

There is another sense, then, in which there are alternative strategies facing national governments. These involve MNEs as major players, but not necessarily as unilaterally dominant players. This kind of national autonomy is clearest in the case of economically advanced nations. Bailey *et al.* (1994), in their review of relations between MNEs and governments, point to major limitations on inward foreign investment, most notably in post-war Japan. Despite a slow trend toward liberalization, the evidence is that Japan has only eased barriers against foreign multinationals when circumstances were deemed to be in Japanese interests. Liberalization remains controlled through a system of administrative guidance that itself reflects the key role of government policy in Japanese capitalist development.

More liberal approaches to inward foreign investment are evident in other places, especially in Britain and the USA. Elsewhere, especially in France, governments, while tending towards liberalization, have nonetheless intervened selectively to block both foreign take-overs of, and joint ventures with, French businesses, (Bailey *et al.* 1994, pp. 64–75). This in turn reflects widely articulated French concerns about problems such as the foreign ownership of key industrial sectors as well as perceived adverse effects on MNE penetration on employment and the economic vitality of regions. This argument about national variations is confirmed by Reich's (1989) study of contrasting national responses in Western Europe to the regulation of foreign investment in the automobile industry.

In all of this, the terms upon which MNEs operate are subject to negotiation and sometimes veto wherever governments have decided that the balance of costs might exceed that of benefits. It is nonetheless increasingly the case that governments regard national interests and those of most MNEs to be broadly complementary. This is scarcely consistent with a picture of unilateral domination, although this is not to say that undue MNE pressure is not sometimes put on politicians, as in the case of the Lockheed and ITT bribery scandals in Japan (Martinelli 1982, p. 92).

What then of the developing world? An earlier generation of critics tended to emphasize the victim status of Third World economies and governments in relation to multinationals. For the poorer countries, it was argued that small sets of MNEs could dominate an entire nation, as in the case of fruit companies in Central America or copper mining firms in parts of Latin America. The more general argument proposed by Frobel *et al.* (1980) was that a New International Division of Labour (NIDL) had been created based upon the systematic exploitation of developing countries. This was reflected in the use of cheap labour, minimal skill transmission from MNEs to local workers, and a lack of long-term commitment to sustained investment. Governments in this scenario exercised little bargaining power. Instead, their role was to maintain authoritarian labour market policies that suited the exploitative economic regime. The prospects for democracy are even worse, insofar as political élites and multinationals have a shared interest in political authoritarianism.

This victimology of Third World domination by Western MNEs, backed up by market-orientated regulatory institutions such as the IMF, has come under critical attack for a number of reasons. First, the success of a number of Third World countries in East and South-East Asia in breaking out of dependency and asserting their autonomy has, as discussed earlier, undermined any notion of dependency as a permanent condition. This in turn challenges the very concept of the Third World as a homogeneous group of underdeveloped nations unable to exercise any kind of sovereignty. Second, and following on from this, comes evidence of the complex bilateral nature of the interaction between developing states and external transnational actors such as MNEs.

It has been pointed out that the principle of juridical sovereignty of states, inherited from the pre-1939 interstate system and reaffirmed in the Charter of the UN, means that all states have the capacity to regulate their domestic polity, to set rules, and so forth. The decisive point here, however, is not so much the existence of formal rules about MNE activities that developing states may, from time to time, establish, as the effectiveness of such rules. Krasner (1985), for example, argues that the capacity of such states to bargain varies according to their size, relative military capacity, and wealth, and the type of economic activity involved. For example, states with a significant home market, such as India, may bargain more effectively over the terms of MNE entry than those without.

Krasner also argues that states may strike better deals with MNEs involved with raw materials than with those involved in manufacturing (1985, pp. 183–5). Providing developing states are rich in marketable raw materials in the first place, they are in a stronger position to bargain about the terms under which these are extracted than about the terms under which manufacturing investment is brought in. This is because raw-material-based MNEs may have few alternative sources of raw material supply, and once established, it is hard for extraction-based MNEs to threaten to exit. Manufacturing-based MNEs looking at production sites may have a range of alternatives to choose from, while such operations are easier to exit from.

In addition, some aspects of technical expertise and market knowledge are easier to acquire (for example, in sectors such as mineral extraction) than in the high-technology aspects of manufacturing, where MNEs closely guard intellectual property rights. This is one reason why developing countries have done better in sectors such as oil production, where the developing countries of OPEC now play a major role, than in manufacturing. In 1970 MNEs owned 94 per cent of crude oil production; by 1980 this had fallen to less than 50 per cent. Whereas MNEs in the 1940s and 50s controlled Middle Eastern oil production through concessions imposed on weak states (for example, Standard Oil of California and Texaco dominating Saudi Arabia, and BP dominating Iran), this concessionary regime has been replaced by the OPEC system, which represents a greater rather than lesser measure of sovereignty.

Aside from the OPEC case, however, Krasner's argument about the bargaining position of raw material suppliers seems exaggerated. Work by Moran (1974) on the Chilean copper industry, and Girvan (1971) on the Caribbean bauxite industry, points in a different direction. The suggestion is that MNEs' control over distribution and marketing can offset any leverage that the poorer developing countries may possess by virtue of the physical location of raw materials within their jurisdiction. In this sense, it is not at all clear that countries rich in raw materials are necessarily in a better position that those in which manufacturing is located.

A somewhat different line of argument about Third World domination by MNEs is that a relatively small proportion of multinational investment has gone to developing countries, reflecting the fact that MNEs are not solely driven by a search for low-cost labour. This stems, at least in part, from the recent developmental shift towards an information economy based on higher levels of value-added production (Castells 1993, p. 37). Undoubtedly, the 1980s and 90s continue to see some countries and regions expand economically on the basis of low labour costs, such as the *maquiladora* industries in Northern Mexico or the region around Bangkok. Nonetheless, within the broader context of the information economy, there is declining scope for national competitive advantage based purely on low-wage factories producing for world markets. The problem facing the poorer developing countries is, in one sense, as much one of neglect as one of exploitation by the powerful, one of too little MNE investment rather than too much, but also one of inadequate access to technology transfer and training.

Sklair (1991, p. 87), points out that governments in developing countries have generally scrambled to attract multinationals rather than keep them away. This may reflect a belief that the net benefits of MNE investment are positive for the recipient country, especially for those able to secure incomes higher than would otherwise have been the case, whether as suppliers, investors, wage and salary earners, or corrupt officials. Whether such a judgement about net benefits is entirely justified is, however, not easy to determine. It is especially difficult to strike a balance between the costs and benefits of such MNE investment as has taken place in the developing countries, especially those whose bargaining power is relatively weak. The complexities of this question, as discussed by Sklair (1991, pp. 87–91), cannot be addressed here. What seems clear enough is that foreign investment is of major significance in any development strategy, that MNEs generally benefit more than developing countries from the way in which investment takes place, and that the positive impact of foreign investment is often far less than is claimed. At worst, MNE penetration of local markets often puts local producers out of business or inhibits the entry of domestically owned competitors into sectors of MNE domination. Positive effects on local suppliers or through the training of local personnel vary so considerably from case to case (Dror 1984; Grunwald and Flamm 1985; Sklair 1988, 1989) that it is hard to make any secure generalization (Sklair 1991, pp. 89–90).

The significance of this discussion for present purposes is not to attempt to resolve general questions about the economic impact of MNEs but rather to evaluate the extent and limits of autonomy that developing countries may possess in relation to MNEs. In the light of new evidence reviewed above, there has recently been a reappraisal of earlier arguments that nation-states remain weak or powerless victims in the face of MNE dominance. Castells (1993, pp. 27–8) identifies three strategies open to governments in an era of MNE penetration. These involve (a) traditional international trade in primary products within the existing division of labour dominated by advanced countries, (b) import-substitution industrialization, attempted in Latin America in the 1960s and 70s, and (c) the more recent and largely Asian export-orientated manufacturing strategies of the 1980s. The latter involved either manufacturing exports from domestic firms as in South Korea, Hong Kong, and Taiwan, or exports from MNE operations outside the country of origin, as in Singapore and Malaysia. It is a strategy that has proved remarkably successful compared with the other two options. The availability of this strategy and the development of national development strategies on this basis indicate the possibility of government autonomy in the setting of national goals and the implementation of national strategies.

Whether in the advanced economic nations or in the developing world, the older model of MNE dominance over nations seems too simplistic. It may be conceded that governments have few alternatives but to deal with MNEs if they wish to optimize levels of economic growth, employment, and government revenue. Many of the terms of the bargain are, however, up for negotiation, and governments hold some cards, especially if they can deliver high levels of political stability, as well as infrastructural and fiscal support. Even within the developing world, there are many settings in which the nation-state is far from dead or powerless, especially where development alliances between government and local capital are possible.

One underlying reason put forward for this is that MNEs need nation-states for the performance of certain key functions. This applies not merely to the home base and country of domicile, but also to other outside countries. Martinelli (1982) sees multinationals' dependence on government as an illustration of the more general proposition that markets do not, by themselves, solve all problems with which they are confronted. These include the long-run stability and legitimation of a market-based system. States in the 19th century were required to provide rules to regulate excessive competition and also structures to encourage social consensus in the face of economically generated conflicts, for example between capital and labour. In the second half of the 20th century, similar state functions were required. These included the post-1945 restabilization of Europe under US hegemony.

Martinelli's general argument is that MNEs 'need strong states and stable societies' capable of defending property rights, securing the free flow of factors of production, and legitimizing capitalist social relations (1982, p. 86). The implication is that the pursuit of these functions gives governments a certain autonomy in relation to MNEs. This autonomy rests not only on pressure to solve problems left unresolved by the market, but also on the basis of domestic political opposition to MNEs. This may come from local producers or interest groups that feel threatened by their operations, for example organized labour or environmentalist groups. As a result, a range of policies has emerged to limit MNE autonomy, including controls on inward investment, incentives to domestic industry, and product standards for environmental protection. Such limitations are, however, conditional in scope. That is to say, they rarely go so far as to threaten a capital 'strike', involving MNEs in the wholesale abandonment of their investments.

Martinelli and others argue that MNEs and the nation-state need each other, and that the relationship between the two allows for significant elements of bargaining between them. Such power as the nation-state possesses in this kind of model derives from failures of the market to resolve issues such as economic stability and the legitimacy of a social order, based primarily on capitalist property rights. This approach is a useful one, but it fails to consider wider aspects of the modern nation-state that are not explicable simply in terms of the vicissitudes of the market and the capitalist economy. In other words, states may exist for reasons other than the problems and conflicts generated by capitalism. Martinelli's argument is, in this sense, excessively functionalist, in that it presumes that whatever the state does must in some sense be functional to problems of the global capitalist economy.

The discussion of multinationals and the nation-state was designed, in part, as a critique of views that announce the demise of the nation-state under the impact of the global economy in general and of multinational business in particular. Certain aspects of national sovereignty, but not the institution of the nation-state itself, have undoubtedly been eroded by economic globalization. The reasons for the resilience of the nation-state may be partly a response to problems of the market as an all-encompassing social institution. However, they extend further to the wider historical development of the nation-state as a multifunctional institution involved in military, political, and social, as well as economic affairs.

The historical dynamic of the nation-state

There are a number of different ways of understanding the historical emergence of the nation-state. One is to focus on the issue of sovereignty. In this perspective, our attention is directed back to 17th-century Europe, to the emergence of concentrated monarchical power and to the development of a system of nation-states sovereign in relation to each other. This approach is typified in international relations theory.

A major problem with analyses of this kind is their somewhat one-dimensional view of sovereign powers. As Michael Mann (1993) has recently pointed out, most of the key functions of the modern state developed subsequently to sovereign powers in foreign policy. Prior to the 18th century, in his view, states did comparatively little apart from conduct war and diplomacy, and administer overarching forms of internal repression. While this argument underestimates the political economic scope of 17th-century mercantilism, the thrust of Mann's general argument stands. In short, 'the sovereign nation-state is very young' (1989, p. 116), most of its powers and capacities being forged and consolidated in the 18th and 19th centuries, as far as Western Europe is concerned. Meanwhile, the 20th century has seen what Roland Robertson refers to as the universalization of the statehood as a political form, in the aftermath of the break-up of dynastic empires and successful revolts against colonialism.

In the European case, Mann points to the consolidation of the state's military powers in the 18th century. The state's role was expanded during the 19th and early 20th centuries with the extension of citizenship rights and the provision of economic and social infrastructures for industrial society in areas such as communications and mass education. During the 20th century, further extensions of welfare state function have been combined with macro-economic planning activities. While neo-liberalism within Western nation-states has significantly reversed some of the latter developments in the past two decades, state activity is still expanding in other areas, as in the social regulation of personal relations affecting men and women, children, and abortion. Meanwhile, nationalist feeling, or at the least a strong identification with the national community, remains highly significant.

Mann's argument, then, represents a second approach to the historical emergence of the nation-state. The emphasis here is multidimensional, emphasizing a range of state functions, in contrast to one-dimensional emphases on the sovereign power of nations in relation to one another. His underlying argument is that the modern state fuses a range of functions together within a 'single caging institution' (1989, p. 118) and that this institution is still in a sense maturing rather than being in the last gasp of senility and decrepitude. While certain state functions may grow or recede in importance, the institution itself is in healthy shape.

One further indicator of this is the general reluctance of states to submit conflicts with other states to the dispute resolution processes of transnational authorities such as the UN (Held 1991, pp. 212–13). This reluctance derives from states' continuing assertion of the sovereign right to make war. This represents a further illustration of Mann's emphasis on the military powers and capacities of the nation-state.

There are, however, two reservations to be made about this overall judgement on the continuing resilience of the nation-state. The first concerns the question of regionalism. European regionalism and the EU, of which the vast majority of Western European nations are members, is indicative of new, although not historically unprecedented, developments that affect states within its territory. While member nations have voting and certain veto rights, the EU, as was argued earlier in this chapter, has developed significant areas of transnational sovereignty of its own, in such matters as trade liberalization and product standardization, and the single European market, requiring the free movement of goods, and is attempting future extensions in matters such as movement of persons across national boundaries and monetary union. Consensus across such issues is by no means complete, reflecting continuing areas of national resistance (for example, by Britain on the issue of a European currency). A considerable degree of constraint on the sovereignty of member nations has nonetheless been obtained by consent. This indicates that the nation-state, however mature, holds no monopoly over economic policy or legal functions.

Mann goes on to argue that, beyond these economic areas, the European nation-states retain effective political sovereignty in most areas of social policy, public order, communications infrastructure, and the regulation of personal life. This suggests to him that European regionalism has largely been constructed to promote the interests of European capitalism against the challenges of the USA and Japan, leaving the individual nation-states with a broader range of functions that do not necessarily stem from problems arising from the operations of markets or global economic competition. It is arguable that the less highly developed regional trading blocs of NAFTA and APEC reflect the same kind of concern to promote regional economic interests rather than any more profound shift to transnational political organization.

This economistic approach to European regionalism has merit, but it is equally arguable that the EU has moved some way beyond economic policy-making. This is reflected both in the human rights and regulation of personal life issues discussed by Weissbrodt (1988) and Held (1995), and also in the Social Chapter, concerned with social justice and welfare. Mann's defence of the resilience of the nation-state is, at least in respect to Europe, somewhat exaggerated.

A second reservation about any theory of the robustness of the nation-state concerns its applicability outside Europe. While the post-colonial world has seen a massive expansion of statehood outside Europe, this has not always proved institutionally stable. There are undoubtedly a number of examples of successful state formation, as in South East Asian countries such as Indonesia, Malaysia, Singapore, and Thailand. In such cases, success has been based on a mix of strong economic and cultural infrastructures in civil society, together with strong modernizing state institutions.

At the other end of the spectrum, however, there is evidence of post-colonial state collapse, as reflected in Rwanda and Somalia. Here, the Hobbesian problem of order has overwhelmed state structures with few infrastructural capacities, largely as a result of internal ethnic or communal divisions rather than global capitalism. Most other state structures rest somewhere in between these two types. Here, state élites typically struggle to construct the capacities to secure internal social order and economic development in the face of disputes with neighbouring states, as in the Iran–Iraq war, ethnic division, seen in Central Asia, and poverty, which is a highly generalized condition. At the same time, many also experience problems of excessive military expenditure and predatory authoritarianism, reflected in corruption and human rights abuses.

While multinationals and transnational regulatory bodies may sometimes collude in or compound certain of these problems, they are by no means the underlying source of such problems of ineffective state formation and a weakly constituted civil society. Such problems may rather be traced both to colonial and precolonial history, and to the rapid process of decolonization after the Second World War. Jackson (1990), in particular, argues that decolonization created what were, in many cases, essentially 'quasi-states'. These emerged in a radically altered post-war interstate system. In this, post-colonial statehood depended on the international recognition of juridical statehood alone, rather than on effective claims to exercise statehood on the basis of the capacity to exercise effective power. Whereas statehood in past history depended on interstate as well as intrastate power struggles, in which some actual or would-be states survived and others succumbed, for Jackson, the post-war epoch of egalitarian rights of national self-determination has created post-colonial states that 'are not allowed to disappear juridically... [and which]... cannot be deprived of sovereignty as a result of war, conquest, partition or colonialism as frequently happened in the past' (1990, p. 23). The result has been the creation of weak states, recognized juridically and admitted to equal formal membership of the club of nations on the same basis as others, yet unable to exercise substantive sovereignty in the sense of taking full advantage of their formal sovereign independence.

Table 4.1   The creation and disappearance of states, 1816–1973

Time period	States created	States disappearing
1816–1876	24	15
1876–1916	12	1
1916–1945	16	7
1945–1973	81	1

Source: Adapted from Thompson and Krasner (1989, p. 207).

The recent juridical robustness of the nation-state is reflected in statistics of state creation and disappearance assembled in Thompson and Krasner (1989). Table 4.1 indicates a contrast between a pre-1939 pattern of disappearance as well as creation, and the post-1945 process of state construction. While the table takes the story up to 1973, further phases of state formation have taken place with the collapse of Communism and the development of post-Communist states.

There is little doubt, then, that effective nation-statehood remains the political form to which most developing countries, and many minorities within Western states, aspire. This in turn reflects the wish to have some kind of autonomy and effective sovereignty. Such aspirations may be found among peoples or nations that lack states, such as the Kurds or Chechnyans, as well as in national minorities within Europe, such as Basques and Scots. The general conclusion, therefore, is that while the state institutions and capacities of developing countries are often weak and undeveloped, effective nation-states possessing elements of sovereignty in domestic affairs still remain a major goal. This aspiration is as robust in the developing world as the fact of effective state capacity is in Europe, the USA, and the advanced economic countries.

The nation-state and multiple challenges to state sovereignty

To resume our general argument, it is clear that the historical dynamic of the nation-state is very far from being played out. Yet it is also clear that the world that nation-states inhabit is changing, that globalization is a major source of change, and that many aspects of globalization are altering the roles and relationships of nation-states to each other and to other organized interests within the global political system. Such changes may involve the erosion of traditional ideals of absolute state sovereignty within particular boundaries, yet they dispose neither of the idea of sovereignty as state autonomy from external coercion nor that of sovereignty as a bargaining resource that political élites may use in negotiation with external interests.

This process of shift towards ever more conditional forms of sovereignty may be analysed following the work of David Held (1991, pp. 212–22) as comprising the four main elements outlined in Table 4.2.

Table 4.2   Challenges to state sovereignty

1. The global economy	Multinational companies
	Global capital markets
2. Transnational bodies	Economic regulatory bodies, for example World Bank, GATT/WTO
	United Nations
	European Union
3. International law	Legal conventions recognized by national courts and states
	United Nations and European conventions and charters
4. Hegemonic powers and power blocs	NATO and former Warsaw Pact

Source: Data from Held (1991, pp. 212–22).

With the end of the Cold War (Holm and Sorensen 1995), the fourth of these components has become far less salient to the global polity. Superpower conflict no longer constrains national sovereignty in the way it once did. Nonetheless, NATO is far from dead, as the Balkans crisis in the mid-1990s has proved. What Held calls 'the internationalization of security' remains a significant issue. This tends to limit national sovereignty, whether of nations whose armed forces may be committed to NATO missions, those nations that may become the target of such missions, or those third parties who may wish to support target nations. At the same time, the limits to sovereignty are generally inversely proportional to the military capacity of those involved, especially on the NATO side. For the most part, and under peacetime conditions, however, it is the first three challenges that represent the greatest limits on national sovereignty.

We now extend this discussion further to consider the place of the nation-state within the emerging global polity. While the nation-state is far from finished, there is good reason to doubt that states hold the monopoly of power within the politics of globalization. A number of theorists now see globalism as a multi-actor system rather than an inter-state system, but who are the main actors, how do they interrelate, and what new types of global political interdependency are emerging? Is World Government a genuine possibility, or are moves toward a global polity still dominated by bargaining between parties for whom self-interest still overrides internationalism.

5

Towards a Global Polity?

Public debate may still be hostage to the outdated vocabulary of political borders, but the daily realities facing most people in the developed and developing worlds... speak... differently... Theirs is the language of an increasingly borderless economy... [in which] the primary features of the landscape – the traditional nation-states begin to come apart at the seams. (Ohmae 1996, p. 8)

Introduction

Globalization is often seen, as in Kenichi Ohmae's comments above, primarily in economic terms. The mobile forces of capital, labour, technology, and information are presented as moving relentlessly to and fro across political and cultural boundaries, threatening the integrity of the nation-state and of national cultures as they go. Nations and cultures, so the story goes, are faced with massive challenges to their very existence unless they can find some effective form of national resistance.

The message of Chapter 4, in contrast, is that borders still matter. This is not because ideals of absolute sovereignty are a viable alternative to globalization. Instead, it is because most global economic actors have so far felt the need for some kind of stabilizing framework of rules and public support structures beyond the networks generated through market transactions. Even in an age of deregulation, most actors continue to look to states to provide or underwrite such supports. The nation-state, in this sense, is not coming apart at the seams, but it is becoming increasingly implicated in wider sets of relationships with other nations, MNEs, and global NGOs operating across political boundaries. It is this latter response that we will consider in this chapter, asking how far a global polity has emerged and what form any moves towards political globalization have taken.

Discussions of the contemporary nation-state, and the role of nations within international affairs, can no longer be conducted on the basis that nations and global economic institutions constitute the only players in the game. Two other types of player must be taken into account. The most obvious and tangible, as we have noted in the previous chapter, are the transnational political and legal institutions surrounding the UN on an international scale and the EU on a regional scale. Beyond these formal political and legal institutions, there exists a second type of transnational player, namely the international NGO (INGO). Less familiar than the institutions of the UN and EU, this broad and somewhat unwieldy category is sometimes deemed to include MNEs. However, in a more restricted definition, it may be taken to include a range of sociopolitical, human rights, professional, and charitable bodies, ranging, for example, from Amnesty International and the International Commission of Jurists, to the International Committee of the Red Cross, Médecins sans Frontières, and the International Jesuit Refugee Service. Such movements have risen to such prominence as activists on a range of contemporary political issues that some analysts now speak of the emergence of a new 'international civil society' (Ghils 1992). This view is nonetheless a controversial one, requiring further scrutiny in relation to the extent of INGO influence on the formal polity of national states and transnational political and legal institutions. In other words, how far does the global polity remain state centred?

The changing global context of political activity

Defining who the main players are within global politics is one way of establishing the relative importance of nations within world politics and of the existence or otherwise of a new global order. However, before considering this issue, there remain some important points to be made concerning globalization and the process of global politics. These take us back to the issue of global interdependence raised in the previous chapter.

The first issue concerns the impact of changes in communications and information technology on political events – what might be called information interdependence. The development of satellite broadcasting technology, for example, has contributed to a simultaneity in the coverage of political events, in which events in one part of the globe can be watched on television in all other parts. This is reflected in the rise of global news, symbolized above all by the American CNN channel, described by its founder Ted Turner as 'the town-crier of the global

village'. The most striking instance of simultaneity may be found in the
Gulf War of the early 1990s, when the timing of major events in the War
was staged at prime-viewing times in Western capitals, especially in the
USA. War could be both brought into the living-room as a global spectator event and managed in order to promote the public relations objectives of the protagonists, both American and Iraqi.

The technological capacity for simultaneity is part of the expanding
capacity of global communications to convey information. Such flows
of information cannot be regarded as neutral and objective transmissions of fact, as critics of the global media point out (Stam 1992). What
counts as newsworthy is the product of standards of selectivity on the
part of broadcasters, as well as of strategies of news management
adopted by powerful interests such as governments and MNEs. Writing
of Gulf War media coverage, Stam speaks of the invitation of viewers
to become spectators in the technological dominance of the Western
military: 'we were also encouraged to spy, through a kind of porno-
graphic surveillance, on a whole region, the nooks and crannies of
which were exposed to the panoptic view of the military (and the spectator)... The military view literally became our view... For the first
time the media embraced the purposes and the visual technology of the
warrior state...' (1992, pp. 102–3).

Whether television transmission of world events amounts to top-
down ideological manipulation, as proposed by some media critics, is
debateable, since producer management of issues is not necessarily
able to control the way in which news is interpreted by those who
receive it. News is undoubtedly managed selectively and cannot therefore be regarded simply as neutral and objective fact. It is nevertheless
arguable that the net effect of global communications changes has
been to expand popular access to and awareness of world events. To
this extent, overt political events in a single country or even small
town may be said to have become globalized, in that the rest of the
world will soon hear of them.

A very striking example of the globalization of political awareness
and the complexity of viewer reception is provided by the Moroccan
sociologist Fatima Mernissi (1993). She reports on the reception of
major European events, such as the fall of the Berlin wall and of the
Romanian Ceaucescu dictatorship, in North Africa, as follows:

> I remember the day when a fishmonger in the Rabat medina left me standing with
> a kilo of marlin in hand while he rushed to the neighbouring shop which had a TV
> set, to hear the announcer report the capture of Nicolae and Elena Ceaucescu.

Mernissi claims that this event and the fall of the Berlin Wall, as reported in global TV media, were interpreted and welcomed by many Moroccans as universal symbols of the collapse of despotism, with implications for democratic struggles within Morocco. These democratic impulses were not, however, reported in the Western press, which narrowed its coverage to an obsessive search for examples of anti-Western fundamentalism for the Islamic Other.

As Mernissi reports it, the Rabat fishmonger, having seen the exciting events, bought a television set for himself, largely to receive global news. Westerners, regarded hitherto as brutal colonizers, had become slightly more credible as a result of recent political upheavals as forces for good. Then came the Gulf War and massive disillusion with the West. Two weeks after the start, the fishmonger sold his television and donated the money to the Red Crescent to buy supplies for Iraq.

This story reflects both the global impact of communications technology in widening access to information and the capacity of television viewers, in this case Moroccan merchants, to make their own judgements about the meaning of events rather than being dominated by Western television newscasting strategies or military news management.

The globalization of political processes may be regarded as a further stage in the development of what Giddens (1990) calls the disembedding of contemporary society from localism and parochialism. It is a process whose effects stem not only from communications transmissions over large distances and across borders, but also from processes of international migration whereby transnational linkages and information networks keep diaspora populations in touch with events across the globe.

Greater popular awareness of world events, however distorted by media or parochial prejudice about other nations or cultures, represents a change in the conditions under which major political actors operate. As recently as 1914, in an era before television, radio, and mass diffusion of the telephone, the governments of the major states were still able thoroughly to dominate domestic opinion in relation to decisions about going to war. Other parties could be represented as the aggressor, and there were virtually no alternative sources of popularly available information. On the outbreak of hostilities, anti-war sentiment evaporated and took a year or two to revive on a significant scale.

In the contemporary situation, governments at war or involved in controversial human rights areas still seek to monopolize access to information, but it is harder to achieve blanket control. This occurs inasmuch as the parties in any conflict have access to global telecommunications media, and critical commentary is more widely entrenched in Western media circles and social movements such as Amnesty International and Greenpeace International.

The contrasts in popular access to global political information between 1914 and the early 1990s should not be exaggerated. Independently sourced information that challenges prevailing official views is often scarce and usually has actively to be sought out. The global newsgatherers typically rely on well-resourced mainstream news channels and services, rather than on cash-strapped independents for their information. Nonetheless, the overall point remains. However imperfect flows of information may be, governments can no longer take either domestic or international political decisions in an information void, filled solely by their own propaganda.

Technology may have expanded access to flows of information, but is this the same thing as informed access to knowledge, consistent with the idea of government by informed discussion? Should we be so optimistic about the information revolution? This question has been raised by Sartori (1989) and Ionescu (1993) in connection with the problem of growing complexity and overload in information flows, available to citizens and to governments alike. This stems not only from new communications technology and increasing global interdependence in economic and political life, but also, according to Ionescu (1993, pp. 224–5), from limits to the cognitive capacity of science to produce an accessible understanding of the causal processes of the natural and social worlds. The effect is to produce undercomprehension and cognitive incapacity.

Ionescu asks how national policy-makers can understand, let alone explain to others or debate in an informed manner, the complex processes of a globally interdependent world. 'How,' for example, 'can a congressman from Vermont explain if it is a good thing to link Toshiba, Siemens and IBM, in a worldwide trilateral monopoly for the production of "brain chips" and what the effect of such a monopoly would be on the American company, or on world trade?' Alternatively, 'how can the MP for Rutland [in the UK] obtain an objective answer from his constituents on the advantages and disadvantages of the lowering of interest rates of the Bundesbank, even if he succeeded in explaining to them, and to himself, how they could affect their welfare?' (1993, p. 227). Other examples from a range of different policy areas abound.

The challenges posed by Sartori and Ionescu suggest that the complexities of global interdependence set cognitive limits to political capacities to understand and explain what is happening within global society. This may constrain capacities to respond with the wisdom of understanding, but it does not necessarily constrain action on the basis of moral judgement or assertions of political will. A good deal of the actions of politicians representing nation-states within the global polity may take this form. Yet beyond this, there has also been a shift towards the establishment of organizations based on non-elected expertise and institutional autonomy within the UN, Bretton Woods, and, more recently, EU bodies. This represents a feature of the global polity, which is neither totally swamped by uncontrolled information flows, nor necessarily or easily subsumed to the interests of nation-states as politicians define them. This point will be pursued in more detail below.

A third, related set of arguments about the changing global context of political activity centres on those types of economic and political interdependence that link the fate of all nations with one another. There are several sides to this. One is the familiar point that all nations are profoundly affected, to a greater or lesser extent, by continuous international processes such as the mobility of capital and information, as discussed in previous chapters. Another is that events or crises in one country or set of countries typically have wide-ranging implications in others. Tony McGrew (1992, p. 1) cites the following example. When Iraq invaded Kuwait on 2 August 1990, the headline in a local newspaper in the English industrial city of Coventry read 'Iraq invades Kuwait – bus fares to rise'. The interdependence here occurred through the connection between invasion, a disruption of oil supplies, a rise in world oil prices, the increased cost of oil-powered transport, and a rise in bus fares. A final, less obvious side to interdependence is that international agreements involving multilateral treaties or declarations are typically fine-tuned to accommodate the varying interests and sensitivities of the parties to them (Parry 1993).

One consequence of interdependencies of this kind is captured in the much-cited observation of US President Clinton at his Inauguration on 20 January 1992, to the effect that 'there is no clear division today between what is foreign and what is domestic'. In other words, domestic politics and foreign politics can no longer be set apart, as two autonomous areas of political life, with largely separate agendas peopled by different bodies of specialists and different pools of expertise. Economic, social, and environmental questions are no longer simply matters of domestic politics, as distinct from the world of political diplomacy.

Intensified interdependence seems to be a fact, but how exactly is it to be analysed? Rosenau (1980) has attempted a more systematic approach to the nature of contemporary interdependency. This focuses on the relative shift over time from issues to do with military control, territoriality, and national legitimacy, to a range of social, economic, and environmental issues in which nations share concerns and must co-operate to find solutions. Such problems include pollution of the natural environment, population pressure on resources, and economic inequalities, such as those between North and South. For Rosenau, such problems cannot be resolved by military means but through technical and scientific solutions embodied in political decisions.

Analysis of the interdependent actions of the various players in the different countries of the world is necessary to reach such solutions. Thus 'the actions of innumerable farmers... are central to the problem of increased food production, just as many pollution issues depend on choices made by vast numbers of producers, energy conservation on millions of consumers, and population growth on tens of millions of parents' (Rosenau 1980, p. 44). In addition, actions in one area, such as food production, affect those in another, such as birth rate.

It is a further characteristic of these processes that they are typically decentralized through the actions of large numbers of people and involve non-governmental as well as governmental organizations. They are, therefore, less amenable to governmental action and redress alone, however crucial that involvement may be in terms of the mobilization of resources. This in turn means that the redress of such problems requires not only intergovernmental co-operation, but also the involvement of other parties, of which Rosenau singles out professional experts.

In the remainder of this chapter, we shall explore the nature of contemporary global interdependence, as posited by Rosenau. We shall proceed first to look at institutional developments such as the UN and EC, and thence to INGOs. The underlying issue to be examined here is the nature of these transnational political institutions. Are they simply to be seen as creatures of nation-states, or do they have an autonomy from nations, in which case how far do they represent a new form of global politics, different from that which went before?

The internationalization of the state and the UN

The contemporary nation-state is typically and increasingly involved in a range of 'multilateral forms of international governance' (Held and

McGrew 1993, p. 271). Some of these, like the UN General Assembly, are multipurpose bodies, while others have a more specific remit. This ranges from trade in the case of the WTO, (formerly GATT), through health under the auspices of the WHO, to the weather, as with the World Meteorological Organisation, and designated species fisheries regulators such as the International Whaling Commission (IWC).

As is well known, the UN was established in 1945, in the aftermath of the Second World War and upon the ruins of the League of Nations, founded in 1919 after the First World War. Both of these initiatives were responses to what might be termed the globalization of war, by which is meant the transformation of warfare from limited regional conflicts between small sets of nations to intercontinental struggles involving far larger numbers of states, the political and economic consequences of which affect all states and regions. Such developments reflect *both* the spatial expansion of 19th-century Western capitalism and colonialization that intensified the global interdependence of states and regions, whether in Europe, the Americas, Africa, or Asia, *and* changes in military technology that assisted the more powerful nations to wage war on a transcontinental scale.

The two world wars demonstrated that questions of security and peace were a concern of all states, one that the existing machinery of intergovernmental relations, bilateral treaties, and multilateral security pacts had proved inadequate to regulate. The UN was, then, in large measure, a response to this failure of international security. Its Charter began with the words 'We the peoples of the United Nations are determined to save succeeding generations from the scourge of war'. Yet the UN was conceived in an even wider sense, inasmuch as wider social and political issues such as human rights were included within the new organization's Charter and foundational Declarations. Alongside the UN Security Council, charged with preservation of security through peace, stood the General Assembly, part of whose powers included not only the discussion of questions of human rights, but also the capacity to develop international Conventions on such matters (Cassese 1992). These 'law-making' powers have subsequently been extended to cover a vast range of human rights areas and have in their turn spawned a complex set of UN agencies.

The reference here to law-making should, however, be read in a particular sense. UN Conventions on human rights or on the rights of particular groups such as women, children, or refugees do not represent transnational legal initiatives that are binding on all nations but rather initiatives that emerge from a majority of member nations, which can only ultimately be implemented by judicially sovereign nations if they so wish. Influence and pressure may be placed on members who refuse or whose support is not translated into action, but this is as far as it goes. Such methods of achieving compliance may often fail, but they are not necessarily without effect.

The period of post-1945 international political and social reconstruction that resulted in the foundation of the UN was, of course, also the same period that saw the establishment of global regulatory organizations such as the IMF and World Bank (see Chapter 3). Both of these processes may be regarded as aspects of globalization, but neither represents nor was intended to function in a manner that fundamentally usurped the sovereignty of nation-states in the name of a new global order. In the case of the UN and its agencies, as with the Bretton Woods arrangements, the system that emerged made sovereignty less absolute and more conditional on transnational regulation, but the system remained founded on nation-states as the major players in the new global polity.

The political and normative agenda involved in the establishment and subsequent functioning of the UN and its agencies is proof of the influence of particular nation-states or sets of nation-states. Not surprisingly, the nations that emerged victorious from the Second World War, namely the US, USSR, and UK, played the most significant role in the negotiations that led to the establishment of the UN (Russell and Muther 1958; Cassese 1992). The primary concern here was international peace irrespective of issues of social justice, and the UN Security Council's mandate and veto privileges for the victorious wartime nations has preserved this focus ever since.

While Western interests dominated deliberations in the early years, excluding Communist China as a 'non peace-loving nation', for example, the steady expansion of new members as a result of decolonization reduced this influence over time, especially in those bodies such as the General Assembly based on majoritarian voting procedures. The inclusion of increasing numbers of former colonial nations in UN membership has meant a shift in the UN agenda from initial Western concerns for peace and stability, to a greater emphasis on global social justice and human rights (Mazrui 1990; Cassese 1992). This agenda is not restricted to the largely rhetorical theatre of the General Assembly, but is also evident in the various social and cultural committees of the UN.

Conflicts over access to and political participation within transnational institutions have been redefined by many in socioeconomic rather than geopolitical terms. The vocabulary is one of North–South conflicts based on inequalities of wealth and power rather than conflicts between Western and non-Western polities. Within the UN, such conflicts are reflected in conflicts over human rights.

In response to the human rights violations of the Second World War, the UN Charter of 1945 spoke of 'faith in fundamental human rights, in the dignity of the human person, ...[and]... in the equal rights of men and women and of nations large and small' (cited in Weissbrodt 1988, p. 7). These commitments were reaffirmed in the Universal Declaration of Human Rights in 1948. Over the subsequent 45 years, what has come to be known as the UN 'human rights regime' has been established (Alston 1992). The provisions of the Declaration have been refined in Covenants and codified in multilateral treaties, while procedures for implementing and monitoring human rights have been institutionalized within a complex set of committees, centring on the Human Rights Committee, set up in 1976 under the International Covenant on Human Rights (Opsahl 1992).

Within these complex structures, conflicts between the developed North and most other states have occurred over the meaning and institutionalization of human rights. For the first 20 or so years of the UN human rights regime, the emphasis was more on the civil and political rights of individuals, reflecting Western liberal-democratic traditions. Social and economic rights were either ignored (Donnelly 1981) or subsumed within civil and political rights, as if the former were the sole and effective route toward the latter. With growing post-colonial participation in the past 25 years, the shift has, in contrast, been towards a greater emphasis on the social and economic rights of groups or nations, regarded in an important General Assembly vote of 1977 as the precondition for effective political rights. Human rights violations and abuses cannot, however, be interpreted merely as rhetorical battles between nation-states, since human rights NGOs have played a major role in bringing violations to international notice. No government, be it in the developed or the developing world, is immune from criticism on human rights issues, either from outside or from dissidents from within.

Conflict over the meaning of human rights throws into doubt any theory of the emergence of some kind of universalistic human rights framework within global politics, to which all parties subscribe. The reality is rather different. In the first place, countries within the developed North seek to use UN bodies to encourage the emergence of liberal-democratic rights in authoritarian regimes within the developing South. In parallel with this, developing nations seek economic and social rights to freedom from poverty and economic exploitation for their nations, by calling for the North to divest itself of its unequal share of power. Meanwhile, dissidents within the South criticize their own governments over lack of liberal-democratic freedoms, and critics in the North point to their own governments' complicity in human rights abuse in supporting authoritarian regimes overseas.

Does a global polity really exist?

If the UN is not grounded in any clear kind of agreement on universalistic normative principles about key issues such as rights, does this mean that no effectively *global* or *transnational* polity exists? Criticism of the UN for its lack of effectiveness as a transnational organization extends beyond rights to a range of other issues, including international security and peace. The global political agenda, in this sense, has by no means been redefined in purely social terms.

The criticism of the UN's post-1945 record in delivering security with peace is twofold. First, the institutional machinery of the UN was marginalized during the period of the Cold War, effective power residing with the two superpowers and the security alliances of NATO and the Warsaw Pact. This power constellation curtailed the capacity of individual nations to pursue independent or autonomous foreign policies, either through the UN or outside it.

Second, with the end of the Cold War, the hoped-for revival of effective multilateral diplomacy permitting a revival of the UN has not occurred. Instead, it is arguable that the UN has conspicuously failed to prevent civil war and genocide in the former Yugoslavia, Rwanda, and Somalia. Such failures relate not only to logistical inadequacies in delivering appropriate resources quickly enough to trouble-spots, but also, more fundamentally, to rivalries between nations and failures of collective will by the key nations (mostly in the West) to intervene effectively to pre-empt war and conflict. In this sense, freedom from the constraints of the Cold War has not meant that international conflict resolution has been redirected through the UN. The more powerful nations such as the USA and France still reserve the right to mediate on an independent basis in international disputes. Meanwhile, the various national components of UN peace-keeping or crisis intervention forces remain under the influence and ultimate control of national governments rather than the UN.

Negative evaluation of the UN is thus both a matter of inadequate normative consensus about what should be done to secure global peace and justice, and a matter of consistent failure in responding to immediate challenges and crises that require action. The case against the UN as the centre point of an effective global polity, couched in these terms, may look overwhelming. Yet the extreme scepticism of this negative evaluation is unwarranted for a number of reasons.

The first is that the UN, for all its weaknesses, functions as a single global forum for the exchange of views and as a body that attempts to broker and implement solutions to problems as defined by member states and a wider set of NGOs. The existence of such a worldwide forum for discussion and interstate negotiation and problem-solving through the implementation of agreed policy measures, incorporating virtually all the nations of the world, on a limitless agenda of issues, is historically unprecedented. Such a forum may lack the power to coerce national governments into compliance, but it does possess influence and expertise in both political conflict resolution and wider socioeconomic matters.

Within the conflict resolution and peace-keeping arena, for example, the UN has had some successes, such as the transfer to independence in Namibia and the partial success of political stabilization in Cambodia. Bercovitch (1996), in a survey of UN mediation of interstate conflicts, has calculated that, of 355 mediations studied, a successful outcome was achieved on 35 per cent of occasions. This record of successes is significant if not exactly outstanding. However, Bercovitch goes on to make the further point that many of the mediations that failed involve intractable cases of conflicts between nations with long histories of disputation, such as Arab–Israeli warfare, or of countries that are deeply divided with no recognized leadership or authority to secure peace, as in Somalia or Rwanda. In a sense, therefore, it is the most difficult cases that get to the UN, which is trying to mediate conflicts in which the parties themselves are poles apart. Here, the UN acts as mediator 'of last resort' and, in this sense, is unlikely to achieve a spectacular success rate.

The UN performance of mediation functions may be seen as a component part of a certain type of global polity. This scarcely lives up to the Utopian dreams of world peace held by some of the UN's founders. It is more akin to the conception of world order described by Roland Robertson (1992) in Figure 2.1 as a global *Gesellschaft*, based on the 'weak' ties of interstate dependency rather than on any 'stronger' sense of world government. In this context, it should be remembered that at least part of the disillusionment with the UN is precisely related to the failure of Utopian hopes that a world government, able to rise above nation-states, would materialize (Righter 1995). In this sense, a good deal of criticism of the UN takes the form of a failure of expectations as much as of a failure of effective political intervention.

The problem with using a 'world government' yardstick to judge UN performance, whether in conflict mediation or any other area, is that it treats the achievement of a global polity as mutually incompatible with the continuing autonomy of nation-states. This broad-brush approach gives insufficient attention to the complex and more fine-grained relations between the UN and its member-states or to subtle shifts in the practice of national sovereignty that have occurred as the UN has itself evolved.

Within a global *Gesellschaft,* we may expect states to wish to maximize their self-interest and to enter into collective arrangements with other states where interests suggest this as the optimal course of action. In so doing, however, further subtle changes in the direction of more conditional forms of national sovereignty have emerged, as we have already seen in Chapter 4. Rosenau conceives of these in terms of a normative shift from UN action taking place 'at-the-convenience-of-states', to the more muted principle whereby 'states-are-sometimes-obliged-to-go-along' (1996, p. 237). Two examples of this shift are cited. The first is the decreasing use of the veto in the Security Council, signifying less readiness to push sovereign national interests to the limit. The second is the widespread appeal of nations for the UN to monitor domestic elections. This has occurred in South Africa, Mexico, and Latin America, and widely in the countries of the former Soviet Union.

The conception of a global polity based on nation-states exercising conditional sovereignty, insofar as they accept the procedural rules of UN mediation and conflict resolution, provides one dimension of the contemporary global order. Yet the UN, in line with the broad aspirations of its Charter, has extended its scope well beyond issues of peace, security, and mediation, to include matters of economic development, social justice, and human rights, including the rights of women and children, and the issue of the natural environment. These topics involve governmental and intergovernmental debate within the central forums of the UN, but they also typically involve an increasingly complex and wide-ranging set of consultative, technical, and administrative institutions. These have the capacity to set standards and to monitor the performance of individual nation-states in meeting such standards.

A second major dimension to the existence of this kind of global polity is the development of a set of specialist UN agencies, such as the WHO or the UN High Commission for Refugees, with their own bureaucratic structures, accumulated bodies of expertise, and, in many cases, regulatory or interventionist capacities. Surrounding these institutions are thematic conferences, sponsored by the UN and its agencies, on issues such as population, women, social development, and the environment.

How and why has this extension of global political organization emerged? Part of the answer has already been suggested, in terms of the extension of UN membership to newly independent post-colonial nations with their own agendas of development and justice. But this is not the whole answer. What also requires explanation are the reasons why sufficient numbers of the nation-states that are members of the UN have been prepared to countenance an extension of the UN's scope.

One important point made by Rosenau (1980), as noted above, is that nations have come to see that many issues do not have military answers that can be resolved through the exercise of coercive power. Issues of economic development or environmental pollution, for example, involve the decentralized actions of many individuals, as well as governments, and hence are not amenable to military coercion. They are also typically issues in which the interdependence between nations affects what goes on in any one nation.

Contemporary nation-states typically find themselves faced with increasing numbers of problems that cannot be resolved on a national basis (Keohane 1984; McGrew 1992; Held 1995). The difficulty here may either be that individual nations lack the technical or financial resources to address problems such as poverty or economic modernization, or that nations face common problems, such as security or environmental protection, that require the joint action of all to produce effective results. Both types of difficulty may, of course, be involved in the one issue, as in the case of the environment. Here, expert technical knowledge about how best to address pollution problems is equally as important as collaboration between governments to implement change.

Such bodies can never operate independently of nation-states, but they have over the years developed significant elements of autonomy. This is evident not only in information-gathering and global agenda-setting, but also in the establishment and implementation of a range of interventionist and regulatory actions. Autonomy is also heightened by the access to and close working relationships of such bodies to a range of non-government organizations. In the case of the human rights area, for example, these include both professionally based organizations such as the International Commission of Jurists and broad-based social movements such as the Anti-Slavery Society and Amnesty International.

Close working relationships between national UN delegations, UN agency officials, and NGOs have grown up since the UN's inception. In some respects, these linkages build on even older precedents such as the humanitarian campaigns of the International Committee of the Red Cross, founded in 1863, or the peace and social reform work of the Women's International League for Peace and Freedom, begun in 1916. Such activities were designed to pressure nations into greater co-operation to achieve peace and humanitarian standard-setting in the international arena. They contributed to the earlier set of instruments such as the Geneva Conventions of 1864 for the Amelioration of the Condition of the Wounded and Sick in Armies in the Field, and the Hague Conventions of 1899 and 1907, limiting methods of warfare, and to further supplements to the Geneva Convention in 1949 and 1977 (Weissbrodt 1988).

NGOs were present at the San Francisco Conference in 1945 that drafted the UN Charter and were envisaged under Article 71 of that document as playing an important consultative role in the deliberations of the UN's Economic and Social Council (ECOSOCC) (Suter 1996, p. 258). This consultative role has been played out over the years in bodies such as the Commission on Human Rights and the Commission on the Status of Women. It has also expanded as the number of NGOs has grown and as the UN's agenda has widened, in part at least due to NGO pressure. NGO prominence in processes of agenda-widening has recently been evident at the Earth Summit in Rio, held in June 1992, and the Beijing UN Women's Conference in September 1995. In 1909, according to Held and McGrew (1993), there were 176 NGOs operating in the international arena. By 1989, this figure had risen to 4624 (Held and McGrew 1993, p. 271).

NGOs are not a uniform or homogeneous set of institutions. In some contexts, their principal role has been to provide political pressure to stimulate greater concern, as in a variety of environmentalist campaigns on issues such as acid rain or whaling. In other contexts, they may offer expert opinion geared to international standard-setting or the monitoring of compliance with UN conventions. The latter activity is especially important in the human rights area, where expert NGOs such as the International Commission of Jurists and Amnesty International have provided advice and information relevant both to human rights standard-setting and to the monitoring of countries' compliance with treaties they have signed (Weissbrodt 1988; Opsahl 1992).

The emerging picture of the global polity presented here is a rather complex one, for several reasons. First, as pointed out throughout this chapter, there are multiple actors, and not only nation-states, involved. Second, national sovereignty remains intact in an ultimate juridical sense but is increasingly conditional upon compliance with a range of transnational regulatory regimes. This reflects increased international interdependency and the growth of problems that nation-states believe (or are pressured to believe) can only be effectively addressed through international co-operation and transnational agreement. To elaborate this argument in a more concrete way, we will now look at an important case study, that of environmental protection.

Environmental protection: a case study in the operation of the emerging global polity

Concern for the adverse, and possibly disastrous, impact of human activity on the natural environment has grown to become one of the leading issues in national and international politics at the end of the 20th century. The German sociologist Ulrich Beck (1992) has argued that the character of risks facing humankind has shifted with the advent of industrial society from naturally induced disasters to risks and hazards generated by human society. In addition to the ultimate threat of annihilation by nuclear weapons, there is a long list of other socially generated environmental problems such as ozone depletion in the atmosphere, industrial pollution and acid rain, chemical pesticides, and the depletion of natural resources through overfishing and inappropriately intensive agriculture. Many of these problems compromise or threaten to compromise the food chain, as recently dramatized in the 'mad cow disease' crisis, apparently originating from inadequate management practices in the animal feed industry. Such risks are also typically cross-border problems that implicate many if not all nation-states.

The concern often expressed about the transborder character of environmental problems is that they are beyond the regulatory outreach of nation-states. This is disturbing since so much environmental hazard is tied up with processes organizationally concentrated in the hands of multinationals. Problems arise not simply from the intensive use of hazardous industrial technologies, but more fundamentally from economic transactions that put profit and immediate economic cost minimization above broader social objectives and wider kinds of social cost. For example, multinationals have, in certain cases, located environmentally hazardous production processes in countries or regimes with lower regulatory standards, such as Mexico rather than the USA, or operated to lower standards in developing countries than in developed ones. The 1984 environmental health disaster at the Union Carbide pesticide plant in Bhopal, India, which killed at least 2500 people, is one of the most tragic instances of the multinational exploitation of low regulatory standards. Longer-term cumulative hazards apply to practices such as climate-damaging deforestation in Latin America and South-East Asia, in which local capital and developing government support and complicity compounds the impact of multinational operations.

Many environmentalists go on to argue that the failure to address environmental problems prejudices the long-term survival of the human race on the planet. Whether or not such Doomsday predictions are valid, it is clear that environmental thinking has a strong and intrinsic tendency to think globally. However localized particular instances of environmental damage may be, they are typically subsumed within a broader global framework of thought. This is largely because of environmental interdependency, whereby damage or problems created in one area have a wider effect elsewhere, unimpeded by territorial boundaries. Thus greenhouse gas emissions primarily from the northern hemisphere have contributed to, among other things, the depletion of the ozone layer over the South Pole, which has in turn contributed to increased levels of skin cancer in Australia. Again, the fall-out from the Chernobyl nuclear disaster created adverse effects on the health of people and animals in many other parts of Northern and Western Europe as well as the Ukraine.

International involvement in environmental protection dates mainly from the period since 1972 when the United Nations Conference on the Human Environment (UNHCE) was held, leading to the establishment of the United Nations Environment Program (UNEP). Over half of the 140 multilateral environmental treaties signed since 1921 date from the period since 1973. Further intensification of UN involvement took place in the early 1990s with the United Nations Conference on Environment and Development (UNCED), or Rio Earth Summit, held in 1992. This not only laid down conventions on biodiversity and greenhouse gas emissions, but also adopted a programme of action to achieve the principles of appropriate environmental behaviour laid down in the Earth Charter. This agenda looks impressive but has been subject to severe criticism from the outset as a document without the teeth to secure change. It nonetheless remains important to establish exactly how such a global environmental standard-setting agenda came about and how far national governments and other powerful interests are really prepared to comply with environmental protection regimes. What, in other words, does a case study of environmental protection tell us about the emergent features of the global polity?

One of the most valuable research-based studies of such questions is 'Institutions for the Earth', a collaborative project headed by Haas, Keohane and Levy (1993). This deals almost entirely with the period before the Rio Earth Summit. The environmental challenge is disaggregated into seven particular subfields, namely oil pollution from tankers, acid rain, stratospheric ozone depletion, pollution of the North and Baltic Seas, mismanagement of fisheries, overpopulation, and the misuse of farm chemicals.

It should be emphasized that this choice of seven problem areas is deliberately skewed to matters that have received significant levels of institutional involvement. It is designed, in other words, to permit testing of the impact of institutions. There are clearly other environmental areas, such as deforestation or species extinction, in which international institutional involvement has been less significant and in which environmental outcomes may therefore be expected to be worse than in the seven chosen cases. Within these limitations, the importance of the 'Institutions for the Earth' project is that it analyses how institutional regulation arises, what problems it faces, and the extent to which these have been overcome.

The impact of international institutions on the seven chosen areas is investigated through a three-phase model. This focuses first on agenda-setting, whereby environmental concerns are identified. Next comes international policy formulation, which turns concern into policies for collective application. Within this second phase, particular emphasis is placed on the 'contracting environment', that is, on the structure of incentives and sanctions affecting individual governments' willingness to agree to policy change. The third and final phase is one of implementation primarily through national policy development. This in turn centres on the capacity, both scientific and financial, of governments to take action.

One of the main findings of this study is a lack of uniformity in responses to the various environmental problems. In some cases, such as oil pollution and fishery mismanagement, it has been very hard to raise government concern through international negotiations. In others, such as ozone depletion, concern has been successfully mobilized and policies formulated, leading to implementation strategies in the form of reduced chlorofluorocarbon (CFC) emission levels. What is not clear, as yet, is how well nations are actually complying. In other environmental areas, such as acid rain and maritime pollution, the position is more ambiguous, with plenty of rhetorical concern and new policy regimes, but still uncertainty about whether the effects of such actions will actually remedy the underlying problems.

Blanket diagnoses of inexorable environmental doom or institutional success may be premature and ill-founded, but what exactly is it that explains the variations in response identified here? As far as governmental responses are concerned, it is coalitions of national governments that are in the main ultimately responsible for implementing change. Whether individual governments do respond is partly a question of whether they perceive environmental problems to be worthy of action, how they understand the connection between such problems and national interests, how far they are pressured by powerful domestic interests, whether the international institutional setting offers incentives to co-operate with other governments in global regulation, and whether governments have the capacity to act.

One of the major findings of this study is that campaigns by NGOs and/or scientists may play a major role in raising the concern of governments. In the 1970s, for example, scientists were the first to raise the problem of ozone depletion, while NGOs took the lead in publicizing the problem of chemical pesticides. Individual governments may also quickly take up issues and become leaders for change, as in the key roles of Norway and Sweden in developing recognition and more effective regulation of the problem of acid rain. More typically, however, within Western democracies, it is only when domestic political pressure mounts (sometimes in conjunction with the added commitment of individual lead nations) that most governments take action. However, as Levy *et al.* (1993) point out 'the salience to domestic publics in the West of issues of ozone and acid rain has been much greater than that of international oil pollution and the pesticide trade' (p. 408). Where public pressure is not forthcoming, as in the latter case, environmental action is far harder to achieve.

International institutions may also heighten the concern by amplifying public pressure on laggard governments. This may take the form of public exposure before international meetings at which representatives of other nations are present. In the 1980s, for example, public exposure of the UK government's lack of action on issues of North Sea pollution and acid rain succeeded in stimulating political responses and policy developments. The presence of NGOs prepared to speak out on controversial issues at meetings of bodies such as the Long Range Trans-Boundary Air Pollution (LRTAP) has made it increasingly difficult for recalcitrant governments to simply ignore problems.

Why then do governments obstruct certain kinds of environmental protection regime but not others? Rowlands (1995) has compared environmental regulation in two major areas, namely ozone layer depletion caused by the production of chemicals such as CFC gases, and the climate change resulting from greenhouse gas emissions. He argues that there has been greater success in regulating types of chemical production such as the use of CFC gases in aerosols than in regulating greenhouse gas emissions. The explanation of this contrast is complex. One reason for greater success in the ozone depletion regulatory area was the greater degree of scientific consensus compared with the greenhouse gas area. In this latter case, scientists have been more divided and slower to reach consensus on the problem of global warming. This made it easier for many nation-states to resist or dilute arguments for action on the global warming question, both before and after the 1992 Rio Earth Summit.

Yet scientific learning and the degree of scientific consensus are not the only relevant variables here. According to Rowlands, another reason for greater progress in the ozone depletion area is that the vested economic interests of private corporations were, in significant respects, less hostile to regulation in the ozone depletion area than in the greenhouse gas area. In the case of CFC production, for example, American chemical producers certainly resisted regulatory measures, such as the banning of CFCs in aerosols. Yet over time, US corporations, led by Du Pont, were more easily able to shift production to non-CFC alternatives compared with European producers, led by ICI, who had a greater proportion of their investment within the chemical industry tied up in CFC production. Once profit opportunities were identified in alternative technologies, the interests of American producers shifted to support the regulation of aerosol CFCs in order to achieve a competitive edge over European producers still committed to the older technology. This shift in corporate strategy helps to explain why the US government was more supportive of CFC aerosol bans than were European governments and the EU.

In the greenhouse gas debate, in contrast, the USA not only has a huge investment in fossil fuels through a reliance on coal, electricity, and gas, but also has a higher-cost and less efficient energy industry compared with that of Europe. The resistance to greenhouse gas regulation on the part of the private economic interests involved has been far more significant, and the US government position accordingly more hostile, rejecting any kind of binding agreement on greenhouse gas emission. Similar resistance is to be found on the part of other economic interests and governments implicated in fossil fuel burning, such as the OPEC oil cartel or leading coal exporters such as Australia.

Obstacles to government involvement in improved environmental regulation may also emerge from difficulties in the contracting environment and/or a lack of capacity to implement change. In the former case, the contracting environment that governments and intergovernmental agencies face may not be suited to the enforcement of regulation. If individual states cannot be assured that other states will collaborate in regulation, they may not be prepared to take action to protect the environment, even though they recognize that a problem exists. This applies especially in cases where nations share the use of common resources, such as international fisheries. In the case of fisheries management, the scientific evidence on overfishing did not lead to effective management owing to difficulties in preventing cheating by some countries on quotas imposed by international agreement. It was only when the more effective device of exclusive economic zones was agreed, allowing more effective policing, that the climate of distrust was at least partially overcome and more effective steps were taken to manage stocks.

While international bodies may increase governmental concern by providing and disseminating scientific information, their role in enhancing the contractual environment may be crucial to achieving policy development. Intergovernmental bodies serve here as bargaining forums that may remove obstacles to compliance with environmental regulation. This may happen through improved iterated bargaining procedures in which nations build up trust in each other or through the sharing of the costs of monitoring agreements once they are made.

A final set of issues affects the translation of policies such as the development of new rules of environmental protection into practice. This centres on the technical, organizational, and financial capacity of governments to effect reform. Such issues are especially important for those developing countries or post-Communist countries in Eastern Europe whose abilities to implement much-needed environmental policies are restricted by a lack of resources. Here, international institutions have provided both expert and financial advice to governments and other bodies.

Expertise has been brought to bear on issues such as agricultural pesticides through the Food and Agriculture Organisation (FAO), while the International Maritime Organisation's World Maritime University offers training to ship captains in the application of environmental regulations. An area in which financial assistance has been forthcoming is that of ozone depletion. Here a fund exists to help less developed countries find alternatives to CFCs. There are, however, significant general problems with arrangements of this type. First, the financial support is often very limited. Second, in a number of areas such as maritime oil pollution, there has been little upgrading of the responsive capacity of developing countries.

We have dwelt, at length, on the issue of environmental protection, both for its intrinsic importance to the social ecology of globalization and, above all, as a case study in the operation of global politics. What is striking about the evidence from this case study is the simultaneous persistence of nation-states as key players, with the emergence of a wider multi-actor (although imperfect) system of environmental regulation, with which increasing numbers of nations have been prepared to comply in some form. The point here is neither that all environmental problems are now being addressed through effective compliance with regulation, nor that such regulations as exist are optimal for the environment. The argument is rather that, in the space of less than a century, from a time when the League of Nations was reluctant to get involved at all in environmental issues, there now exists a significant if incomplete global institutionalization of environmental protection. This comprises international organizations – governmental and non-governmental – as well as norms about the desirability of environmental protection. The link between organization and norm is provided through a regime of rules, in whose design the key players have the opportunity to participate and to which national governments may comply.

The particular case study of environmental protection may, in these respects, be taken as an exemplification of a wider model of global politics, to which we now turn.

Conceptualizing global politics

A key question that has both engaged and perplexed commentators is whether or not a world order exists, and if so, what form it takes. This issue has become a matter of considerable rhetorical significance in the light of George Bush's announcement of the emergence of 'a new world order' after the end of the Gulf War. This remark has prompted both scepticism among those who see only anarchy and disorder and opposition from those who agree that there is order but see it lacking in social justice. One conceptual difficulty here is that the term 'order' has both sociological and normative connotations, and the two are often hard to separate. Many commentators are, for example, loathe to describe what they see as an unjust system, built on massive North–South inequalities, as orderly in any normative sense.

A number of attempts have, nonetheless, been made to identify the major social regularities and patterns of the global political order. McGrew (1992) has very usefully identified three major paradigms, namely realism and neo-realism, liberal-pluralism, and neo-Marxism, that are relevant to this exercise (p. 22). These are differentiated according to types of dominant actors, political processes, and forms of order involved.

Realist approaches, for example, take nation-states and intergovernmental organizations to be the dominant actors, and interstate bargaining and conflict to be the principal political processes at work within a global polity. This essentially interstate system is regulated primarily through the balance of power. The emphasis that this approach gives to the robustness of the nation-state and interstate bargaining is important, especially in the light of premature declarations of the death of the nation. At the same time, global politics is clearly not composed simply of nation-states. Other types of actor are involved, ranging from the MNEs and economic regulatory bodies that McGrew associates with neo-Marxist thinking, to the wider range of UN social agencies and non-governmental bodies dealing with human rights and social justice, included in the longer list of dominant actors developed in liberal-pluralism thought.

If realism has the demerit of too narrow a view of the dominant players, its state-centred view of the political processes of the global polity is also vulnerable to criticism by the neo-Marxist emphasis on the political economy of the global division of labour constituted through MNEs as well as nation-states. Neo-Marxist global political economy, with its emphasis on capital accumulation and class in the analysis of global investment and the operations of the IMF and World Bank, is an important corrective to narrowly realist depictions of global politics in terms of international security issues. A further more particular advantage of liberal-pluralism is that it encourages a more multidimensional account of political processes than does neo-Marxism.

Global political issues such as human rights and environmentalism are thereby recognized in their own terms rather than as moments in the global conflict between capital and labour.

What liberal-pluralism adds to both realism and neo-Marxism is an alternative to solely Hobbesian interest-based, conflict-centred models of global order, be these between nations or classes. While liberal-pluralism may in turn be criticized for being insufficiently conflict-centred, it has merit in exploring the shift to consensual processes of global politics, especially where normative influences are evident, as in aspects of environmental politics, reviewed above.

A final set of issues concerns differing conceptions of global order. Here, the realist conception of the interstate system is a necessary but insufficient model of global politics. It is hard to see how global socio-economic inequalities can be accounted for without greater emphasis on neo-Marxist political economy, especially as it affects the terms upon which nations are involved in trade, investment, and technology transfer. The alternative and wider liberal-pluralist case in favour of global management or regulation as an increasingly overarching political framework depends on the argument that the neo-Marxist critique of realism is still too narrow, one-dimensional, and reductionist. In other words, not all global political decisions are to be explained in terms of the operation of a single capitalist logic. Whether and how nuclear weapons proliferation, human rights, or environmental protection is regulated depends on more complex processes in which a range of political as well as economic interests are at stake, in which global capital does not have unilateral sway, and in which a range of governmental and non-governmental actors are involved.

The comparison of these three paradigms yields a number of general insights. These encourage us to picture global politics in terms of a multiplicity of linkages that operate across political and cultural boundaries. These are not simply intergovernmental processes, but are also the multiplicity of interconnections linking NGOs, (both commercial and non-profit-making), social movements, and individuals. These link producers with consumers, scientists and professionals in various countries with each other, extended families spread across diasporic migrant chains, members of worldwide Churches, sporting groups preparing for the Olympic Games, and the Treasuries and Education Departments of different nations and regions, as well as bodies such as the WHO and Amnesty International.

The breadth of these linkages may be better grasped by contrasting two models of global politics, outlined in Figures 5.1 and 5.2, based on the work of McGrew (1992). In Figure 5.1, a simple model of global politics as politically centred interstate relations is presented. Here, each circle represents a nation-state divided into governmental (shaded) and non-governmental (plain) segments. The linkages are exclusively between governmental state-based bodies, both national and international. This contrasts with the more complex polyarchic and decentred cobweb image depicted in Figure 5.2. Here, global political interaction is represented by the complex sets of arrows linking NGOs, such as corporations or social movements, and individuals, with each other as well as with governments, in addition to the intergovernmental linkages of the state-centred model. What the cobweb image of Figure 5.2 successfully evokes is the complexity of a global political structure that is very far from being exclusively state centred and intergovernmental.

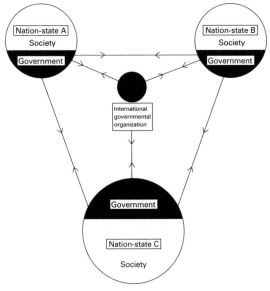

Figure 5.1   Global politics as interstate relations

Source: Adapted from McGrew (1992, p. 6).

An example of such webs in action concerns the Century Zinc mine project in northern Australia, owned until very recently by the Anglo-Australian multinational mining giant Rio Tinto. The attractiveness of

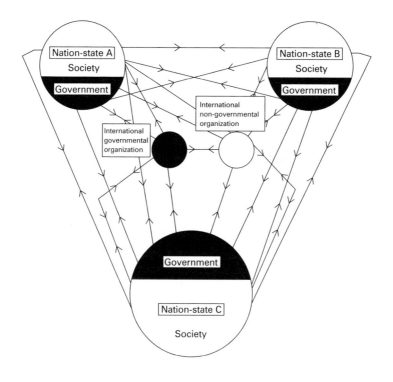

Figure 5.2   Global politics: the multicentred cobweb image

Source: Adapted from McGrew (1992, p. 13).

this project is that the zinc ore is of a chemical composition that is better able to meet more stringent EU environmental regulations governing atmospheric pollution, recently implemented in the Netherlands, site of a major European zinc smelter. The company wished to bring the Australian mine on stream by the middle of 1996 to comply with the regulations but found that an Aboriginal land rights claim had been placed on the land where the mine would operate. The dilemma for the company was that the European regulatory framework demanded a rapid agreement on meeting the new environmental standard, but the Australian legal determination of the land rights claim was likely to be lengthy. Having initially tried to combat the Aboriginal campaign by lobbying for the legislative protection of mining rights, the company then changed tack and agreed to negotiate. Meantime, the Dutch deadline for compliance was extended. As lengthy negotiations with traditional Aboriginal owners continued, Rio Tinto cut its losses by selling the mine to Pasminco, another large producer, providing the land rights claims could be settled. This took place in mid-1997.

This case has been cited in support of the idea of webs of regulatory influence, involving both governmental bodies at national and international levels, and non-governmental bodies, both corporate and organized within social movements. In this case, the regulatory strands involve both environmental issues and the rights of indigenous peoples.

Concluding remarks

As indicated at the outset, this chapter, like the previous one, has been concerned primarily with the place of the state as a political institution and apparatus of power within the rapidly evolving sphere of global politics. While we have argued that state sovereignty is highly conditional on global patterns of interdependence, the state as a political institution is far from being submerged, either by global capitalism or by transnational political organization. To leave the matter here would, however, be to ignore the other half of that modern amalgam the *nation-state*, namely that pertaining to the nation as a political and cultural community.

While global politics is very much a contemporary reality, it is also very clear that nationalism and the politics of national identity are equally significant aspects of the contemporary world, from the Balkans and Eastern Europe to many parts of the Western and developing worlds. The institutional robustness of the nation-state stems, in large measure, from its instrumental value as a power container able to secure political security and socioeconomic stability conducive to business and expanding citizenship rights. Yet it is also arguable that the nation-state draws much of its contemporary resilience from its symbolic significance as a source of political and cultural identity. This raises the possibility that nations and nationalism are, in certain senses, forms of resistance to globalization as much as institutional components of the global order. This line of argument is pursued in the next chapter, where the primarily economic and political discourse of the past three chapters is extended into more explicitly cultural directions.

6

Nationalism and Ethnicity: Obsolete Relics, Antiglobal Trends or Key Components of the Global Field?

The dynamics of the late 20th century world have confounded social scientists and political actors alike. Conventional certainties and widely held predictions about the future have been undermined as social change takes on new characteristics or seems to return to features of an older world thought to be obsolete and outmoded. Among the prime examples of this process are the revival of nationalism and the robust persistence of ethnicity.

At first sight, these two often interrelated trends seem to run counter to processes of globalization inasmuch as they emphasize the necessity and desirability of boundaries between groups rather than a single borderless world. Their continuing presence seems to contradict claims that globalization is an unstoppable process dominating nations and eroding local allegiances. Many commentators assume that the contemporary eruption of apparently primordial loyalties and hatreds represents a major limit to the process and scope of globalization. Many also see the revival of nationalism and ethnicity, in part at least, as resistance to a global world where boundaries are permeable and all is in flux. National identity, especially where it is overlaid with a sense of ethnic solidarity, offers some kind of stable anchor for identity and political security in an age where impersonal global capital predominates. It is thus well worth considering whether political and cultural processes and institutions are less easily globalized than economic ones, and if so, why this should be.

Nationalism and the nation-state

Contemporary nationalism, in one shape or form, is evident on almost every continent, defying the projections of both Marxism and modernization theory. Whether in Western Europe, the Balkans, Central Asia, Africa, or Latin America, the appeal to nation as a source of cultural identity and political security has, on most occasions, proved more powerful than the claims of social class. In addition, nationalism, in certain of its manifestations, also threatens the liberal-democratic model of a secular society of free-standing individuals able to secure their interests through the market and citizenship rights. In particular, the association between nationalism and racism or extremist forms of ethnicity, reflected in the 20th-century tragedies of genocide and what has recently been called 'ethnic cleansing', has shaken the complacency of Western commentators who thought that the end of the Cold War automatically meant the triumph of liberal-democratic politics.

The wide range of contexts in which nationalism has arisen and the different forms it has taken are evident from even a cursory inspection of the history of the past 250 years and academic commentaries on the topic. Nationalism has been conceived, for example, as political or cultural, unificatory or fragmentating, ethnocentric or polycentric, and progressive or reactionary. Leaving these binary conceptual distinctions aside for the moment, it is instructive to note the distinction between three contemporary types. The first involves the association of nationalism with *democratic struggles* against autocracy and monarchical dynasticism, often with a strong internationalist tone, as in the American and French Revolutions of the late 18th century. The second is connected with *anticolonial struggles* against European powers by political movements in Africa and Asia, seeking to project a sense of the national community beyond tribalism. Post-colonial nationalism has sometimes projected wider transnational aspirations, as in Pan-Arabism and Pan-Africanism. The third comprises *antiliberal and chauvinistic* forms of nationalism. In this, nationalism is linked not with claims about the common aspirations of some wider entity, such as humanity or the African peoples, but with the exclusive and often racist claims of a particular people, defined as culturally distinct from and often superior to others. It is this version of nationalism that may in extreme forms be used to license genocide and 'ethnic cleansing'. Well-known examples include the Nazi Holocaust against the Jews and the more recent interethnic conflicts in the Balkans involving Serbs, Croats, and Bosnian Muslims.

Each of these examples has a complex history of its own, and the place of nationalism and ethnicity in each also varies. Yet the underlying logic to all such cases is that identity, political loyalty, and political action are based on membership of a national community. Where differences arise is, first, in how a nation is conceived, and second, in how a nation is seen to articulate with both transnational and subnational social groups.

As indicated in earlier chapters, the institution of the nation-state represents an amalgam of two entities: the state as a set of political institutions, and the nation, conceived of as the political and cultural community of a people. These distinct entities have often been confused and conflated, leading to notorious difficulties in defining exactly what a nation actually is. Walker Connor regards the shorthand use of the term nation to refer to either or both of the following:

- a sense of peoplehood
- a political institution.

This has contributed to a 'terminological chaos' in discourses on nation and nationalism (Connor 1987). One example of this is the failure to distinguish between nationalism as loyalty to the state and nationalism as loyalty to a nation or people.

Failure to distinguish the two for purposes of analysis has created several problems. One is that many people are able to identify with the nation as a cultural and historical identity without necessarily identifying with the current political institutions embodied in the national state. One could be a staunch Greek nationalist under the dictatorship of the colonels without supporting the Greek state of that era, just as liberal-democratic German nationalists under the Kaiser could support and identify with the nation while criticizing the monarchist form of state. A second problem is that states can be established without necessarily being attached to strong bodies of nationalist feeling. This often occurred in the post-war process of decolonization, when the same arbitrary borders that colonial powers imposed on the territories they annexed were subsequently used as the boundaries for new postcolonial states even though they typically encompassed a range of tribal and ethnic groups. In Europe, too, it is clear that nations such as the UK are not composed of a single people or ethnicity. The UK contains the Scots, Welsh, and Irish as well as the English, while Spain contains Basques and Catalans. For Connor, only a minority of nation-states, such as Iceland, Japan, or Norway, are sufficiently homogeneous to be described as nation-states.

Connor uses evidence of this kind to dispute as facile the conventional proposition that the world is composed of nation-states. The world may well be divided into states based upon claims of exclusive juridical sovereignty within a given territory. However, such entities are more typically multi-ethnic or multinational, in the sense of being composed of a range of peoples. The typology of relations between states and peoples given in Table 6.1 is therefore proposed. Here, states vary according to the number of peoples within them, the number of peoples whose homeland is within some part of the state, and the particular impact of immigration on patterns of state-building. Mestizo states, for example, are a category limited to Latin America based on a population of those with joint European-Amerindian ancestry, contrasted with multihomeland multinational states, such as Nigeria and the former Soviet Union, containing the homelands of many peoples.

Table 6.1   A typology of relations between state and nation

Type	Characteristic	Examples
Nation-states	Extremely homogeneous	Iceland, Japan
Multination-states	Ethnic diversity	
1. Unihomeland	Ethnic mix due to immigration, but claimed as home by only one group	Srilankan Sinhalese Malaysian Malays
2. Multihomeland	Ethnic mix, but claimed as home by more than one group	Former Soviet Union Nigeria
3. Non-homeland	Ethnic mix due to immigration, but no group sees the territory as the homeland	Caribbean states such as Guyana or Trinidad-Tobago
Immigrant states	Integration of ethnic mix into a single nation, without that being a historic homeland	USA
Mestizo states	European-Amerindian mix	Latin America

Source: Adapted from Connor (1994, p. 77–84).

Another set of definitional and conceptual problems stems from the emotionality and normativity of terms such as 'national' and 'nationalism'. This normativity is reflected in Ernest Gellner's minimal definition of nationalism as a 'principle which holds that the political and national unit *should* be congruent' (1983, p. 1) (emphasis added). The proposition that polity and nation should coincide is deep-seated but also profoundly contested. For some, nation is a sublime and sacred entity; for others, it is one fundamental root cause of violence, suffering, and illusion. We are dealing here not simply with ostensibly neutral social science concepts, but with matters that are charged with high levels of emotional force and embedded in often deeply held values. Nations in this sense typically have moral and aesthetic personalities, both to adherents who identify nations with positive values and all that is beautiful, and to opponents who associate nationalism with all that is bad, evil, irrational, and ugly.

These simple dichotomies born of political commitment and intense social psychological engagement do, however, skew the analysis of nationalism to only some of its more powerful exemplifications. Michael Billig (1995) has recently issued a cautionary warning against stereotyping nationalism as extremism, gripped by intense emotion, and embroiled in violent pathological modes of political action. To think solely in these terms, he claims, is to neglect more mundane or banal forms of nationalism, embedded in the everyday life of nations that are more politically settled and peaceful, such as the USA or many parts of Western Europe. The national flags that hang almost unnoticed on public buildings symbolize this latter form of nationalism and stand in contrast to 'hot' activist forms of nationalism, in which flags are waved in the course of conflict and political mobilization. While the Irish tricolour is waved as a gesture of nationalist defiance of British sovereignty by many Catholics in Northern Ireland, the same flag hangs on public buildings in the Irish Republic as a more mundane symbol of nationhood, along with national symbols on bank notes, currency, and advertising logos. Each is a variant of nationalism, but the latter forms tend to be neglected by predominantly liberal theorists of nationalism who see in it only irrational pathology and atavistic social aspirations.

Notwithstanding this array of difficulties, analysts of nationalism have taken a range of positions on the relationship between the two parts of the amalgam of nation-state.

Theories of nationalism and the nation-state

John Hutchinson (1994) has distinguished between primordialist, modernist, and ethnicist interpretations of nationalism. The primordial position argues that nations represent ancient 'natural' loyalties that originated in the mists of time but which have nonetheless driven the recent historical emergence of the nation-state. Herder, the 18th-century German theorist of nationhood, and Bagehot, the 19th-century English political commentator, both, in their different ways, saw the nation-state arising from the aspirations of a people (or Volk), implying that peoples create and have a right to create political institutions. Nations come first, states come next, albeit in organic union with each other.

The attractiveness of this argument is that the appeal to historical roots is exactly how nationalist movements understand and present themselves to the world. Hence the trappings of tradition and inherited myths that attach to such movements. The problem with this view is that national consciousness appears to be a comparatively recent phenomenon, one which in many, although not all, respects post-dates the formation of nation-states. Both Mann (1986) writing of England and Braudel (1988) of France make the point that in late medieval and early modern times, most inhabitants of these two countries did not conceive of themselves as English or French, nor did they speak a standard language. Until the French Revolution of 1789, there was no national French flag, while the language of the Declaration of the Rights of Man was spoken by only a minority of the population (Billig 1995, p. 25).

The further back in history one goes, the greater the degree of mixture and complexity that arises in the background constituents of groups that may today regard themselves as a people with a continuous historical integrity. This is reflected in an ironic remark attributed to Israel Zangwill that if we 'turn time's cinematograph back far enough... the Germans are found to be French and the French Germans'. By this, he means that the French nation was constructed on lands settled by the Germanic Franks, Burgundians, Visigoths, and Normans, while modern Germany comprises lands in which Celts as well as Germanic tribes settled. Even in the mid- to late 19th century, there is evidence to suggest that many Europeans, especially those from rural and less educated backgrounds, identified primarily with local or regional entities rather than with the nation (Weber 1976). Most late 19th-century migrants to the USA identified themselves in the official migration documents, 'as Neapolitan, Calabrian and the like, but not Italian... Gorali, Kashubi, Silesian and so on, but not Polish...' (Thernstrom 1980, cited in Connor 1994, p. 221).

Such criticisms have given credibility to an alternative approach to the analysis of nations and nationalism that may be termed modernist. For analysts such as Gellner and Hobsbawm, nationalism is a modern phenomenon linked with processes such as the rise of the nation-state, industrialization, and the development of modern capitalism. In spite of its apparent appeal to the past, nationalism is seen as an invented tradition, fostered more by intellectuals and manipulated by political élites and special interest groups. These are the key mechanisms behind groundswells of spontaneous popular enthusiasm rather than the reawakening of ancient traditions. Hobsbawm (1990) cites the following instructive comment by the 19th-century Italian nationalist Massimo d'Azeglio on the achievement of Italian unification: 'We have made Italy, now we have to make Italians' (1990, p. 44). The implication is that national feeling has now to be created by those political actors and nationalist intellectuals who had driven forward the unification process to military and *realpolitik* success. What pre-existed this process, as far as the populace was concerned, was regional and/or local affiliation embedded in regional languages and dialects.

Gellner (1983), in a much quoted discussion, sees nationalism emerging when the institution of the state has already emerged in stable form. Its emergence is connected with the transition from what he calls agroliterate to industrial societies. In the former, there was no tendency to connect political power with cultural boundaries. For Gellner, privileged élites typically accentuated their distinction from the remainder of society without recourse to cultural imperialism or the cultural homogeneity of the political unit. There was no need for such congruence where hierarchy prevailed, and most of the population was 'laterally insulated' from each other in agricultural communities (1983, p. 9).

Industrial societies, in contrast, depend on much higher levels of standardization in technological competence and communication. One response to this is the drive to create a standardized national language. At the same time, the commitment of industrial societies to perpetual growth within a specialized division of labour requires high levels of literacy, which can only be delivered by centralized systems of education. Socialization takes place outside local intimate social relations. This creates problems in finding some new principle of social integration that can tie together the new industrial state with the cultural order in a way that is suitably standardized. For Gellner, nationalism is such a principle. Thus it is not to be seen primordially as 'the awakening of an old, latent, dormant force, though that is how it does indeed present itself. [Rather] it is... the consequence of a new form of social organization, based on deeply internalized, education-dependent high cultures... (1983, p. 48). In the longer term, however, once industrialization is achieved, the intensity of nationalism declines.

One potential problem with Gellner's approach is that his model works better for Western than for Eastern Europe or the post-colonial states. Here, as Hutchinson (1994, p. 21) points out, nationalism predates industrialization. Gellner had himself considered this kind of objection in attempting a typology of nationalisms (1983, pp. 88–109). This investigated the effect of variations in the structure of power, access to education and literacy, and levels of cultural unity on varieties of nationalist experience. One distinction drawn was between the conditions under which nationalism emerged in Western and Eastern Europe. In the latter, where industrialism was less well developed and access to high culture limited, as in the Hapsburg lands of Central and Eastern Europe, nationalism tended towards ethnically driven fragmentation and Balkanization. In the West, in contrast, where industrialization developed more rapidly and literacy was more advanced, unificatory forms of liberal nationalism were more evident.

Whether this analysis of diverse forms of nationalism leaves Gellner's general theory intact is, however, debatable. This is partly because he has to dilute the bold proposition that the state precedes nationalism in order to deal with cases where the reverse is true. However, it is also because of underlying difficulties in holding to an entirely endogenous approach to nationalism, in which the conditions for its emergence in any particular location are related solely to the modernizing characteristics of the territory within which it emerges. Gellner recognizes that a broader cross-national focus is required in certain residual cases, as in the diasporic nationalism of groups such as Zionist Jews, but fails to develop the point very far to look at nationalism as a paradoxical force that both moves across borders to animate new groups while also creating or reinforcing other boundaries.

Gellner's argument is only one a number of versions of modernism, another being Eric Hobsbawm's emphasis on the nation-state as the most suitable political framework for the development and reproduction of modern capitalism rather than industrialization *per se*. Hobsbawm is also critical of Gellner's excessively top-down approach to nationalism, preferring to see it as a 'dual phenomenon', that is, the product of both popular aspirations 'from below' as well as capitalist development and state-building 'from above' (Hobsbawm 1990, p. 10). Such developments do not, however, return us to an emphasis on the primordial as found in Herder or in the propaganda of many nationalist movements. For modernists, they lead us rather into issues to do with the invention of tradition and the recasting of older traditions into nationalist form.

The idea of the invention of tradition, historically elaborated in Hobsbawm and Ranger (1983), proposes that the seeming age-old myths and rituals of nationhood are comparatively recent inventions rather than primordial sentiments existing in some kind of unbroken line of succession from the dim and distant past. Hobsbawm, for example, in his own work notes that institutions such as national anthems, national flags, and the personification of nations in symbols such as Marianne (France) or the Yankee Uncle Sam were invented as 'entirely new symbols and devices' in the period since the 1740s (1990, p. 7).

Some traditions, of course, depend on older materials, although even here the extent of accretion and discontinuity is significant. In Britain, for example, myths of King Alfred or King Arthur and the Knights of the Round Table, as episodes in the history of the English or British race, represent retrospective reconstructions of a speculative history that is very much mythical. Whether or not such figures existed – the evidence for figures such as Arthur being very slender (Williams 1994) – and whether they perceived themselves as English or British is beside the point. What is more salient is the way in which mythical stories about their deeds and exploits have been reinvented and recast, to be later woven into a broader story seeking to establish the ancient character of nationhood and its intimate connection with institutions such as monarchy and Christendom, or values such as courage and honour. In the case of the myths of Arthur and knights such as Lancelot, these have been appropriated by late medieval Cistercian monks as spiritual figures, by the English Tudor kings to assist in legitimizing a secular claim to the throne, and by 19th-century poets such as Tennyson to celebrate a more recognizably British nationalist past (Williams 1994). Aspects of 19th-century stories such as the Holy Grail, the Round Table or the magician Merlin are not there, so to speak, in the earliest original, but over time become accretions tying in with aspect of the reinvented story that suit a succession of religious, secular, and nationalist purposes.

Nations, as Benedict Anderson (1983) has pointed out, function as 'imagined communities'. By this, he means that those who identify with a particular nation will never meet in a face-to-face way with all those others who are attached to the nation. Rather, they rely on images of the nation as a people, such that 'in the minds of each lives the image of their communion' (p. 6). For Anderson, this process of imagining was historically dependent on the invention of mechanical printing and the mass production of the printed word in vernacular rather than arcane priestly languages (for example, Latin). This renders nationalism a relatively modern development of the past 350 years. The common features of the imagined nation are its bounded nature, its sovereign freedom within a bounded territory, and finally its constitution as a community, regardless of other marks of difference, such as wealth or status, that may differentiate its members. Unlike Gellner, Anderson sees nationalism as a rather more gradual product of social change. His analysis is also less trapped within a primarily endogenous framework in which nationalism emerges primarily within a distinct territory, having characteristics determined by factors such as the political structure and cultural make-up of the territory concerned. Instead, Anderson is more open to the influence of cross-border flows of nationalist feeling and political mobilization, as in his development of the idea of 'long-distance nationalism' to refer to the operation of diasporic nationalist sentiments under increasing conditions of global mobility of people, technology, and cultural representations.

This move beyond an endogenous framework has been taken furthest in Robertson's concept of the global field. This draws our attention to the process whereby, once some peoples have achieved the status of nation-state, combining political institutions with a sense of national community, all those who see themselves as peoples have sought out the status of a nation-state. In this way, national minorities within the former Spanish, Austro-Hungarian, Ottoman, French, or British Empires have sought national self-determination, with many cross-currents and linkages between them. Nationalism and a sense of peoplehood, in cases such as the peoples of 19th-century Latin America or 20th-century Africa and Indo-China, have both predated state formation and drawn on wider transnational currents of thought and mobilization. In the immediate post-war period, for example, the contact of West African troops serving in Asia as part of the Allied war effort assisted in transmitting the momentum and confidence of Indian nationalism to parts of the British Empire in Africa, notably the former Gold Coast, now Ghana. We shall return to the paradoxical connections between nationalism and globalization later in this chapter.

Modernist accounts of nationalism have provided a valuable and convincing critique of primordial theories. They have also offered considerable insights into certain connections between aspects of modernization, such as capitalist development or printing and literacy, and nationalism. They are nonetheless vulnerable to the criticism that they go too far in emphasizing discontinuity with the past and the novel character of nationalist feeling. This line of critique has been advanced by so-called ethnicist theorists of nationalism, foremost of whom is Anthony Smith (1971, 1986, 1990).

One of the most striking difficulties with the modernist position is to explain why individuals and social groups should still adhere to national feeling and national symbols in a modern, secular, and global world. How is it that individualism and self-interest, qualities associated with capitalism and liberalism, do not carry all before them? It is one thing to argue that capitalist institutions such as multinational companies need states to perform certain support functions but quite another to explain why states also become attached to a sense of nationhood based on political community. Even if it is argued that nationalism is fostered and manipulated from above by politicians, intellectuals, and the media, it still remains unclear why this particular form of loyalty and identity should be chosen as a basis for adherence. Why not adherence to something smaller, like a city, region, or industry, or something larger, like the world as a whole? If capitalism operates increasingly through global investment, production, and marketing strategies, why not organize ideological adherence to a global pattern?

In answering these questions, it is instructive to review the modernist argument that nationalist traditions are invented. This may well be true in a number of senses, especially inasmuch as there are few if any primordial loyalties that can be traced in any kind of unbroken lineage from the distant past to the present. To say this is not, however, to say that there are no long-run continuities between older forms of cultural allegiance and identity, and contemporary forms of nationalism. Ethnicity, considered as allegiance to ascriptive ties of history and place, may be one such linkage that spans either side of the supposedly 'Great Transformation' dividing the modern from the premodern. To think in this way is to dispute the proposition that processes like the Industrial Revolution or the French Revolution transformed the premodern world in some fundamental way that obliterated all previous allegiances and identities.

If the origins and development of nationalism predate the 18th century, how far back in history should analysis go? While modernists such as Benedict Anderson (1983) emphasize 16th- and 17th-century developments like innovation in printing and mass publication, there is a strong case for going much further back into the ancient world. Anthony Smith has argued that nationalism emerges where social groups face profound threats, be these from warfare or some other social and spiritual crisis. Warfare has been an endemic aspect of world history that clearly predates the modern world. The crises created by warfare and other threatening processes do not in and of themselves create nationalism or ethnic allegiance. However, the search for a common cultural base around which to mobilize in cases of threatened invasion or colonization encourages the formation of stronger ascriptive loyalties of place and kinship. These may cohere around a range of broad loyalties, including religion, as well as ethnicity and nationhood. Smith (1971, pp. 153–4) cites the example of the revolt of the Zealots against ancient Roman rule between AD 66 and AD 73 , in the name of both God and the Jewish people. Hutchinson (1994, p. 24) cites the example of the Armenians and Georgians living on shifting borders between warring Christian and Islamic states, who have retained a strong loyalty combining ethnic and religious components well into the modern period.

These examples indicate a sense of peoplehood way back in history, embedded for the most part in religion and ethnic identity. Such cases are deployed by Smith to support the argument that nationalism may have a long history connected with religious tradition and ascriptive ties of ethnicity. It is not, in this sense, a modern invention. Culture in the modern period has not then been a *tabula rasa* on which any kind of content may be inscribed. While many changes are evident in forms of nationalism between the ancient and modern worlds, and while much may be put down to modern cultural invention, this does not entirely dispose of continuity. The underlying point is that the nation has emerged, sometimes over a very long time period, out of ethnocultural feelings and sentiments that become embodied in myths about origins and in senses of a common heritage. These components of ethnocultural community, for example in the traditions of Jewish or Armenian people, persist over longer time frames than modernists suppose.

This persistence may, according to Smith, be embodied in a range of aesthetic and religious cultural forms as well as military and administrative practices. Religion is especially important as a bearer of group identity, insofar as the feelings and practices of a people are expressed and codified in forms of writing such as holy books (Smith 1986). Modern creators of the nation may seek to reinterpret or invent new senses of nation, but they do so in a context of popular attitudes and traditions that set limits to top-down manipulation by intellectuals and élites.

A case in point is the constraint exercized by existing Muslim traditions on the Indian subcontinent on modernizing nationalists attempting to establish a new secular nation-state in the 1930s and 40s. Here the Muslim separatism that led to the establishment of Pakistan was not simply a product of Muslim élite fears that they would be swamped by Hindus in post-independence India. It depended also on a persistent popular cultural tradition on the importance of living in an Islamic society under Islamic religious law (Robinson 1979).

Modern nations, the argument continues, are often built upon premodern ethnic cores, 'whose myths and memories, values and symbols shaped the culture and boundaries of the nation that modern élites managed to forge (Smith 1990, p. 180). This has, however, been obscured by the highly modernist bias built into definitions of nationalism. For many modernists, these centre on the particular forms of the American or French Revolutions that are then generalized into an ideal type. This bases conceptions of nation and nationalism on liberal-democratic ideals of equal citizenship rights within the political community. Smith calls this 'polycentric nationalism', in that it 'resembles the dialogue of many actors on a common stage' (1971, p. 158).

The cost of defining nation and nationalism in this way is that continuities with other ways of conceiving of the political community of a people are thereby ruled out. The cases from the ancient world, reviewed above, are regarded by Smith as an alternative type of ethnocentric nationalism. The commonalities here are not simply that each refers to the unifying principles that define a people but that the ethnocentric type was the historical forerunner of the polycentric type.

It may be observed in passing that this kind of historical sequence helps to explain why it is that ethnic elements of social solidarity may be found even within the political organization of societies committed to civil or liberal universalism as a principle that stands above particularistic associations. As Alexander (1988) points out, the extent of civil integration within any given society is typically limited by the ethnic historical core from which the nation was constructed. Hence the dominance of the White Anglo-Saxon Protestant (WASP) core within the USA and, notwithstanding certain connections between Protestantism and liberalism, the practice of the exclusion of non-WASPs, whether Blacks or non- European migrants, at various points in recent history.

How then to respond to debates about nationalism? The foregoing discussion suggests that a synthetic approach, combining aspects of the modernist and ethnicist arguments, is more powerful than either approach taken alone. Some compromise between the two is necessary, in part because no general theory of nationalism is adequate. While there are cases of inheritance of tradition (for example, the Jewish nation), there are equally cases of invention in which, as Hutchinson puts it, 'would-be nationalists have to concoct a common past out of fragmentary memories or conflictual traditions' (1994, p. 34). French nationalism appears to be a case of the latter process.

Synthesis between modernist and ethnicist accounts thus recognizes continuities as well as contrasts in popular allegiance and cultural identity between the modern and the premodern. It also recognizes that ethnicity has played an important part in the identity of peoples, both historically and in the contemporary world. This emphasis on ethnicity is evident, albeit in different ways, in Smith's approach to ethnohistory, in Hutchinson's work on cultural nationalism, and in Connor's studies of ethnonationalism. Ethnicity is, in this sense, very far from being an obsolete relic. Yet what is it that makes the connection between ethnicity and nation so powerful and enduring?

Ethnicity and nationhood

We return now to the question of why it is that nationhood and nationalism have been the form that much political allegiance and identity have taken in the making of the modern world. The answer is complex, relating both to the functions of nationalism as a form of cultural and political mobilization of a people against some kind of (usually) external threat, and to the attractions of the nation as a cultural symbol rooted in a sense of distinctiveness and boundedness. Ethnicity is one important way in which distinctiveness is conceived and boundedness is established.

As with other key terms, no commonly shared definition of ethnicity exists. One reason for this is that ethnicity is both a form of self-ascription, that is, a way in which people describe themselves and their identity, and a form of classification, by which groups are classified and constructed by others. In any particular case, the two may not coincide. Observers and classifiers, for example, may describe sets of people by ethnic labels or identify behaviour as being motivated by ethnicity when those concerned do not recognize or accept such forms of classification. Banton (1994), building on this point, argues that it is especially difficult for observers to distinguish between behaviour that is based on nationality and that based on ethnicity. Actors' definitions of the situation are therefore a necessary component of any analysis of the perceived operation of ethnicity. Such accounts do not, however, make sense by themselves, but also require attention to the economic and political context in which social action takes place.

One way of tackling some of the problems of distinguishing ethnicity from nationality is by distinguishing between two contexts in which ethnicity operates. The first is, so to speak, endogenous, that is, where appeals to ethnicity rest on historical claims by a people over a territory on the basis of historical and cultural descent. This is typically connected with ethnonationalism, in which conceptions of nationhood and membership of the political community are co-terminous with membership of a bounded ethnic group. Examples include the secessionist forms of nationalism that have challenged multi-ethnic empires, such as the now defunct USSR or the former Yugoslavia, or challenges by Scots or Bretons within more stable political units such as the British or French nation-states. In such cases, the appeal to ethnic identity rests largely on historical connection with a particular territory with which a cultural group claims a more or less continuous attachment over a significant period of time, often as a cultural minority within a larger political entity.

However, the appeal to ethnic identity also arises in a second context, namely as an immediate consequence of cross-border and global migration, where countries of settlement, such as the USA or Canada, become more multi-ethnic as a result of the mixing of populations. International migration, as indicated in Chapter 3, has been and continues to be a major component of globalization, virtually all nations and regions being involved in complex webs and long- as well as short-distance migration. Migrant ethnicity, as distinct from ethnonationalism, typically occurs outside the national homeland, as for example among Indo-Chinese in Australia or West Indians in Canada.

If we accept for the moment the contrasts between these situations, it would seem that ethnicity plays a somewhat different role in each. In the former, it is connected with national self-determination and nation-building, reflecting the claim that each people has a right to a national home or nation-state. In the latter, ethnicity may function both as source of cultural integrity and identity for minorities in a new and often hostile environment, and as the basis for expanded citizenship rights (Soysal 1994) within a multicultural political framework. This may be true, but it may still be insufficient as an answer to the question 'Why ethnicity as opposed to some other cultural identification?'

Another way of approaching the attraction of ethnicity as a cultural principle is clearer to see if the initial distinction between ethnonationalism and migrant ethnicity is relaxed. The case for doing this derives in part from the ubiquity of migration across boundaries within history (McNeill 1986) and the consequent typicality of multi-ethnic culture contact and settlement patterns throughout history. Human history over the very long term has seen massive population movements. Virtually all those who consider themselves settled in a particular place, even to the point of asserting aboriginal primacy, generally migrated, be it several centuries or several millennia ago, from somewhere else. While this sometimes meant occupancy of previously unpopulated land, it increasingly meant cultural contact, conflict, sometimes genocide or expulsion, but also often fusion with other groups, which were themselves often to split again, sometime later to compete as rival ethnicities. The peoples that recently fought each other in the Balkans over issues of ethnic purity and national self-determination once came from the same cultural stock.

In all these contexts, ethnicity, defined in Smith's terms, as an *ethnie,* or people with a bounded sense of identity and history, has functioned as a way of differentiating social groups from others who are felt to threaten or oppress them. This applies both to settled occupiers of land threatened from invaders and competitors from outside, and to migrants threatened by majorities from within. The social psychology of threat, including death in battle, rape, enslavement, and forcible removal from a territory, unemployment and poverty as the result of economic competition, or migrant assimilation to the cultural mainstream, generates an intense search for new meanings and new anchors for culture and personality.

Ethnicity offers higher levels of security against threat than do many others sources of identity and allegiance, because it offers members of a group symbolic as well as material forms of gratification and security. Such symbolic qualities include the security of a place in history and a sense of descent through history, as well as emotionally charged symbols of contemporary identity that typically appeal both to values of courage and vitality in opposition to enemies, and to the mythical stability of a natural order free from conflict and uncertainty. This order is often overlaid with religious associations, which not only reinforce ethnic group membership, but also add an appeal to transcendent religious principles to the other symbolic gratifications of ethnicity. Sexual representations of ethnic and ethnonational sentiment, as Mosse (1985) has noted in the case of nationalism, also play a key role here, both as metaphors for the courage and fertility of the cultural stock, and in terms of the capacity of groups to reproduce themselves over time.

Alternative affiliations find it hard to compete. In the case of class, for example, it is arguable that the promise of material security has rarely been enough to undercut the wider appeal of ethnicity and ethnonationalism, especially in a crisis. The failure of proletarian internationalism to prevent the First World War is a striking if tragic case in point. Peasant-based movements against imperial domination in recent Asian history were generally only successful where economic grievance was allied with national sentiment (Johnson 1962). Adherence to the city-state, an older model derived from the Hellenic past and reinvented in Renaissance Italy, has in contrast been unable to match the material security promised by the nation-state, on the basis of a larger home markets and modern developments in military technology rendering cities too small and vulnerable to be competitive.

In this general model, which draws in large measure on Smith, ethnicity, either alone or in conjunction with nationhood, acts as a means of promoting and retaining identity and security in situations of challenge, destabilization, and crisis. The connection with nationhood and the nation-state is clearly greater for the modern period and operates in several ways. First, there are liberal-democratic nation-states, which define citizenship in terms of membership of an ethnic community, notably Germany, where *jus sanguinis*, or law of the blood, still prevails. Second, there are peoples lacking a national home, such as Palestinians and Kurds, who base their claims to a nation-state on historic ethnonational rights, similar to the claims by Zionist Jews before them.

Third, and rather differently, even those migrants who settle as cultural minorities in a new society may retain links with the homeland, in terms of what Benedict Anderson (1994) refers to as long-distance nationalism. This involves a close connection with events in the homeland. Mechanisms of continuing contact involve the diffusion of cultural contact and political currents through newspapers, religious communities or via the telephone and e-mail, as well as by return visits. Long-distance nationalism includes the figures of German and Australian 'Croats' lending support to homeland moves to establish a separate nation-state on the ruins of the old Yugoslavia, and Massachusetts Irish assisting the IRA, as well Ukrainians and Tamils in Toronto, and Albanians in Ravenna, all maintaining a stake in various kinds of homeland ethnonationalist politics. Long-distance nationalist migrants who are scattered across the globe in a number of locations in this manner take on the characteristics of a diaspora (Kotkin 1993).

Ethnicity and multiculturalism

A general model of the enduring appeal of ethnicity has been sketched above, based largely on the symbolic functions performed in contexts of crisis and threat. One serious qualification of this argument is, however, necessary before we proceed further. This concerns the material as well as symbolic advantages that accrue to the membership of ethnic groups. Ethnicity is not, of course, a phenomenon of exclusively symbolic significance. This is true in several contexts. The first is where the ethnicity of majority of powerful groups is used to secure economic and political advantage in business, the labour market, and governmental positions. The second is where ethnic differences within a population are used by third parties, be these employers or colonial administrations, to divide and rule, undercutting class unity by treating ethnic groups differently or manipulating existing tensions for advantage. A third case, worthy of further comment, is the recent development of a politics of ethnic identity and recognition, associated with multiculturalism.

Multiculturalism is a term whose meaning varies considerably, to the point of such conceptual confusion that it can mean opposite things to different commentators. One reason for this is that the same term has been used to refer to a range of different issues arising in somewhat different historical and political contexts (Rex 1995). What is common to all instances of multiculturalism is the context of a multi-ethnic state, usually the product of processes of culturally diverse population movement, whether through enslavement and transportation, refugee settlement, or voluntary migration. Discourses of multiculturalism have, in this context, been most highly elaborated in countries of the New World, notably the USA, Canada, and Australia. Yet the meaning of multiculturalism within these settings varies dramatically from the post-Civil Rights emphasis on cultural separatism in the USA, to issues of social justice and cultural integration *within* the liberal-democratic polity of Australia.

In the USA, multiculturalism has been primarily associated with the politics of ethnic and racial identity and entitlement, and with moves towards ethnic or racial separatism, with particular reference to educational curricula and affirmative action programmes. Such moves have occurred in a context of radical disillusionment with the gains from the Civil Rights movement epoch. The specific terrain of debates on multiculturalism as separatism has been the politics of educational provision and curriculum content (see the debate between Ravitch 1990, 1991, and Asante 1991). While some critics of separatist multiculturalism have found a liberal-democratic multiculturalism more acceptable, other critics have been more uncompromising. Educational separatism, for example, has been criticized by some liberal-conservatives as both a violation of principles of social equality and as socially divisive (Schlesinger 1992). Such criticisms arise from the perception that special advantages are given to particular persons for particularistic rather than universalistic reasons. The effect is to magnify social division and in some respects to encourage and magnify lines of cultural advantage.

This line of criticism may be countered, at a theoretical level, by the claim that liberal universalism is not socially neutral, privileging certain dominant groups over others. The strong implication is that liberalism (in the European sense of the word), with its emphasis on the rights and obligations of the rational individual citizen, rests on assumptions about social life that are at once too abstract and seriously incomplete (Young 1989). Individuals are not social atoms, and the ideal of free-standing rational individuals has been criticized as being gender blind (Pateman 1988) as well as indifferent to cultural difference. Such debates reflect an uneasiness with any kind of social theory or moral philosophy that is too distant from the constraints and choices faced by real world actors. They also reflect a particular way of understanding the contemporary global context. This is based not on the global dominance of the Western liberal-democratic individualism, as predicted by modernization theory, but on a diverse set of challenges to that model. These come from a range of voices, including racial and ethnic minorities, post-colonial intellectuals, and feminist movements, many of them bound up in transborder processes of population movement linked to slavery or global migration.

Multiculturalism based on multi-ethnic population movement is a characteristic of most New World societies of mass migration and settlement. Echoes of particularly American discourses of multiculturalism may thus be found in places such as Canada and Australia. Nevertheless, the focus of multiculturalism outside the USA has generally lacked the particular US context of unresolved Black–White relations and the political agenda of Afro-Americans developed against a history of slavery. Pressure for ethnic separatism may be found outside the USA, notably among the French-speaking Quebecois of Canada. Nonetheless, in both Canada and Australia from the 1970s onwards, proponents of multiculturalism have focused far more upon the responsibility of public policy to mediate between an overarching framework of universalistic standards common to all and recognition of the specific needs of particular groups or individuals within such groups (Australian Council on Population and Ethnic Affairs 1982, Hawkins 1989, Office of Multicultural Affairs 1989, Richmond 1991). Multiculturalism has been elaborated by many precisely as an culturally inclusive form of liberal-democratic politics that seeks to unify rather than divide. This nonetheless adds to conceptual confusion, inasmuch as liberal-democrats in different countries may find themselves either for or against multiculturalism depending on how it is conceived.

Multicultural policies and programmes, in the Australian, Canadian, and North American cases, in spite of such differences of historical and political context, do, however, have some common significance for the more general discussion of ethnicity. This stems from ethnicity becoming a specific target for government attention in redistributive social policy formation. At this point, ethnicity ceases to be simply a matter of the self-ascribed identity of groups and individuals, and becomes something that is politically and administratively defined as much from above as from below. We have already come across the idea of the invention of national and ethnic tradition from above as a means of political mobilization and state formation. The more recent case of multiculturalism and the politics of ethnic identity represent another instance of ethnicity becoming embedded in the broader processes of political determination.

A number of US commentators have argued that there are very material as well as symbolic advantages to the possession of an ethnic identity. These draw in part on the argument that ethnicity has a dual character, functioning both as a source of identification for members of a group and as a label utilized by others to represent a group. This external labelling affect may, of course, often be negative, as in forms of stereotyping that represent ethnic or racial groups in pejorative ways. However, it may equally be positive, in the sense that what are perceived as groups are both socially recognized and regarded as having political rights and entitlements, whereby ethnic identity is a recognized basis for the receipt of economic or social welfare resources. Glazer (1983, pp. 318–19), writing in the context of Black–White relations in the USA, makes a point of wider significance, namely that where law 'names groups... because the groups are named, individuals inevitably become beneficiaries or non-beneficiaries of law specifically because of group membership'.

Nagel (1986) sees ethnicity not as a form of primordial expression but rather as a combination of the ascriptive labelling of a group by others and a strategic opportunity for those so identified to choose to maintain or take up a particular identity that is politically recognized. Such an identification enables those thus identified to compete for economic as well as political resources. In the US context, this may be recognition as an official minority, entitled to particular labour market, small business, or educational advantages.

A situational account of ethnicity, then, must take note of both material and symbolic issues, as understood by members of ethnic groups and wider social structures alike. With this proviso about the interpenetration and inseparability of material and symbolic issues, we now return to the broad thrust of this chapter. Here, it has been argued that ethnicity retains considerable cultural influence because it effectively addresses problems of political crisis and insecurity, with deep-seated symbolic promises of order and security. This model may now be applied to the issue of globalization. Has globalization created a sense of cultural crisis and insecurity, and if so, is this why we currently see a revival of ethnicity and nationalism?

Globalization, nation-state and ethnicity

In Chapters 4 and 5, it was argued that the nation-state cannot be regarded as being in decline or overrun by globalization. This is in large measure because global capital is mostly not of an anarchic variety and still requires state functions to be performed. We may now add a second reason, to do with the nation rather than state part of the amalgam that is the nation-state. This concerns the robustness and persistence of national identity and nation-focused sentiments, often, although not necessarily, in conjunction with ethnicity. The revival of nationalism augurs well for the future of the nation-state as a political form with popular support. But why has this been forthcoming?

One line of argument recently developed is that the revival of nationalism and ethnicity, and, one might add, fundamentalist religion, is to be interpreted as resistance to the disruptive, impersonal impact of globalization. The logic behind this argument is that culture is far harder to globalize than is the economy. One indicator of this is the spectacular failure of Esperanto as an international language. While there has been an overall decline in the number of languages in the past century, this in no way signals a convergence toward one world language. Instead, there are a set of world languages, notably English, but also Spanish, French, German, and Chinese.

Anthony Smith (1990) has argued that culture is hard to globalize because globalization destroys the particular attachment to history and place that gives meaning to the lives of individuals. Global culture has been attempted, in the form of standardized consumer styles found in McDonald's or Coca-Cola, but these offer few meaningful or enduring attachments. For Smith, the attraction of national cultures as forms of social solidarity is that they are 'particular, time-bound and expressive' (1990, p. 178). Their appeal is thus bounded to those who claim the reality of a common experience that others do not and cannot directly share. This may comprise shared memories of a collective history, a sense of continuity across generations, and some sense of a common destiny. The implication of this argument is not only that cultural identity is hard to globalize, but also that the very persistence of national identities and images speaks to the deficiencies of global identity as an anchor for meaning and security in the lives of individuals.

The persistence of national identity should not, however, be regarded as an entirely even and constant phenomenon. Its significance is more accurately seen as episodic, achieving its greatest significance perhaps in times of crisis, such as war, when insecurity and pressures of boundary-setting tend to be more intense. Simon Schama (1991), in discussing the historical emergence of an idealized sense of homeland, points to parallels between British and German art in the most uncertain days of the Second World War. Thus:

> Frank Newbould, the greatest virtuoso of the patriotic poster... projected an image of the country, as... sweet and pure – rolling downs, lyrically lit, gently peopled by loyal dogs and obedient sheep, a stone-walled village, nestling... at the base of undulating hills... Across the North Sea, the Third Reich had an equally powerful sense of landscape and people... painters... produced works that drew on ancient allusions to work and redemption (plowing and growing)... together they created a mystical definition of homeland... (p. 11)

Globalization as a process of (both perceived and very real) change, taking place across political and cultural borders, is perhaps as overtly challenging as war. Threats of global economic restructuring leading to job loss, a declining sense of national economic sovereignty in an interdependent world, perceptions of declining social cohesion associated with mass culturally diverse migration, and the sheer pace of unfamiliar technological change, nonetheless all create an atmosphere in which security and identity are felt by many to be under threat. As with war, although for different reasons, symbols of stability and order may become attractive and may, of course, be manipulated by powerholders, as occurs in wartime, to maintain particular kinds of political and cultural order. Nationalism, in the sense of cultural identity and association with both history and place, thus remains a fundamental means of responding to globalization, as it is to war. It is obviously very far from dead, and Smith clearly establishes the core of one argument for why this should be so. What is not so clear is whether contemporary nationalism is necessarily to be seen as a reaction against globalization *per se* and whether the global and the national should be seen as warring principles, locked in a conflict that one or other will win, even if only for a limited period of time.

To assist in resolving these questions, it is worthwhile recalling an alternative perspective developed in Chapter 1. Here, global developments are seen as one element in a complex 'field' (Robertson) in which global and national, universal and particular interact and are mutually interdependent and self-constituting. One way of describing this is in terms of glocalization. This approach emphasizes paradox and interpenetration rather than any kind of simple clash between the global and the national, or the economic and the political or cultural.

One pertinent example of this is the paradox that the institutions of the nation-state and nationalist consciousness have been globalized, in the sense of being diffused across all regions of the world. All who claim to be peoples expect rights of self-determination as a nation and recognition as a nation-state, with a seat at the UN. In this way, one may speak of the globalization of particularism, that is, of the model of nationhood as the embodiment of the specific claims of particular groups with a discrete history and identity of their own. The paradox is that the institutions of the nation-state and nationalism have been diffused across existing boundaries and borders, typically leading to the collapse of imperial and colonial borders while concurrently redrawing fresh boundaries as new nations are formed. At the same time, the form that nationhood and national consciousness takes in these various settings varies markedly, such that we may speak of the particularization of nation-state building.

One important way in which nation-states vary is in how membership of the nation is conceived in terms of the formal requirements of citizenship. Within recent European history, as Brubaker (1992) points out, a major distinction is evident between French and German conceptions of nationhood and citizenship. In France, this has centred on political understandings of nationhood, based upon birth (*jus soli*) (and/or permanent residence) within French territory. This approach is more conducive to the political inclusion of diverse cultural groups, as citizens at least, than is the alternative German model. Here, in contrast, understandings of nationhood have been more culturally centred on the German people and German ethnicity (*jus sanguinis*), whose integrity predates that of the German nation-state. This focus is far less conducive to the integration of diverse cultural elements into German nationhood, as contemporary second-generation Turkish 'guest workers' have found. The former model is also to be found elsewhere, of course, as in societies of European settlement such as Australia and Canada, in contrast with the greater cultural focus in contemporary Serbia and Croatia.

Conceptions of nationhood may thus vary considerably. Nonetheless, there remains a more general paradox involved in the revival of nationalism of whatever kind in the epoch of globalization. The paradox is that globalization has assisted in constituting a world of discrete nations and nationalist politics by diffusing models of political organization, even while much nationalism has arisen as a reaction against larger political forces. Such forces may be described as aspects of globalization, as in the case of Western colonialization and global capitalist economic domination. The nationalism of the former colonial nations of Africa and Asia, for example, may be read as resistance to aspects of capitalist or Western globalization. However, in other cases, the external force against which nationalism reacts may be better described as regional in character. This applies in the case of political Empires such as the old Soviet Union, or multinational or ethnic states like Great Britain or the old Yugoslavia. The recent nationalism of Latvians, Ukrainians, and Chechnyans, for example, is related to the regional political dominance of the old Soviet Union. In yet other variants, the recent nationalism of Serbs and Croats, or Scots and Welsh, is related more to grievances associated with the terms of their incorporation into wider national political entities. Regionalism, in its transnational rather than subnational sense, has also prompted various kinds of national counter-reaction within the EU. Tensions over European and national sovereignty have been reflected in the troubled reaction to the terms of the Maastricht Treaty and to particular issues of policy or law, such as the management of 'mad cow disease' or the legitimacy of the corporal punishment of children. Nationalism here, following Billig, may take mundane as well as politically explosive forms, expressed in parliaments and court houses as well as in the streets.

In this way, one cannot regard nationalism as a reaction against globalization *per se*. There are a range of different external entities against which nationalist movements struggle, and these may be national or regional rather than global in scope. In addition, the grievances at the heart of national feeling pertain as much to symbolic value-laden issues, including cultural domination and humiliation, as to material exploitation through global economic mechanisms.

There is, however, a further major line of objection to seeing the current world in terms of fissures between the global and the national, and between global capital and national political culture. This objection might be labelled in a shorthand way as the problem of cultural pluralism. The difficulty here is that contemporary identity takes many forms, some of which differentiate different groups of people from each other, some of which are evident as multiple identities within particular individuals. Such identities may be local, national, regional or global, or a combination thereof.

The following example may help to establish the face-value nature of this problem. It concerns migrants to Australia from particular Greek Islands, who may see themselves simultaneously as Greek and Australian, may have taken out Australian citizenship, but may also see themselves as part of the Greek diaspora around the globe, with family in the USA as well as Greece and Australia. Yet they also simultaneously identify with their island of origin. Let us further disaggregate the category 'they' by generation and gender. While those who first migrated were both Greek, the children born in Australia may have intermarried, perhaps with an Anglo-Australian, perhaps with a Serbian migrant to Australia, who is also part of the Orthodox church. One member of the family may have returned permanently to Greece. Maybe an Anglo-Australian wife has returned with her Greek-Australian husband to Greece (see the testimony of Bouras 1986). Now let us introduce the question of salience of identities. Is ethnicity and nationality the strongest identity for the group of individuals involved? Do the younger generation identify more with global youth culture, around secular icons such as Kurt Cobain or Michael Jordan, than with symbols of Greek heritage? And would this change if Greece became involved with war with Turkey, just as the Croatian heritage of second-generation Croatian-Australians became more intense with the break-up of the former Yugoslavia (Skrbis 1994).

Such considerations can be replicated many times with other examples from other groups and places around the globe. The point of this example is to throw into doubt the simple idea of a polarization between global and national identities, and to reinforce Robertson's sense of the complex interpenetration of global, national, regional, local, and individual elements within the global field. The choice here is thus nowhere near as simple as deciding how far globalization is creating global people or, as a reaction, reborn nationalists.

When Smith argues that the idea of global culture lacks the specificity and historicity that individuals require to find meaning and security in their lives, he gives insufficient attention to the ways in which the global and the national or local may co-exist in people's lives. Global culture is taken to be a singular postnational identity and caricatured as a syncretic commodity, constructed out of bits from here and there, but decontextualized so that it can be packaged and sold in a standardized form. This way of dismissing the possible development of global culture has some force, but it is liable to the counter-criticism that it neglects the possibility of particular global cultures forming, linked initially to particular origins but diffusing outward in space and time. Syncretization and hybridization may thereby create viable cultural forms to which individuals may attach meaning and value. From this viewpoint, the dichotomy between the global and the national or ethnic is too crude and simplistic.

We have focused so far on the presumption that globalization is a destabilizing, unsettling, even threatening experience, and that nationalism and ethnicity may in part be appropriate reactions to such difficulties. But what if aspects of globalization are received positively or blended with subglobal identities and cultural practices? Is this happening, and if so, is it leading to a new cosmopolitanism? These are the issues to which we now turn in Chapter 7.

7

What is Happening to Culture? Homogenization, Polarization or Hybridization?

Those who analyse globalization in terms of the capitalist world-system and the activities of powerful multinational companies generally assume that economic globalization creates a version of cultural globalization in its own image. In contrast, for those who see nationalism and ethnicity (in part at least) as resistance to globalization, contemporary culture is far from dominated by the logic of the dominant economic system. Neither of these two interpretations is, however, acceptable to a third school of thought, which sees global cultural forms emerging that are transnational in form yet far from dominated by global capitalism. Beyond this, many other observers point to the ways in which transnational developments are linked with local and subnational cultural processes and identities. So what is really happening to culture, and how are cultural identities and practices articulated with other aspects of globalization?

Such questions are rendered harder to answer by notorious difficulties in defining what is meant by culture (for a further elaboration, see Holton 1992, pp. 182–5). These include the misleading practice of defining culture in terms of elevated forms of 'high' culture, as distinct from popular art and aesthetics. This way of thinking has been rendered obsolete by the merging and synthesis of what were previously thought of as 'higher' and 'lower' activities. One of the undoubted effects of increased demand and mass marketing in so-called culture industries such as music and art has been the blurring of distinctions between high culture and popular culture. The net effect of democratization and the commercialization of culture has been to destroy many of the status distinctions and much of the élitist Romanticism that previously surrounded cultural practice.

A more difficult problem has been created by the tendency to define culture in terms of ideas as distinct from actions. This opposition is in part arbitrary because it severs the recurring feedback loop between thought and action that constitutes human experience. The intimate connection that exists between practical and contemplative or imaginative activities has been denied for a number of complex historical reasons. Not least of these has been a considerable weight of philosophical and religious backing for the proposition that thought represents higher human functions and higher human worth than practical activity in the material world.

In what follows, we take culture to refer to both ideas and practices that have in common the function of providing meaning and identity for social actors and which combine cognitive, expressive, and evaluative elements. Culture, then, may be thought of as both a tool box of practices (Swidler 1986), which help us to understand (for example, science and religion) and act upon the world (for example, technology and prayer), and a source of emotional symbols (for example, national identity) and values (for example, freedom and justice) by which we orientate and justify our actions. The presumption is both that cultural practices, in the broad sense sketched above, vary more or less between social groups, and that these variations may be related to other aspects of social change.

The nature of such influences is, however, interactive, that is, culture may be both a cause of change elsewhere and profoundly affected by change. Here, we strike against a third problem in the analysis of culture, often found among economists, whereby culture is seen as the conservative limit on economic change. The argument, here, in contrast, takes up Eisenstadt's (1992) point that culture may be either order-maintaining or order-transforming, and a more subtle claim from anthropology that the same cultural practice may be used to justify both change and stability.

Having clarified what is meant by culture, we now turn to the more substantive analysis of the relations between culture and globalization.

Globalization, cultural dominance, and cultural homogenization

Arguments connecting globalization with cultural dominance may take a number of forms. These have often emphasized cultural homogenization of various kinds. The anthropologist Claude Levi-Strauss, for example, in lamenting the global challenge to local cultural variation, argued that 'humanity is installing itself in monoculture; it is preparing to mass-produce culture as if it were beetroot' (1955, p. 37). A very popular version of the homogenization argument contends that globalization means Westernization, and that global processes function to impose Western cultural imperialism on the non-Western world. Such Western traits are taken to include capitalism and the profit-centred market economy, democratic politics, secular thought embodied in scientific reason, individualism, and human rights. These ostensibly Western developments have a strong normative and value-laden significance, many Western commentators approving homogenization of this kind, while critics both outside and inside 'the West' regard such developments as either flawed or, at best, inadequate as a basis for the good society. The alternative value positions against which 'the West', and by implication globalization, are found wanting include values of community, religion, and spirituality.

Fatima Mernissi (1993), the Moroccan sociologist, recounts popular criticism of Western cultural dominance within the Arab world around standardized world-time and the standardized calendar. This critique was prompted, in part, by the organization of the Western allies' Gulf War attack on Baghdad in relation to timetables derived from prime-time television opportunities. Mernissi develops this argument in a wider frame, seeing Coordinated Universal Time and the Western calendar as creating a 'horrible colonization' that is an affront to Arab and Islamic dignity. This is symbolized in the marketing of a Japanese-produced Kabir watch that chimes five times a day at the hour of prayer and a more expensive version that recites different Koranic verses:

> The tiny silicon chip, on which a holy calendar, cyclical by definition is inscribed, is a technological device that denies the sacred vision of the cosmos and declaims the triumph of the electronic age, where profit is the be-all-and-end-all – the age of scientific man, who no longer fears death and draws power from his very mortality, for he has buried his gods long ago, and reduced the earth and the stars to numbers processed by satellite… . (Mernissi 1993, p. 141)

There is no doubt that globalization has assumed a negative, and at times almost demonic, significance in many quarters as Western imperialism – cultural as well as economic. The voices of critics who originate from, live in, or identify with the non-Western world are significant evidence of this, whether or not they are represented in Western scholarly literature. The voices of those who are well represented include the Palestinian intellectual Edward Said. He argues that Western cultural imperialism operates, in part, through discourses of power, whereby the non-Western world is constructed as 'different' in nature, as 'the Other' against which the West is defined. Such discourses suffuse literary as well as political and scientific cultures.

A major example is the construction of the Middle Eastern Islamic world as 'Oriental' in contrast to 'Western Occidentalism' (Said 1978; Hussain 1990). Whereas the Orient is seen as stagnant and unchanging, or aggressive and fundamentalist, the West is constructed as dynamic and innovatory, tolerant and democratic. Western scholars can, in this sense, only get to know the Orient through an exploitative and demeaning form of discourse. In a later study (Said 1993), this analysis was extended to a more general argument about empire and culture, applicable to the Western thinking on Africa, the Caribbean, India, and the so-called Far East.

The general point made here about cultural construction is that it asserts difference as a basis for cultural domination. The net effect is a generalized kind of discourse, in which the drive to power overrides the search for truth and caricature replaces subtleties of conceptualization. In this way, according to Said (1993, p. xxii), populations and voices that link Westerners and *their* 'Others' are ignored or marginalized, overlaps in their experience are discounted, and 'the interdependence of cultural terrains in which colonizer and colonized co-existed and battled against each other through rival geographies, narratives, and histories' is missed. One strength of Said's argument, is thus that both Westerners and *their* 'Others' have been drawn into and implicated in globalization in recent centuries, through an exploitative imperialist process, which by 1914 meant that Europe held 85 per cent of the land surface of the Earth, whether as colonies, protectorates, or dependencies, or by some other mechanism.

One general difficulty with critiques of this kind is nonetheless that they leave unclear whether careful scholarship can in some sense redeem the situation by undermining such a one-sided and gross caricature of the non-Western world. Critics of Said, for example, claim that Western Orientalist scholarship was more varied than he suggests, that much of it has been positive in orientation towards Islam, and that recent generations of work have increasingly moved away from the

discredited Orientalist assumption that Said and others rightly challenge (for an elaboration, see Hourani 1991, p. 55ff.).

A second, potentially more damaging, problem with Said's argument
is that it rebounds on his own intellectual procedures. That is to say, the
charge of Orientalism levelled against Western scholars can be met
with the counter-charge of Occidentalism as a practice of non-Western
critics (Ahmed 1992). Just as certain Western scholars may have
constructed the Orient as 'the Other', so certain non-Western scholars
have constructed the Occident as 'the Other', regarded in a similarly
pejorative manner. These similarities should not conceal differences in
the political and cultural power accorded to Orientalism and Occidentalism within the global arena, yet they are indicative of similar intellectual procedures and are hence equally liable to the same kind of
intellectual criticism. In this sense, we are left with a titanic battle
between two politically expedient caricatures and the sense that such an
encounter may be intellectually barren. This line of criticism rebounds,
of course, not only on Occidentalists, but also on Western scholars such
as Samuel Huntington (1993, 1996), who portray the world order as
riven by a cultural fault-line separating Western civilization from an
Islamic–Confucian civilizational axis.

Said himself is critical of Afrocentric and Islamocentric as much as
Eurocentric approaches (Said, 1993, p. xxiii). His alternative reaches
for a broader historical approach, which somehow transcends the
immediate political context in which there is temptation to rest content
with 'the radical purity or priority of one's own voice' (1993), and the
voices of one's own 'side' or 'culture'. This alternative to polarized
caricatures is consistent with the approach to globalization as a long-
run historical process suggested in Chapter 2. From this viewpoint, the
West and the world beyond are not two separate and discrete regions,
one of which is the source of globalization and the other the victim of
global processes developed by others. The West and the world beyond
have long been engaged in interchange and interaction as well as
exploitation and conflict, including cultural as well as economic and
political institutions and technologies. Global interchange was already
well advanced before the religious wars (or Crusades) between Christendom and Islam, which led to the cultural representation of West and
East, Europe and Asia, as sharply distinct social regions or civilizations
(Delanty 1995). The terms 'west'/'occident' and 'east'/'orient', or
'Europe' and 'Asia', are indeed cultural constructions, as Said suggests,
that have been imposed on the fluidity and complex interchanges of the
global field.

The modern history of relations between West and East may indeed be largely one of domination and colonialization. Yet this should neither obscure the earlier development of an interrelated Euro-Asian or Central Civilization (see Chapter 2) nor obscure the contemporary re-emergence of the world beyond Europe, with economic advances in Japan, East Asia, and parts of Latin America. Cultural patterns have also been opened up to interchange with global migration, world travel, and a continuing syncretization of cultural styles. The West and the non-West are, in this sense, less and less distinct physical places, even though they still loom large in the imagination as polar opposites. This polarization may be interpreted, however, as an effect of moral and political oversimplification, since it is not at all well grounded either historically or analytically. We shall further elaborate this claim later in the chapter.

Cultural homogenization and Americanization

A less generalized and more empirically specific version of the cultural homogenization argument centres on the Americanization of global culture. This has been advanced by scholars such as Herbert Schiller (1976), drawing on the arguments of those who would defend national cultures against what is seen as American cultural imperialism. These include Jack Lang, French Minister of Culture for much of the 1980s, and significant sections of European and Third World opinion within UNESCO. Criticism of this kind came to a head in 1980 with the publication of the McBride Report, which called for a more open world information order less dominated by US interests (Wete 1988).

The Americanization thesis builds on a number of key elements. One is the theme of predominant American ownership of key resources for the manufacture and transmission of culture, including satellite systems, information technology manufacture, news agencies, the advertising industry, television programme production and export, and the film industry. Cultural homogenization, in this sense, is linked with the predominant role of the USA in the export of television, film, and news information. Prominent examples include the worldwide diffusion of television programmes such as *The Brady Bunch*, *Dallas*, and *The X-files*, and CNN, the global news channel. During the 1980s the USA imported less than 5 per cent of its television programmes, while many other countries, in both Europe and Latin America, imported 25 per cent or more from the US alone (Varis 1988). Meanwhile, Hollywood feature films dominate in the cinema. In 1991 *Terminator 2* was the top grossing film in Argentina, Brazil, Chile, Japan, Malaysia, and Mexico, while *Dances with Wolves* held the top spot in Austria, Denmark, Egypt, France, Iceland, the Netherlands, Poland, Spain, and Switzerland (cited in Barber 1995, p. 308). Locally made films made it to number 1 in very few locations (for example, Finland, and Italy), while in some countries (for example Argentina, Austria, Brazil, Egypt, Greece, the Netherlands, Poland, and the UK), they did not even make the top 10. While there may be a number of reasons for this, not least the greater popularity of US films, we will for the moment pursue the homogenization argument a little further.

A second theme in the Americanization literature focuses on the USA's role in constructing a regulatory framework within culture and information industries that favours US interests. Schiller (1976), in particular, draws attention to the consistent post-war policy of US governments and businesses to challenge other countries' use of governmental control or regulation as a means of protecting aspects of national cultures against US domination. 'Freedom of information' was thus used to break the immediate post-war grip of British news-gathering cartels, to use UN agencies in the 1950s and 60s to disseminate Cold War propaganda, and more recently to undermine attempts by UNESCO to establish a regulatory framework for global communications with priorities other than private profit-making for business. These included increased worldwide literacy and professional education. Wete (1988) argues that the bogey of state censorship was used to challenge almost any kind of regulatory arrangement that did not provide free trade in information and cultural products as an open door to the US culture industries.

A third approach to issues of globalization, cultural homogenization, and Americanization looks at the diffusion of cultural practices across a wider number of settings, moving beyond culture and information industries, to the very characteristics of modern social organization. When George Ritzer (1993), for example, speaks of the 'McDonaldization of Society', he refers not merely to the spectacular worldwide rise of the American fast food industry, but more generally to certain broader cultural traits in the economy, organization, and personal life, of which McDonald's is a manifestation.

McDonald's fast foods, which began in the USA in 1955, opened its 12,000th franchise operation in 1991. In that year, more new restaurants were opened abroad (427) than in the USA itself (Ritzer 1993, pp. 2–3). By 1994 McDonald's had 5,000 restaurants abroad (Fantasia

1995, p. 204), including Moscow and Beijing. By 1995, around 20 million customers were served daily around the world, and 45 per cent of company profits derived from international operations. Ritzer's argument is that McDonald's corporate strategy, based on efficiency, calculability, predictability, and control over both products and the labour force, represents a leading example of the process of global rationalization. This perspective draws on the German sociologist Max Weber's argument that the modern world would see the driving out of personalized value-centred relationships in favour of impersonal technocratic modes of organization, symbolised as an Iron Cage. This has previously been exemplified in Henry Ford's assembly line and in mass-produced and standardized suburban housing but is now reflected in the rationalization and standardization of personal consumption. Cultural homogenization, with the US playing a leading role, is thus embodied in a wide range of social processes.

But do the American origins and Americanized business methods of McDonald's necessarily mean the Americanization of consumers? It is important here to avoid the trap of assuming that any message sent is necessarily received in the manner intended. How far, for example, do McDonald's customers patronize the chain simply because it is cheap and convenient? Against this kind of utilitarian motivation, there is some evidence that the experience of McDonald's in countries other than the USA is perceived very much in American cultural terms. Stephenson (1989), in a study of Dutch patrons of McDonald's, for example, found that Dutch patterns of sociability, including presentation of self and queuing behaviour, became altered to fit Americanized informality. For Fantasia (1995), writing on France, it was precisely the informality and lack of status hierarchy associated with self-service that appealed to the primarily young clientele.

Treated increasingly as an American cultural icon rather than merely as a business, the prefix 'Mc' has quickly become attached to a range of other cultural products and processes, such as the 'News McNuggets' that characterize the US daily paper *USA TODAY* or drive-in clinics advertized as 'McDoctors'. For Benjamin Barber (1995), McDonald's is a component part of the global consumer capitalism, of fast food, fast computers, and fast music, the 'Mc' prefix now being applied to the global system – 'McWorld'.

One criticism that may be levelled at the Americanization thesis is that it is capitalism rather than Americanization that is becoming globalized. Many aspects of capitalism, such as mass production, the Taylorist scientific management, or McDonald's-style consumerism may be seen as originating largely in the USA. Yet management techniques and mass marketing are not an American invention (Pollard 1965), nor have practices such as Taylorism remained unaffected by modifications and innovation elsewhere. In Japan, for example, Taylorism imported form the USA (Warner 1994) has subsequently been modified and reformulated from a market-based to an organizationally based practice. The Toyota 'just-in-time' system of work organization, total quality management, and quality control circles, while drawing in some respects on the American legacy, have emerged under Japanese modes of innovation to be exported back to the USA (Lillrank 1995). Another recent example of modification and re-export is new product development in the fast-food business involving French-inspired innovations such as the 'croissanterie' (Fantasia 1995, p. 202).

The net effect, then, is global interchange and some convergence towards similar types of business organization and economic culture, rather than Americanization *per se*. This in turn suggests that the mechanisms behind convergence are not solely the product of a single national source, even allowing for the hegemonic or near-hegemonic significance of the US for much of the post-war period. Rather, kinds of interchange similar to those found in previous epochs of world history have continued, even if in a more intensified form. The sources of cultural influence with respect to the economy and to other aspects of social life are in other words diverse rather than unitary with respect to national or regional origins.

One reason for this is that standardized global supply cannot necessarily dominate or manipulate world markets, which remain steadfastly diverse. As we have already seen in Chapter 3, multinational companies have encountered limits to mass marketing. These are not necessarily insurmountable, but they have led to a greater emphasis on niche marketing and an acceptance of variation. One example of this is variations made to the marketing and content of Music Television, generally known as MTV, to different youth markets in the USA, Europe, and Asia. MTV, which features as one element in Barber's spectre of McWorld, has found it necessary to vary the mix of musical styles and programme format to satisfy different tastes (Sturmer 1993). Another example is the deliberate use of the marketing of diversity in campaigns of the clothing manufacturer Benetton (Giroux 1994).

A general proposition worth restating at this point is that the global field is multicentred rather than dominated by a single centre. This applies in the cultural domain as elsewhere. There is no single dominant centre, in spite of the dominance of the USA or certain American symbols in particular markets and sectors, such as fast food and many aspects of youth culture. One aspect of this multicentredness is that, for many locations, it is not Americanization but some other force that is perceived as threatening. As Appadurai (1990, p. 295) points out, 'for the people of Irian Jaya, Indonesianism may be more worrisome than Americanization, as Japanization may be for Koreans, Indianization for Sri Lankans, Vietnamization for the Cambodians, Russianization for the peoples of Soviet Armenia', and so forth.

Such fears, especially for small nations with large neighbours, are clearly linked to political as well economic and cultural imperialism. In this respect, the thesis that the nation-state is far from dead, advanced in previous chapters, is reinforced. Fear of invasion across borders is, in some of the areas listed by Appadurai, as powerful if not more powerful than anxiety about economic penetration or cultural concern about Coca-Colonization.

Another more positive aspect of multicentredness within the global field emphasizes that which attracts rather than that which generates fear. If we ask what people in different locations identify with, the answer is not necessarily Coca-Cola and McDonald's. One reason for this is that much of the influence of the cultural centres of former imperial nations remains intact in spite of political independence for former colonies. Significant elements in the populations of France's former African or Caribbean colonies, for example, still look to Paris, be it for cultural style, intellectual sustenance, or both. However, they do so largely on their own terms rather than in a slavish imitation of French models.

This is evident in Jonathan Friedman's (1994) study of the *sapeurs* (literally, those who dress elegantly) of the former French Congo. To be a *sapeur* in Brazzaville is to seek prestige, beginning with the import-ation of European goods and then going to live in France itself. The subsequent return should be with Parisian *haute couture*, whose labels are sewn on the outside of clothing as a badge of status. Meanwhile, the Coca-Cola that is consumed is not the bottles locally produced under US franchise but the Dutch-made imported cans. What is going on here, according to Friedman, is neither American Coca-Colonization, nor Francophilia *per se* but the channelling of pre-existing traditions of prestige accumulation in new and exaggerated directions (1994, p. 107). For those who make it to Paris, the typical squalor of eking out a living there, the fate of so many post-colonial migrants in First World cities, possesses few intrinsic satisfactions, for it is the Brazzaville audience that is more salient.

Emphasis on the multicentredness and complex flows of cultural interaction and challenge within the global field has not gone unnoticed among those who think of the global order as a world-system or global-system. The challenge facing system theorists is, however, to determine what implication multicentredness has for the system as a whole. Put simply, is it indicative of system instability and disorder, or is it quite consistent with continuing system resilience and orderliness?

For Friedman, mounting evidence of cultural challenge to modern Western cultural identity is indicative of the end of the cultural hegemony of the modern identity based solely on the familiar set of practices such as individualism, an orientation towards achievement, and democracy. Like all previous dominant cultures, Western modernity is subject to a cycle of rise and fall. Multicentredness reflects the incapacity of modern Western institutions to provide adequate cultural supports to answer questions about the meaning of life and to secure a sense of identity. This encourages a cultural pluralism, which, while not turning its back on all that is modern or Western, starts to reconsider the value of tradition, of holistic rather than atomistic thought, and a range of ethnic, nationalist, religious, and indigenous identities. Just as the world-economy has become multicentred, creating increased competition and instability, so now is culture subject to high levels of decentralization.

The emphasis on disorderliness is, however, challenged by Wallerstein's world-system approach to culture. He sees culture as 'the idea system of the capitalist world economy' (1990, p. 38). The functions and substance of culture are to be understood not as expressions of a unitary homogeneous capitalist culture but rather as varied ways of coming to terms with the conflicts and tensions of that system, and of giving legitimacy to that system. For Wallerstein, an array of cultural ideologies has arisen, ranging from racism and sexism to the idea of universalism. All are regarded as conservative ideologies that serve to perpetuate a world order characterized by systemic inequality and exploitation. However, the hierarchical notions of racism and sexism differ significantly from the more inclusive notion of universalism. While the former, in his view, justify hierarchy and inequality, the latter appeals to the idea of a single world and the dream of a global humanism wedded to progress. Hierarchy helps capitalism to divide and rule, and to use patriotism and patriarchy to undermine antisystemic resistance to capitalism. Meanwhile, universalism offers the promise, but not the reality, of a better harmonious future.

Such arguments are liable to the criticism of reductionism, reducing all cultural forms to a top-down form of dominance in which challenge to the system is impossible. However, they are equally problematic in view of their highly generalized and speculative character, standing somehow above the day-to-day interaction of human actors and the operation of concrete institutions. A more typical approach to cultural homogenization, as we have seen, has been to get closer to everyday social life, in particular to processes such as the consumption of goods and the reception of media messages. These indicate the continuing salience of capitalist power and social inequality, but they equally suggest that power is far from unitary and that economic power does not necessarily dominate all aspects of politics and culture. Cultural pluralization, in particular, reveals that human agency and resistance remains a significant element in social life that cannot be subsumed into the singular logic of capitalism.

For all these reasons, Wallerstein's response to the cultural challenges facing the world order is rejected as one-dimensional and inadequate. Yet having said this, there still remains considerable scope for establishing what additional forces lie behind the dynamics of social change. If resistance to economic globalization is one of these, it is clearly not the only one. While some are busy re-erecting political and cultural barriers, others are clearly selecting aspects of globalization that suit their purposes, even if this also means a considerable element of indigenization or fusion of global and national or local elements.

One response to this complexity is to think of the world order in terms of polarization rather than homogenization.

Polarization, not homogenization

The polarization thesis, advanced most recently by Barber (1991, 1995) and Huntington (1993, 1996), albeit in markedly different forms, is built on a realization that the dynamics of the contemporary world are far from dominated by a single logic. For Barber, the polarization, as we have indicated, is between McWorld and Jihad, between the forces of global consumer capitalism and those of retribalization, between Disney and Babel, between commercial artifice, technology, and pop culture on the one hand, and narrow self-righteous faiths that generate war and bloodshed on the other. For Huntington, the polarization is between civilizations in general, and between the West and an emergent Islamic-Confucian axis in particular. This is, however, culture based rather than fundamentally to do with economic arrangements or political power. The spectre that this generates is one of 'global civilizational war'.

Behind these two passionate studies there clearly lies a strong normative and value-laden agenda. For Barber, the problem of polarization between McWorld and Jihad is that they are both hostile to democracy, the former by virtue of unaccountable global economic power, the latter through violent fundamentalist disregard for difference and dissent. In Huntington's case, in contrast, there is no room for moral equivalence between different civilizations and clear-cut support for the moral superiority of the Western way. Huntington's study is nonetheless far more than simple moral assertion, for its intention is to ground the argument presented in empirically based scholarship.

Notwithstanding the broad canvas and bright colours with which polarization theory operates, there is at least some awareness of what Roland Robertson would see as interpenetration between the two separate logics. In Huntington's case, this is rather fleeting, as in the comment that even extreme anti-Westernizers do not hesitate to use global technologies such as e-mail, cassettes, and television, a list to which might be added both Western military technology and Western medical technology. Barber is, in contrast, far more open to the extent of interpenetration and interchange. Thus:

> Iranian zealots keep one ear tuned to the mullahs urging holy war and the other cocked to Rupert Murdoch's Star TV beaming in *Dynasty*, *Donohue*, and *The Simpsons*... Chinese entrepreneurs vie for the attention of party cadres in Beijing and simultaneously pursue KFC franchises... the Russian Orthodox church, even as it struggles to renew the ancient faith, has entered a joint venture with Californian businessmen to bottle and sell natural waters... Orthodox Hasids and brooding neo-Nazis have both turned to rock music to get their traditional messages out to the new generation... (Barber 1995, p. 5)

Beyond this, Barber identifies Jihad within McWorld in a number of senses. These include both the provincial and separatist movements of Europe and also the American Jihad of the Radical Right (1995, p. 9). Fundamentalism is to be found in Christianity (Marty and Appleby 1991) and in ethnic nationalism, rather than simply in certain currents of Islam or among Arabs. Meanwhile, Islam is not synonymous with Jihad, interpreted as militant aggression, for, as Barber points out, there are clearly 'moderate and liberal strands in Islam' (1995, p. 206), even as defined by Western norms. For Barber, then, far more than Huntington, there are soft edges to global polarization.

Taken overall, polarization theory has a number of strengths. First, it draws attention to key elements of cleavage in the contemporary post-Cold War world that are not associated with socioeconomic divisions between capitalism and socialism, and are thus not of class warfare. The lack of connection between political economy and global cleavage is greatest in Huntington's vision, where culture and civilization loom largest. Recent examples of the civilization fault-line between the West and the Islamic-Confucian axis include conflict over human rights and the Olympic Games. At the Vienna Conference on Human Rights in 1993, according to Huntington, China and her non-Western allies outsmarted the West by diluting the Vienna statement on Human Rights principles to allow their effective short-circuiting by individual nation-states. Later that year, in contrast, Sydney rather than Beijing won the International Olympic Committee's approval to hold the year 2000 Olympic Games, voting being 'almost entirely along civilisational lines'.

A second strength of polarization theory is that it draws attention to an irreducible divergence of cultural and to a lesser extent political practice within the world order. All is clearly not converging to a specific Western model as homogenization theory has supposed. Long gone are arguments that ethnicity, nationalism, or religion are somehow withering away in the face of economic development and secularization, or at least of merely transitional significance in preparing the way for a modern social order. The resurgence of Islam is the most visible manifestation of this process but by no means the sole exemplar.

Third, the emphasis on culture as a key element in the social order is valuable, at least in principle, as a corrective to assumptions that the world is primarily economically or technologically driven, or that the interstate system of *realpolitik* exerts a pre-eminent influence on the dynamics of change. These assumptions, as we have seen in previous chapters, still dominate many bodies of specialist literature as well as the beliefs and actions of many participants within the processes that scholars seek to understand and sometimes to influence.

Beyond this, however, doubts about polarization begin to arise. One major line of criticism, already foreshadowed, is that notions of separate and discrete civilizations vastly exaggerate and overinflate cultural and other differences within the global field. Such differences exist, but they are often local, national, or regional in form. And whatever differences are evident, they are not distributed between autonomous free-standing civilizations or cultures but are the product of long and complex histories of interaction and interchange. Put another way, the same kinds of criticism that apply to primordial theories of ethnicity and ethnonationalism apply equally to primordial theories about distinct civilizations. Just as nation-states and national cultures borrow and indigenize elements from the external world, so too do the major component parts of entities that Huntington regards as civilizations. Key social institutions through human history, such as markets and trading networks, technological innovation, or religious communities, span the so-called civilizational divide. Capitalism is as alive in the East as the West, and the interaction between the two has a long although recently intensified history. Christianity, which originated as an Oriental religion, and which has many non-Western adherents, largely through colonization processes, cannot claim to be a primordially Western religion, while different versions of Christianity lead in quite different social and political directions, from fundamentalism to global community-building. Islam is similarly varied, with adherents in Europe and many Western cities, through processes of colonization or migration, with internal differences between Sunnis and Sh'ites, and with many voices, including that of peace and community as much as that of Jihad.

The controversial issue of human rights is perhaps an acid test for Huntington's civilizational cleavage. Here, as we have seen, the argument that China and many Islamic states watered down the 1993 Vienna UN conference commitment to human rights looms large. This particular confrontation was, of course, part of a more consistent opposition to the implementation of human rights by non-Western coalitions within the UN Commission for Human Rights in Geneva. Such defensive actions may, in turn, be seen as reflecting a far worse contemporary human rights record in the non-Western than the Western world.

To leave the matter there is, however, to neglect the existence of pro-human rights thinking and action within the non-Western world. There is no doubt that Chinese and most Islamic governments reject the view that universal human rights should override national political and religious traditions. There is equally no doubt over the strength of popular religious or anti-Western fundamentalism in many such countries. On the other hand, there are voices in both China and the Islamic world that take a different view. These may be politically repressed, as in Tiananmen Square, or may find it difficult to organize in nations without rights of free assembly, but they are present.

The sociologist Bassam Tibi (1994) symbolizes the tension within Muslim countries in his account of the 1993 Vienna Conference. While diplomats from Muslim countries were arguing on the conference floor in favour of the specific character of their culture and against the universality of human rights, 'human rights activists from Muslim countries – like Iran and the Sudan – were drawing attention to the severe violations of human rights in their own countries, acting in the basement of the Vienna Centre...' (Tibi 1994, pp. 277–8). This resistance may well be in the minority, in part for fear of persecution. However, it is clear that considerable internal debate exists in both Islamic and Chinese circles about human rights.

Such debates focus, in part, on the compatibility of Islamic or Confucian thinking with European-derived notions of individual human rights. Tibi notes the views of the Sudanese legal scholar Abdullah An-Na'im, student of the executed reformer Mahmoud M. Taha, and the Egyptian judge Muhammed S. al-Ashmawi that the Islamic *Shari'a* or holy law is not adequate to prevent totalitarianism. Such arguments draw on the liberal Islamic proposition that the *Shari'a* is a construction of Muslim jurists and hence not a divine text of the standing of the Koran. For Na'im, this requires a fundamental reform of Islamic law so that human rights can be established in the Islamic world. In this process of reform, the interests of humanity in the fate of all human beings are more important than the fact that human rights are of Western origin or that Western countries may not always practise what they preach in human rights areas. This argument depends, as Tibi points out, on the drawing of a distinction between Western hegemony in international affairs and the normative force of universalistic human rights standards.

Tibi goes on to argue that most existing attempts at Islamic reform do not accept that Western individual human rights are compatible with Islam. Instead, an attempt is made to 'Islamicize' the notion of rights. This, however, fails to problematize the relationship between the individual and the state, and is highly evasive on issues such as freedom of religious expression (see, in particular, Mayer 1990). This diagnosis flows from a more general argument in which Tibi (1988) posits a fundamental antagonism between the dominant theocentric cosmology of Islam and the cultural modernity of the global order based on reason and individual rights. This antagonism is not, in his view, quite the same thing as a clash of civilizations. Rather, it represents a clash between a global civilization that recognizes individual subjectivity and a fragmented set of local cultures, trapped in versions of premodernism.

A similar, perhaps even more prominent, debate over human rights is evident within China, as evidenced in episodes of official and unofficial pressure for political reform. Some of the intellectual underpinnings and challenges posed by such moves are reviewed in the collection of essays brought together in Davis (1995). In a manner similar to that of internal debate within Islam, a distinction may be made between those who seek purely Confucian sources of human rights and those more open to the reception of Western versions of liberal democratic universalism. Du Gangjian and Song Gang (1995), for example, argue that aspects of classical Confucianism, such as justification of resistance to authority or of individual moral (as distinct from legal) challenges to government, are compatible with human rights notions, although the Confucian legacy itself is largely undemocratic and élitist. As with Islam, the key problem seems to be the difficulty of making any notion of individual rights compatible with cultural traditions that subsume the individual within collectivities such as the state or the family. To this extent, the human rights challenge appears consistent with Huntington's civilizational schism.

Such ostensibly cultural differences over human rights may, however, be exaggerated and misconceived. For one thing, much official Chinese resistance to human rights draws on Western Marxist hostility to what is called bourgeois individualism. If, as Gangjian and Gang argue, 'Confucian theory finds resonance in modern Marxism' (1995, p. 50), is that because Marxism, like Confucianism, is un-Western, or is it because official Chinese resistance to human rights draws on both Confucian and Marxist traditions? In the latter case, we are clearly dealing with the interpenetration of political as well as cultural practices between West and East, rather than purely culturally centred civilizational conflict.

Christine Loh (1995) adds to the complexity of the issue by challenging the notion that specific cultures have a discrete and more or less unchanging position on human rights. While many Asian Governments at the Vienna Conference used cultural difference as a justification for resisting the application of universalistic human rights principles to their own country, dissidents within the same countries have often been killed or gaoled for supporting human rights. In the cases of Wei Jingsheng, gaoled in China for 15 years for the crime of publishing a pro-democracy newsletter, or Ang Saan Soo Kyi under house arrest in Burma, how are we to interpret their actions? Are they simply pro-Western, often Western-educated dissidents fruitlessly trying to effect political reform in an inhospitable civilizational environment, or are they also members of the same society and heirs to the same cultural traditions as the rulers who gaol them? Or are these alternatives too stark?

Western education and exposure to Western culture may indeed assist in securing adherence to particular kinds of support for human rights. Yet this is clearly not the only stimulus for resistance to torture, arbitrary arrest, and imprisonment without trial, nor the only basis for a sense of social injustice and a commitment to political reform. To suppose otherwise would be to assume that non-Western cultures are essentially incapable of generating dissent or pressure toward greater democracy. The dilemma here is that if any support for human rights is identified with Western influence, the link between the West and human rights cannot then in principle be falsified and is hence a philosophical assertion rather than an empirically secure proposition.

Summing up the argument so far, polarization theory is an attractive alternative to homogenization theory in a world where cultural difference rather than conformity is widespread. Yet polarization theory comes in a number of varieties, not all of which are equally persuasive. Barber's scenario of Jihad versus McWorld has the advantage of integrating economic and political as well as cultural elements into processes of polarization, keeping open a multidimensional approach to global social change. Unlike Huntington, he does not see polarization as primarily driven by culture or by civilizational characteristics. This leaves space for an awareness of the importance of global capitalism, with its technological dynamism, brash consumerism, and unequal power relationships within the new world order and the consequent resistances that emerge around retribalized culture and politics. The West, in other words, is not treated as a beneficient civilization bringing democracy, wealth, and human rights to other less fortunate civilizations. More than that, Jihad and McWorld interpenetrate, at least up to a point.

A bigger problem with both Barber's and Huntington's versions of polarization theory is nonetheless to determine whether there is a more adequate paradigm, which would make better sense of the complexities of global cultural development than polarization, without falling back into the problems of homogenization theory. One obvious candidate here is what might be called hybridization theory.

Hybridization

Each year... the countries of Europe meet in a televised song contest... watched by hundreds of millions of people. There is first a national contest in each country to choose its own entry for the international competition. A few years ago, a controversy erupted in Sweden after this national contest. It was quite acceptable that the... first runner up had been performed by a lady from Finland, and the second runner up by an Afro-American lady... Both were thought of as representing the new heterogeneity of Swedish society... What was controversial was the winning tune, the refrain of which was 'Four Buggs and a Coca-Cola': Bugg, like the name of the soft drink, was a brand name for chewing gum... Of the two, Coca Cola was much the more controversial, as it was widely understood as a central symbol of 'cultural imperialism'... what drew far less attention was that the winning tune was a Calypso. (Hannerz 1992, p. 217)

This anecdote contains within it many of the elements that have gone into the development of a body of theory that emphasizes cultural hybridity, creolization, or syncretism within global culture. In a variety of ways, this approach emphasizes cross-cultural borrowings and intercultural fusion and blending to create hybridized or mixed cultural forms. All this somehow occurs in a world where Coca-Colonization or global capitalism is an ever-present but not all-determining force, and where nationalism, ethnicity, or some other kind of quasi-tribal affiliation is not the exclusive source of cultural identity.

This situation has been constituted through flows of people, ideas, and cultural styles across political and cultural boundaries. These, it may be added, are sometimes violently forced, as in slavery, which brought Black African musical traditions to the Americas, and sometimes market driven, as in voluntary migration in search of work, which has vastly extended the cultural diversity of many European, North and South American, Middle Eastern, and Australian nations and cities. Hannerz's examples include the migration of people and musical styles as well as of commodities to Sweden.

For Hannerz, there exists a global cultural ecumene defined, following Kopytoff, as a 'region of persistent cultural interaction and exchange' (1992, p. 218). Instead of thinking in terms of distinct cultures within the global field, this ecumene includes subcultures of the whole, that is, entities with only 'fuzzy boundaries' separating them from each other. Another word for this process is creolization, defined by Hannerz as 'a process where meanings and meaningful forms form different historical sources, originally separated from one another in space, come to mingle extensively' (1992, p. 96).

Against those world-system approaches which think in terms of cultural diffusion outward from a metropolitan political economic core to the Third World periphery, Hannerz sees a far more complex intersection of intercultural relations, in which religious connections do not necessarily follow economic connections, and in which different

cultural influences such as film, or music, or literature do not follow
each other. US influence may be strong in personal computer software,
fast food, and types of popular music, involving cores such as Silicon
Valley, New York corporations, or the grunge music of Seattle.
However, as Hannerz points out, places such as the Vatican or the Shia
holy city of Qom also organize different aspects of culture within
core/periphery relations. In addition, some countries may have a
disproportionate regional cultural influence, such as Mexico in Latin
America, or Egypt in the Arab world, without exerting a transregional
global influence.

Much of the contemporary evidence in favour of creolization or
hybridization is drawn from the sphere of music. The most overt
example here is the development of self-styled world music, a dynamic
amalgam and blending of various styles. One way of describing the
process of intercultural syncretization is to speak of the indigenization
of Western styles in non-Western settings and the fusion of non-
Western influences into Western music (Roberts 1992). In the former
category is the *bhangra* music of Britain's Asian youth, which
combines Indian music with Western dance-beats, or Algerian *rai*
music based on Arabic chants mediated by the technologies of Western
pop. In the latter category might be included the blending of Western
classical music with Afro-American jazz or the Indian *raga*.

One difficulty that soon emerges in describing the inputs into
hybridized music in this way is that as soon as intercultural contact
takes place, the notion of separate Western and non-Western musical or
cultural sources becomes blurred. Jazz, for example, draws on African,
and African-American as well as European sources, including military
marches and religious music. The impact of the Brazilian *bossa nova* in
the USA, as Roberts points out, also creates conceptual difficulties,
already being built on fusions of Portuguese, African, and indigenous
cultural elements (1992, p. 230). In order to avoid this problem, Simon
Frith argues that 'there is no such thing as a culturally pure sound'
(1989, p. 3).

World music is, in a sense, self-consciously unbounded, and is thus a
particular subset of hybridized cultural practices. Other hybrid forms
set boundaries, but these may be far from co-terminous with the nation-
state or nationally bounded ethnicities. A striking example is what Paul
Gilroy refers to as the Black Atlantic, that is, an 'intercultural and
transnational formation' linking Blacks in Britain and France as well as
the USA and Caribbean. This is a formation that is intermediate
between the global and the local, and which has a dynamic history in

which slavery, colonization, and migration, including the migration of intellectuals and artists, play a part. So too does the crossing of national cultural boundaries by ideas and cultural practices, including music. Mechanisms and symbols of transmission have included the ship and the long-playing record.

While the Black Atlantic is transnational and transcultural, it generates local manifestations that are not identical with each other. Gilroy argues that Black British cultures 'have been produced in a syncretic pattern in which the styles and forms of the Caribbean, the United States, and Africa have been reworked and reinscribed in the novel context of modern Britain's own untidy ensemble of regional and class-oriented conflicts' (Gilroy 1993, p. 3). When North London's Funki Dreds (itself a hybridized name) made their record 'Keep on Moving', for example, this was initially produced in England by English-born children of Caribbean migrants and then remixed in a Jamaican dub format in the USA by an African-American, including segments of records made in the USA and Jamaica.

Music plays a key role in accounts of global hybridization, but how important are musical practices as indicators of trends in global culture? Gilroy's analysis of music within the Black Atlantic suggests that they have considerable importance for groups that do not privilege rational cognition above aesthetics, or separate social and political commentary from cultural performance. In addition, the very fluidity of syncretic cultural forms may be very important to sustaining identity in an epoch of globalization. Thus 'music and its rituals can be used to create a model whereby identity can be understood neither as a fixed essence nor as a vague and utterly contingent construction to be reinvented by the will' (1993, p. 102). From this viewpoint, Black music is not to be read as the authentic product of some fixed and essential Black identity but is instead a dynamic cultural resource for a group whose fate and future has been profoundly affected by globalization. If it is bounded, it is not so by nation or Black culture but by the experience of slavery, racism, and migration.

If Frith has argued that there are no culturally pure sounds, we may question, by extension, whether there are any culturally pure institutions, nations, and communities. Are not all social arrangements – from languages such as English and political institutions such as democracy, to cultural practices such as the contemporary English Christmas – constructed out of a variety of elements with complex origins across time and space. The sociological answer may broadly be 'yes' for most of human history, yet we are left with the difficulty that many wish to re-erect boundaries that others find it advantageous to ignore, permeate, or burst through. While Gilroy's Black Atlantic is transnational, in other parts of the global field, national, ethnic, and other kinds of cultural boundary are being re-erected to the point of promoting or enforcing purity by various means. Western publishers, as Griswold (1992) has shown, prefer Nigerian novels to focus on village and rural themes, thereby contributing to the representation of Africa as tradition bound and satisfying the African roots market. Meanwhile, there remains support for bounded primordial constructions of cultural identity, as we saw in Chapter 6, both among White and Black, Western and non-Western. The difficulty, then, is in deciding how far cultural syncretization and hybridity extend *as a form of cultural identity* and what their limits are.

One debate that is germane to this discussion is that over issues of deterritorialization and cosmopolitanism. Here, global mechanisms of colonization, transportation, migration, and cultural interaction across political boundaries are seen as leading to a loss of singular territorially based cultural identities and a shift towards cosmopolitanism. The nature of this shift is, however, controversial, in part because cosmopolitanism is a rather loosely defined term. It sometimes refers to little more than having a world outlook or extensive experience of tourism. For Hannerz (1990), cosmopolitanism is more usefully defined as openness towards different and divergent cultural experiences, to the extent that intercultural competence as well as intercultural experience ensues (p. 239). Cosmopolitans are therefore distinct from exiles who want to return home or short-term tourists, especially those who are collecting experiences of cultural difference as an experience of the exotic or authentic. Above all, Cosmopolitans are not Locals, whose perspectives are circumscribed even when they travel.

Alternative ways of thinking of cosmopolitanism are in terms of those whose economic and political activities as well as cultural affiliations involve significant transborder dealings. This would include those in occupations with high levels of mobility, such as diplomats, sailors, academics, and managers of multinational businesses, as well as those involved in chain migration networks. Intermarriage across cultural boundaries may also stimulate cosmopolitanism. The global economic processes of both business activity and political economic regulation, described in Chapters 3, 4, and 5, all create opportunities of this kind. However, opportunities for cosmopolitanism may narrow as much as broaden the mind and may be equally as consistent with monoculturalism and localism as with more open expressions of interculturalism.

There are thus very good reasons to be sceptical about the extent of cosmopolitanism. Deterritorialization is also a somewhat problematic idea. Take the case of diasporic communities. While Gilroy, in the case of the Black Atlantic, may well speak of a 'new topography of loyalty and identity in which the structures and presuppositions of the nation-state have been left behind' (1993, p. 16), it is equally clear that other more politically centred diaspora are enmeshed in long-distance nationalism, as discussed in the previous chapter. In both cases, some kind of territorial identity emerges, be it nationalistic, as in the case of Croats and Zionists, or more diffuse, as in the case of Black Rastafarians in London or Black Muslims in New York.

For Gupta and Ferguson (1992), for example, processes of deterritorialization are typically linked to processes of reterritorialization. Even for migrants and those uprooted by colonization and migration, imagined communities are reasserted in new locations. Thus:

> India and Pakistan apparently reappear in postcolonial simulation in London, prerevolutionary Tehran rises from the ashes in Los Angeles, and a thousand similar cultural dreams are played out in urban and rural settings all across the globe... While actual places and localities blur, ideas of culturally distinct places become more salient as displaced peoples cluster around remembered and imagined homelands, places or communities, in a world that seems increasingly to deny such firm territorialised anchors in their actuality. (Gupta and Ferguson 1992, pp. 10–11)

The idea of re-territorialization is thus a useful corrective to popular belief that globalization will create cosmopolitan world citizens and a post-national global culture. This should not, however, obscure the profound ambiguity that the experience of intercultural mixing may create in individual identity. Put another way, whether re-territorialization takes place and what direction it assumes may both be very unclear. This is made very clear in the following account of an 'English' White reggae fan from the culturally diverse area of Balsall Heath in the city of Birmingham:

> There's no such thing as 'England' any more... welcome to India, brothers! This is the Caribbean!... Nigeria!... There is no England, man. This is what is coming. Balsall Heath is the centre of the melting-pot, 'cos all I ever see when I go out is half-Arab, Half-Pakistani, Half-Jamaican, half-Scottish, half-Irish. I know 'cos I am [half-Scottish/half-Irish]... who am I?... Tell me who I belong to? They criticise me, the good old England. Alright, where do I belong? You know, I was brought up with Blacks, Pakistanis, Africans, Asians, everything, you name it...

who do I belong to? I'm just a broad person. The earth is mine... you know we was not born in Jamaica... we was not born in England. We were born here, man. It's our right. That's the way I see it'. (Hebdige 1987, pp. 158–9)

Concluding remarks

None of the three approaches to contemporary culture and the global order reviewed here stands up to critical scrutiny in all respects. Most deficient perhaps is the homogenization theory of global culture. This may well draw attention to power relations in cultural production and representation, but it does not provide a convincing account of the multi-centred nature of power, let alone of bottom-up and not simply top-down processes of cultural development and identity formation. It also operates from assumptions of a singular logic to the contemporary world, flying in the face of evidence about counter-trends that identify competing logics, which generate cultural conflict rather than conformity.

Polarization theory is more alert to divergent trends, in particular the co-presence of global and particularistic national, tribal, and ethnic cultural affiliations. It tolerates a greater level of complexity and successfully recognizes competing logics. The notion of a clash of civilizations remains at best unproven, and at worst subject to the criticism that it oversimplifies and overgeneralizes the nature of contemporary cultural schisms. It is also tends to operate with insufficient regard for interpenetration and areas of common ground between the large-scale entities with which it operates. This leaves out higher levels of complexity and a more fine-grained approach.

The hybridization approach avoids the pitfalls of homogenization and polarization theory by drawing attention to the significance of inter-culturalism for cultural identity, as well as the syncretic historic-making of cultural forms, which social actors may subsequently come to regard as indigenous rather than partly borrowed or blended. Yet the evidence for cosmopolitanism and deterritorialization, in any strict sense, is not convincing. Hybridization theory is also, as yet, rather unclear about the limits of hybridity as a chosen cultural form. The difficulty, then, is how to balance evidence of polarization with other evidence of intercultur-alism and, in a deeper sense, of how to balance a sense of globalization as opportunity with globalization as constraint.

It is arguable that while many of the nationalist and ethnonationalist currents reviewed in Chapter 6 respond to globalization by re-erecting defensive cultural barriers, intercultural connections are in many other respects explicitly welcomed and built into cultural practices. Globalization, in this sense, functions as it has always done as a repertoire of cultural practices, albeit one to which access is mediated though available resources, such as wealth, human rights, and personal mobility, and from which selections and choices may be made under various kinds of constraint. Such constraints include the relative bargaining position of nations, groups, and individuals *vis-à-vis* the suppliers of resources available within the global field. This in turn includes the framework of economic and political regulation, discussed in earlier chapters, that prescribes rules of world trade, intellectual property, or movement of persons. In this process, there are typically winners and losers. The global repertoire is not, then, to be seen as a consumer paradise or a life-enhancing intercultural smörgåsbord, but neither is it a demonic system of top-down system domination. We know this not because optimistic and privileged Western voices say so but because it is consistent with the actions and beliefs of a range of global voices, outside the West as well as within it.

8

Conclusion

You're on earth. There's no cure for that. (Samuel Beckett)

The study of globalization poses major challenges, of both a normative and an analytical kind. The analytical challenges outlined throughout this book centre on the range of misconceptions that have become associated with globalization and their replacement with more plausible alternatives. Thus the globalization process is not a single all-conquering and homogenizing force, driven by the systemic logic of capitalism or Western cultural imperialism. Globalization does not overwhelm nation-states and destroy cultural differences based on ethnicity or some kind of local cultural affiliation. Nor is it a recent phenomenon. In rejecting these propositions, the aim is not, of course, to deny that globalization has profoundly influenced patterns of social change, the capacity of nations of various kinds to determine their own future, or the global distribution of power and inequality. Nor is it to neglect the rapid intensification of globalization over the last century. The underlying analytical challenge, then, is to balance a sense of the dynamic significance, historical periodization, and enduring effects of globalization with a sense of its limits, set by counter-trends.

The normative issues posed by globalization are equally challenging, although they have not so far been discussed in any explicit or sustained manner in this study. If we ask, 'Is globalization a good or a bad thing?', the responses that might be made will clearly be influenced both by the evaluative yardstick that is utilized and by how the globalization process is understood. As we saw in Chapter 2, within the discussion of images of world order, the range of evaluative standpoints from which global-ization might be assessed is enormous. They range from the commit-ment to cosmopolitan ideals of social harmony and community free from conflict, to values of national autonomy and localism. The same values can also lead in different directions. Values of community or democracy, for example, are, for some, entirely compatible with globalization, or at least with particular forms that it can take, while the same values can lead others to a strongly antiglobal position. To be committed to 'green' values of environmental protection and harmony between humankind and the environment leads some to champion localism. Meanwhile, others promote environmental values by participating in global social movements such as Greenpeace International, and transnational organizations such as the WTO or the EU. The slogan 'Think Globally, Act Locally' adds further complexity to this picture by indicating that a global response on one level (for example, knowledge of the cumulative planetary effects of pollution and environmental degradation) may be compatible with a local response (for example, social action) on another. In the normative arena, as in the analytical one, it seems that the global and the local or national not only co-exist but also interpenetrate.

In this concluding section, we draw attention first to a powerful way of reconciling the global and the local, suggested in the influential work of Roland Robertson, before concluding with further comments on normative issues arising from the challenge of globalization to democracy.

Analytical challenges

One of the greatest analytical challenges facing students of globalization is to make sense of the way in which political and cultural boundaries are being simultaneously permeated and re-established, transcended and reinvented by complex processes of social change. Contemporary social life may, of course, be seen in terms of a straightforward conflict between globalizing and localizing trends, yet this seems too simplistic because the same trend may display both global and local aspects. If this is the case, what alternative forms of analysis and explanation are available?

One of the more fruitful alternatives is that provided by Roland Robertson. His culture-inclusive, cognitively centred approach is intended to challenge both the economic determinism of Wallerstein's world-system theory and its undervaluation of human agency. Robertson pursues this objective by rejecting the idea of globalization as a system. His alternative is to reconceptualize globalization as a *field*, (Figure 8.1). Robertson's global field includes *within it* the challenges and contradictions that make the modern world such a paradoxical place. This field is constituted by the complex interpenetration of 'global', 'national', and 'local' or 'individual' aspects of social life that we have analysed in previous chapters.

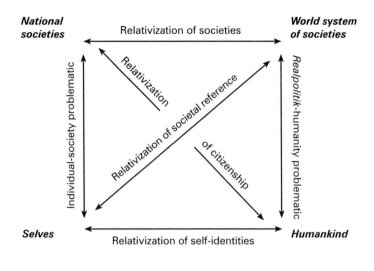

Figure 8.1   Roland Robertson's global field

Source: From Robertson (1992, p. 27).

Robertson's dialectical approach involves seeing globalization as
the 'interaction of different forms of life' (1992) rather than as the
dominance of transnational forces over the national, or the triumph of
modernity over tradition. The 'global' field depicted abstractly in
Figure 8.1 contains, one at each corner of the square, four major
'reference points' in terms of which interaction takes place. Two of
these, namely 'national societies' and individual 'selves', are familiar
elements in modern social theory. What Robertson adds to this picture
is first of all the 'world system of societies' and second 'humankind'.
By the former, he means the system of interaction between national
societies, while the latter evidently refers to conceptions of humankind
as a single entity. These four reference points serve to emphasize the
simultaneous importance of large institutions and the life-world of
individuals within the global field. In this sense, Robertson rejects
those who see the 'global' purely as a macro-level process that
dominates the lives of individuals, who in turn may only organize
micro-level or local resistance to global trends. His global field is,
from the outset, an attempt to bridge the macro–micro divide in understandings of globalization.

Having defined the four key reference points, the interactions between them are represented in Figure 8.1 in terms of six bilateral relationships (depicted by the four interactions along the perimeter and two along the diagonals). The nature of the interaction involved is once again cognitive, in that the parties involved are faced both with tensions between conflicting principles and with opportunities to reconcile such tensions. To make these abstract deliberations more concrete, Tables 8.1 and 8.2 are attempts to work through the logic of Robertson's theory of the global field.

If, for example we start from the position of an individual national society, the ensuing challenges involve interaction with the world-system of societies, with humankind in general, as well as with individual selves. In Table 8.1, the general patterns of interaction involving the nation-state are outlined, and illustrations are provided of the interactive challenges involved in terms of particular features of contemporary globalism. It should be emphasized that the interactions are two-way processes rather than one-sided challenges of adaptation to global developments.

Table 8.1 The interactions of national societies within the global field

Aspect of the global field	Process involved	Examples of interactive challenge
World system of societies	Relativization of societies	Problem of the relative sovereignty of individual nations in relation to that of other national societies as reflected in transnational regulatory bodies and international law. Problem of the capacity of transnational bodies such as the United Nations to gain the adherence of nations to stable patterns of regulation
Humankind	Relativization of citizenship	Problem of the relative nature of national citizenship in relation to global ideas of human rights and environmentalism. Problem of applying general notions such as human rights to the specific needs of particular groups
Selves	Individual–society problematic	Problem of the adherence of autonomous individuals to nations. Problem of the integrity of the self in relation to the surveillance capacities of the nation-state

A similar exercise may be conducted starting with the position of individual selves. This is outlined in Table 8.2. Here the global field embodies new challenges in the relations between individual selves on the one hand, and the world-system of societies and humankind on the other, as well as in the more familiar relationship between individuals and the nation-state.

Table 8.2   The interactions of particular selves within the global field

Aspect of the global field	Process involved	Examples of inter-active challenge
World system of societies	Relativization of societal reference	Problem of the place of individual selves within large-scale interstate and trans-national structure. This problem is symbolized by the remoteness of inter-governmental structures such as the United Nations from individuals, and the highly abstract nature of ideas of global citizenship
Humankind	Relativization of self-identities	Problem of how or whether individuals with local or national identities can relate to notions of humankind as a whole. Problem of whether global consciousness can mobilize particular selves located in a diverse range of social settings
Selves	Individual–society problematic	Problem of the adherence of autonomous individuals to the social collectivity. Problem of the integrity of the self in relation to the surveillance capacities of the nation-state

Tables 8.1 and 8.2 are designed to clarify the thrust of Robertson's concept of the global field and to begin to demonstrate how the general and schematic nature of the concept may be applied to more concrete issues in the contemporary world. They are, at the same time, extrapolations beyond Robertson's argument, in that he has neither fully developed the key concept of relativization nor provided a sustained elaboration of basic global field theory.

Robertson's general approach to globalization has two major elements to it. The first, as we have seen, is its multidimensionality, by which is meant the commitment to seeing multiple aspects of social life – economic, political, cultural, and so forth – together with multiple centres of action and multiple players within the global field. He is not the only writer on globalization to use such an approach (see, for example, Held 1995 and McGrew 1992), but his elaboration of multidimensionality through the idea of the global field is more fertile than other work of this kind in suggesting alternatives to the idea of global society as a system. Unlike orthodox world-system theory, the global field is not dominated by the singular logic of capitalism, nor is it animated by the power of economic institutions or legitimated by a powerful idea-system capable of co-opting antisystemic movements. Rather than having the fatalistic image of a exploitative system that cannot be expected to change much in our own lifetime or that of our children or grandchildren, Robertson sees globalization, for better or for worse, as part of the human condition. More specifically, the global field contains both structures of constraint and structures of opportunity for action affecting all players, be they individuals or nations. In this sense, globalization is far from representing the eclipse of human agency in the face of a system running out of control. At the same time, it is not, of course, beyond the capacity of human agents to make decisions and take actions that impair human capacities to make the most of global opportunities. The ability to wage nuclear warfare or to let population growth run unchecked are two such areas of potential threat.

The second major feature of Robertson's argument is its thoroughgoing dialectical or interactionist character. This is evident not only in the discussion of the four reference points of the global field, but also within his discussion of the relationship between universalism and particularism. While the dialogue and tension between that which is seen as universally significant and that which is particular to the person or local context may, in the most general sense, be a generic feature of all social life, Robertson sees it as intensified under conditions of globalization. In its simplest terms, this intensification arises, in his view, because of the inescapability of the fact that the world has become a single place. Even opponents of globalization, in the name of nation or ethnicity, cannot escape the outreach of transnational processes and institutions.

As the recent Balkans crisis indicates, this is for at least two reasons. In the first place, ethnonational attempts to redraw political boundaries by ethnic cleansing and territorial annexation introduce instability and challenge both into the interstate system of nations and into international economic relations. Although Western powers were slow to intervene in Bosnia, contemporary processes of military, political, and

economic intervention have shown the nations of the former Yugoslavia that there is no prospect of absolute sovereignty over territory.
American and UN diplomacy, the UN military presence, and the
involvement of World Bank and IMF in various aspects of the peace
and restabilization process, all testify to the fact that no nation can go it
alone. A second kind of interconnection between the global and the
national revealed in the Balkans War is that ethnonational struggles
often draw on global networks for support. Assertions of primordial
and historical attachment to territory have clearly been supplemented
by resources of money and people as ethnic diaspora are mobilized to
support the war effort in the homeland. Nationalism has, in this way,
become a long-distance rather than a merely parochial phenomenon.

Although the world is very much a single place, it is one that is
constituted by the paradoxical development of both universalism and
particularism. 'We are in the late 20th century', says Robertson,
'witnesses to – and participants in – a massive, twofold process
involving the interpenetration of the universalisation of particularism
and the particularisation of universalism' (1992, p. 100). This Delphic
observation requires some unravelling before its meaning becomes clear.

Taking the 'universalization of particularism' first, Robertson's intention is twofold. In one sense, this process is taken to mean the explosion
of social difference, as in the revival of ethnicity or the contemporary
proliferation of individual lifestyles. The ubiquity of cultural identification through assertions of difference reflects a situation in which
claims to uniqueness and particularity have become almost limitless.
This has led, according to Robertson, to the expectation that all claims
made by particular groups for particular purposes are legitimate.

The 'universalization of particularism' has a second meaning. This
involves the diffusion of particularistic practices on an increasingly
global scale. A leading example of this is the demand and spread of the
nation-state, as a political institution, across an increasing range of
peoples. Here, the nation-state becomes a universal model of what
political arrangements should look like while at the same time functioning in each specific case to further the particularistic interests of
different nationally bounded groups.

Moving on to 'the particularization of universalism', Robertson sees
this as the process whereby 'the idea of the universal is given
global–human concreteness' (1992, p. 102). What this means is the
translation of abstract entities such as the idea of humanity or of
human rights into conceptions of rights or forms of political mobilization that embrace the particular concerns of specific groups located in

settings that are not exactly shared by others. One way of developing this idea is by considering the relationship of women to the issue of universalism or particularism.

As Robertson points out, a major issue for feminist movements is whether to stress equality with men or to focus on difference. One major strand in feminism has challenged the universalistic claims of modernity as founded on the suppression of gender difference. Concealed behind ostensibly universalistic notions such as individual sovereignty or freedom of contract are patriarchal structures of power that have appeared to offer gender equality but actually constrain women to a private or domestic sphere that lies outside the universalized realm of public life (Pateman 1988). Insofar as globalization reproduces the existing gender division of labour, it too may be seen as suppressing gender equality. But where does this critique lead?

In one sense, the feminist challenge to the quasi-universalistic patriarchal dominance of men might be seen as leading simply to the assertion of gender difference, an aspect of the universalization of particularism. Yet in another sense, following Robertson's argument (1992, pp. 105–8), there is a counter-trend towards women's involvement in the particularization of universalism. This may be seen in moves to apply the universal notion of human rights to women's issues such as abortion or rape, by means of notions such as women's human rights. Women have generally been excluded from the public worlds of global politics and economic management, while also being victims of global processes such as sex tourism and the transnational market in domestic servants (Enloe 1990). At the same time, the resistance to such trends has depended not only on the assertion of difference, but also on the articulation and institutionalization of globally valid rights for women within transnational organizations. These have recently been publicized at the 1995 UN Conference on Women in Beijing.

Robertson's discussion of the universalism/particularism issue is thus both coherent and empirically plausible. It may be distinguished both from modernization theory, which assumed that universalism would triumph over particularism, and from world-system theory, which recognizes the issue, only to foreclose on its analysis by reducing the problem to one of capitalism and its discontents.

We have dwelt on the strengths of Robertson's argument, but what of its limits? One is the uncertain place of the political economy of global capitalism in the schema. Robertson certainly rejects the argument that the logic of capitalism directs culture. As an alternative, he suggests that culture and economy interpenetrate and that this is reflected in the interaction between universalistic globewide consumer capitalism on the one hand, and particularistic demand on the other. This refusal to privilege producers over consumers is attractive in principle since, as we saw in Chapter 3, the power of producers has been exaggerated. Yet the disproportion between multinational power and that of consumers, especially those who lack financial resources and information to make effective choices, is still a fundamental source of inequality, one that has only partly been redressed by regulatory frameworks that seek to address North–South disparities of wealth or, on an individual level, to uphold consumer rights.

This line of criticism connects with a second, namely that Robertson is exclusively concerned with cognitive issues to do with how the globe is understood and how that understanding reflects and embodies the connected issues of universalization and particularism. This focus is very important but is liable, nonetheless, to the criticism that it downplays patterns of institutional power and inequality within the global field. Robertson is aware that global inequalities between North and South influence understandings of the human condition, but what about their effect on the life-chances of individuals and peoples, especially those who lack the resources to enter the market for goods but equally lack a strong nation-state able to bargain effectively within international organizations?

For Friedman (1995, p. 72), Robertson's culturally centred cognitive approach leads him into the trap of suggesting that competing understandings and interpretations of 'global circumstances' actually constitute much of the global field itself. No attempt is made to confront alternative power-centred political economy models 'on their own ground'. In this way, Robertson neglects the post-war global institutionalization of political-economic structures. It is these structures which have constituted many key elements of the global field, including the way in which the 'global', 'national', and 'local' are both organized and understood. The analytical task, is thus to connect issues of global awareness, theorized by Robertson, with issues of global political economy.

There is an extensive literature on the general theoretical task of reconciling cultural and political economic/utilitarian aspects of social life (for example, Habermas 1979; Alexander 1982–84; Holton 1992). Such a project is worthwhile, but it does not form an explicit part of the present study. The analytical approach to globalization adopted here has been one of scepticism towards the claims of any general theory to explain the observable historical, economic, political, and cultural features of globalization reviewed in Chapters 2–7. Reductionist general theories that seek a political-economic or cultural explanation of any global phenomenon seem especially weak. This is because the culture of a particular epoch, group, or nation cannot necessarily be read off from a purely political-economic understanding any more than cultural analysis can explain all patterns of political-economic activity.

The revival of nationalism and ethnicity, for example, presents powerful criticisms of a general political economy approach to globalization. Wallerstein's political economic approach (1984, 1990, 1991), for instance, maintains that nationalism, ethnicity, and cultural particularism may well take on antiglobal forms, yet they function to promote the dominance of the capitalist world-system by undermining class unity and resistance. This broad-brush approach has some merit, but it is insufficiently fine grained to explain cases such as the recent revival of ethnonationalism in the Balkans. Here, nationalism and ethnicity took the form of resistance to regional integration in the former Yugoslavia rather than resistance to globalization, while the effects of civil war have obstructed capital accumulation rather than promoting it.

Table 8.3   Robertson's theory of globalization: strengths and weaknesses

Strengths	*Weaknesses*
1. Avoids the problems of a one-dimensional approach to globalization founded on a single logic, by stressing multidimensionality, complexity, and historicity	1. The general commitment to multidimensionality is not followed through in practice, notably by the failure to connect culture with political economy
2. Avoids a unitary approach to globalization by emphasizing the dialectical interaction of universalism and particularism within the global field	2. The cognitive emphasis tends to obscure issues of power and inequality
3. Successfully introduces culture into theories of globalization	3. Lacks any theory of why different orientations to globalization are present

If we switch our attention from political-economic to cultural versions of general theory, as advanced by Robertson, similar difficulties arise. As indicated in Table 8.3, a third problem with Robertson's approach is its inability to explain why cultural or cognitive orientations to globalization vary. Whether particular groups pick up universalistic cosmopolitanism, particularistic ethnonationalism, various gender-based orientations of a more or less universalistic or particularistic kind, or none of these is not made clear. The most that Robertson claims is that universalization and particularization are the terms within which such orientations are formulated. More than this, we may say that the two poles operating within the global system are mutually constituting. To take one example, particularistic practices are constituted in reaction against the claims of universalistic wholes, as in postcolonial resistance to Westernism, or feminist resistance to patriarchal constructions of modern institutions such as the sovereign individual. Meanwhile, universalistic practices are constituted in reaction to perceived problems with particularism. This is evident in the idea of a transcontextual international law, intended to secure a stable normative framework binding on all individual parties and hence better able to promote conflict resolution and global social order.

To call for a general multidimensional approach to globalization that avoids explanatory reductionism is important. Robertson's concept of the global 'field' is an important contribution to the development of such an approach. Yet general programmatic statements of this kind are little more than broad orientations to analysis. As such, they are no substitute for the fine-grained analysis of particular global processes, events, or historical transformations. As this study has proceeded through historical, economic, political, and cultural aspects of globalization, we have repeatedly seen how general theories about globalization fall down in the face of complex and contradictory evidence that points in several directions. Theories of capitalist global dominance have much explanatory power, for example, but they have proved unable to explain the limits to multinational power set by the robustness of the nation-state and by political and cultural resistance to corporate power. Similarly, theories of global cultural homogenization have much to be said for them, but once again they have not been able to account for the rise of counter-movements emphasizing national difference and the continuing cultural appeal of particular countries or localities.

In the belief that the complex topic of globalization has defied all general theoretical analyses thus far, this study advances a *middle-range* approach. This seeks specific explanations of particulars and looks for the broadest possible patterns, but does not seek to force the complex, paradoxical, and sometimes contradictory phenomena of globalization into a single Procrustean bed of general theory.

Normative challenges

The normative and the analytical are not entirely separate matters, as a vast literature in the philosophy of social science and in cultural studies tells us. Normative questions help to explain why it is that so many scholars have sought to analyse globalization, enter into the prejudices with which the topic is discussed, and influence the way in which concepts are constructed and evidence collected and interpreted. It is hard, for example, to conceive the idea of a capitalist world-system being constructed independently of normative concerns on how far global capitalism has been a force for human welfare and how far a contributor to inequality and exploitation.

The heavy tones of rhetoric that surround the idea of globalization as a 'system' are there, in part, to persuade us of the enormous interconnected reality and power of globalism, well before issues of conceptual precision and empirical evidence are introduced. Within any kind of 'system', big issues are clearly at stake, whether for good, ill, or, conceivably, both. The polarizing political rhetoric enveloping all things global has increased in intensity with George Bush's 1991 declaration, after the official ending of the Cold War, of the coming of a 'New World Order', inviting equally rhetorical rebuttal by those who detect the very opposite, that is, a 'New World Disorder'. Here, order and disorder stand as normatively loaded symbols for what is seen as good and bad about globalization.

Quite obviously, whether globalization is to be seen as good or bad, or is given a mixed reception, depends on what we take globalization to be and which voices or interests are doing the judging. The complex multidimensional approach to globalization developed in the present study rules out any notion of globalization as a unitary process with a single logic, and this in turn sensitizes us to similar complexities in normative debates. For example, many of those who reject economic globalization, in terms of the penetration of market relations and powerful MNEs into national communities, are more positive about political aspects of globalization such as the attempts to secure global human rights or environmental protection regimes. Opponents of multinationals may also sometimes join global social movements such as Greenpeace International. The obverse is also true, in that many economic liberals who welcome unfettered free markets in capital and commodities are socially conservative in rejecting many UN or European human rights initiatives or in rejecting global environmental protection initiatives (Alston 1995). The social multidimensionality of globalization is thus also mirrored by a normative multidimensionality. In this sense, it may be preferable to think in terms of globalizations rather than globalization.

Further normative complexities emerge when we come to consider the voices and interests that come to evaluate global processes. Most discussion about such matters has hitherto been directed towards public political norms, that is, to the future of ideals of democracy and the autonomous nation-state in an epoch of globalization. The place of individuals, families, and households in normative debates over globalization has received less attention in the past, but this is now changing. The advent of the personal computer and the Internet, together with the global expansion of personal consumption and tourism, all raise issues concerning the positive and negative effects of such global developments on human welfare. So too does the expansion of voluntary labour migration and the growth of refugee populations. All such examples raise public policy issues, of course, ranging from consumer rights and questions of personal privacy in electronic communications, to levels of migrant intake and global humanitarian responsibilities. However, they also represent areas in which individual evaluations are made, often repeatedly but in a typically private and less vocal way.

Hirschman (1970) has pointed out that if 'voice' is the typical mode of operation in the public life of democracy, 'exit' is the typical orientation to the 'market'. Since economic globalization is founded on market relations, it is not perhaps surprising that much of the normative orientation of individuals and households towards globalization within everyday life takes place over decisions of whether to enter or exit particular markets. For those whose choices are circumscribed by poverty, such decisions may relate to the purchase of a limited range of desired commodities, many imported or produced locally by global capital. Economic globalization may be evaluated positively insofar as such products (televisions, computers, the Big Mac) are brought within reach. Greater complexities emerge when traditional products (food stuffs and music) are valued more highly. This may mean a rejection of imports or Westernized/Americanized goods and an exit from globalized markets, but it may equally lead to a globalized supply of traditional products and services.

Meanwhile, on the labour market side, foreign capital may increase or decrease access to local employment, depending on the type of activity pursued and the impact made on the existing employment structure. New migrants may be attracted by employment opportunities but may also be seen as taking jobs, reducing the scope for choice.

Global labour market opportunities elsewhere may offer a wider access to alternatives or an escape from a situation with no apparent future. Quiet exit from one country and settlement elsewhere, perhaps organized through kin-based chain migration, represents a specific example of private choices and evaluations of global opportunities. Exit of this kind is, however, increasingly circumscribed by the toughening of immigration policies in the more prosperous countries. This trend has been described by Richmond (1993) as a 'new cultural apartheid', whereby national barriers act to segregate the relatively wealthy and powerful from the relatively poor and powerless.

For those with greater material resources, normative evaluation of globalization depends on how far such resources are seen as threatened or enhanced by the range of global developments. Greater global access to information technology and tourism, or employment and investment opportunities in other places, all of which look positive, may be offset by greater job competition in skilled labour markets and greater instability in globalized finance markets. Tourism may narrow as well as broaden the mind. There is thus no reason to suppose that globalization will produce a significant general shift of middle class norms towards cosmopolitanism, even though some segments of the middle class, such as the geographically mobile, may move in this direction (Hannerz 1990).

To depict a world of private choices, expressing positive and negative evaluations of such global products and opportunities, is useful in the sense that it affirms globalization as a personally and privately enabling as well as a constraining process. Given the contemporary disillusionment with politics in so many parts of the globe, there is, for the moment at least, a strong mood of privatism within the day-to-day life of individuals. This enters into the way in which globalization is approached, utilized, or rejected, quite apart from public political debate about this or that UN decision, or negotiations between governments and multinational companies, the IMF, or World Bank over economic policy or the terms of incoming investment. The private world presented is, however, an incomplete and artificial one, in that it brackets out the institutional framework within which private activity takes place. Exit is, in short, not enough. Voice from time to time erupts or becomes more salient to social groups and peoples. Yet the normative challenges to effective democratic voice posed by globalization are especially difficult and seemingly intractable.

The normative challenges of globalizations are nowhere more acute than in relation to ideals of democracy. The ideal of a self-governing people presumes the capacity to exercise self-determination. The globalization process nonetheless permeates and penetrates those political boundaries that have hitherto defined the territorially based units within which democratic self-determination has been practised, notably those of the nation-state. Questions then arise not only about the future viability of the nation-state, but also on whether new political and legal organization can be constructed that somehow recasts ideals of democracy on a transnational basis, whether this is global as in the UN or regional as in the EU.

We have already noted in Chapter 4 that it is unhelpful to think of the global challenge to democracy at the national level in terms of the loss of some absolute sense of national sovereignty. This has rarely existed and is in no sense a historical or contemporary norm. The challenges that globalization pose to democracy are more to do with increased global interconnectedness and with inequalities of access to power both between nations and between different interests within them. Beyond that, the cognitive complexities of global governance also create additional difficulties for democratic ideals, not least of which are the reliance on experts and the powerful position of epistemic communities of scientists and professionals in relation to citizens.

Observers nevertheless differ on the scope and intractability of such challenges and on the possibility of any successful recasting of democracy to combat the permeability of national boundaries to economic, political, and cultural influences from outside. Benjamin Barber's (1995) analysis of global polarization between McWorld and Jihad is pessimistic for the future of democracy on two counts. First, McWorld, that amalgam of fast food, fast computers, and fast music, corrodes democracy, in Barber's view, through the ideology of *laissez-faire* that leaves little scope for political action in the name of the public good. It also discourages public political participation as 'a culture of advertising, software, Hollywood movies, theme parks and shopping malls hooped together by the virtual nexus of the information superhighway closes down free spaces' (Barber 1995, p. 276). Second, however, the opponents of McWorld, symbolized as Jihad, the holy war of tribalization and fundamentalism, also undermine democracy, albeit in different ways. Principles of democratic process safeguarded by human rights and the rule of law are undermined by a totalitarian politics that represses dissent and open debate.

Barber finds it hard to identify emergent social trends that offer a way beyond the impasse. The potential democratic public remains too fragmented and diffuse for progress to come from below, while attempts at reinventing democracy from above are unlikely to prosper if the surrounding civil society of individuals, households, and voluntary bodies is inhospitable. Confederated political arrangements may represent one political form, able to transcend national differences, but this is still a shaky basis for progress towards a reinvented global democracy and civil society.

David Held (1995) is, by contrast, more optimistic, both in identifying emergent social trends on which a reinvented democracy might be constructed and in redefining what a normative account of such a democracy might look like. The key to his important discussion is the notion of 'cosmopolitan democracy' or 'cosmopolitan governance'. This is presented as an alternative to norms of international relations based on the 17th-century Westphalian model and on the post-war global polity centred on the UN. Neither of these alternatives is seen as offering a solution to the challenges posed by globalization to ideals of democratic self-determination, hitherto centred on the nation-state. The Westphalian sovereignty model is outdated in an increasingly interdependent world, while the UN system is unable to achieve effective compliance with its policies. Both suffer from an inability to reconceive what effective democracy might look like in a global order.

Cosmopolitan ideals, seen as 'belonging to all parts of the world' (p. 227), can be applied to many kinds of social practices, from cultural identity to political organization. For Held, they may usefully be seen as a form of law that is transnational in scope and which refers to the self-determination of all peoples collectively as well as individually. Cosmopolitan democracy in this respect need not be territorially bounded, and even where it is, this need not be restricted to individual nations, as the example of the EU indicates.

Against the criticism that all this is simply Utopian projection, Held makes two moves. First, he argues that cosmopolitan democracy builds on emergent social trends. Foremost of these, as argued above in Chapter 5, is a sense of the global order as a complex cobweb of linkages between governmental and non-governmental bodies. The argument for cosmopolitan democracy rests in part on the 'multiple and overlapping networks of power... which constitute the interconnections of different peoples and nations' (p. 271). Within this context, democratic rights are no longer sustainable within or limited to the territorially bounded world of nations but require a more complex globally organized polity to be effectively exercised. This not only requires a global as well as national and local levels of organization, but must also recognize the diverse cross-cutting communities of which individuals may be part. In this way, Held's second normative move is to detach democratic rights from any necessary relationship with territorial entities, beyond that of the globe as whole. Cosmopolitan democracy, embodied in law, should rather be applicable to all those with an interest in that aspect of human welfare involved, be it health, world security, the economy, or whatever.

Held's optimism is a heartening corrective to Barber's pessimism, and this may have at least something to do with contrasts in the view from Europe as against that from the USA. Held's confidence in the capacity of transnational political and legal arrangements to constrain the actions of nation-states according to a framework of norms seems to draw for many of its examples on the impact of decisions of the EU and the European Court of Justice on certain member states, notably the UK. Beyond this, Held, like a number of other observers, puts more emphasis on the key role of global NGOs in reviving the political activism of civil society, even in the face of McWorld and Jihad. Such NGOs, as we have seen in Chapter 5, do not have the power or the legitimacy of nation-states, but they have succeeded in inducing certain changes in the agenda of politics, for example in relation to environmental issues, and continue to be drawn on for expert opinion in standard-setting and the monitoring of compliance.

Beyond market 'exit' and the democratic institutionalization of 'voice', there remains a third element in Hirschman's analysis, namely the issue of 'loyalty'. This is the element that pertains to questions of normative commitments to community. Barber sees commitment in an era of globalization as polarized between the consumerist seductions of McWorld and the particularistic tribalism and stern moral fundamentalism of Jihad. The suggestion is that polarization of this kind is entrenched, loyalty to a globalized democratic political or legal order being weak.

Held is less concerned to canvass the state of contemporary loyalty in relation to globalization, but he does take up the challenge posed by cultural difference to the ideal of cosmopolitan democracy. The presumption here is that a strong sense of global culture or loyalty to some overarching set of global values is not necessary for the functioning of cosmopolitan democracy. Although Held says far more about the political than the cultural feasibility of global democracy, he argues that the contemporary explosion of cultural difference is not founded on entirely distinct and separate cultural bases. Rather, different cultural patterns are already interlinked through globalization, such that 'sealed cultural diversity' (Held 1995, p. 284) no longer exists. The issue, then, is how such linkages develop, particularly whether opposition, resistance, or mutual accommodation becomes the dominant mode of interconnection.

As we have seen in Chapter 6, the recent explosion of ethnonationalism and the revival of ethnicity in settings of migrant settlement, together with the robustness of more ordinary or banal forms of nationalism, all suggest in their different ways that the project of mutual accommodation between contrasting loyalties is an extremely difficult one. Held's argument is not, however, rebutted by the absence of a widespread global culture with a binding grip on loyalty, as diagnosed by Anthony Smith (1990). While cosmopolitan cultures remain limited in scope, one may expect territoriality, real or imagined, to continue to play a major part in cultural identity. The issue depends rather on the extent to which territorially bound cultural identities lend themselves to mutual accommodation instead of conflict.

Here, the test case remains Europe, where closer integration in terms of markets and political decisions does not depend on any clear sense of European loyalty. The implications of this are ambivalent. In one sense, the EU shows how far transnational relations and institutions can be created to allow mutual accommodation of parties without a strong base of popular cultural loyalty to the framework being created. On the other hand, the lack of such a base and the élitist nature of many EU processes, notably the bureaucratic regulatory institutions centred in Brussels, render the whole edifice vulnerable to national and local resistance. Even if mutual accommodation of interests and cultural orientations should prevail in one crucial region such as Europe, this is no guarantee that similar developments world arise elsewhere. Regional co-operation in North America through NAFTA or in the Asia-Pacific through APEC is still restricted to economic matters, the national decision-making of the various partners still being intact. Beyond this, the cultural diversity included in such arrangements, especially APEC, raises even greater challenges than appear in the European context. Contrasts between European and Asian-Pacific regional transnationalism do, however, alert us to the great unevenness of globalization processes, especially in transnational institution-building. Held tries to allow for this in a stepwise scenario for the construction of cosmopolitan democracy, but it remains unclear whether the future holds stepwise transnational integration, stepwise disintegration, as the reaction against Maastricht takes hold, or a very patchy, uneven cobweb of transnational integration. In any case, the globalization of loyalty seems, for the moment, more remote in comparison with the globalization of voice or of exit.

Such normative debates around globalization, democracy, and cultural loyalty are clearly far from resolution. This applies both to the analysis of emergent social trends and to the coherence of norms such as that of cosmopolitan democracy advanced by Held. While a heavy dose of scepticism may be applied to all such Utopian projections into the future, it is equally the case, as Eric Hobsbawm once remarked, that Utopias may equally prove fruitful as barren.

There is, then, no definitive or even provisional balance sheet to be drawn on where globalization is headed or whether it may be regarded as good or bad. There is, however, no reason that I regard as convincing for seeing globalization in demonic terms as an unstoppable force, a juggernaut driven by technological change, or as a process whose direction is monopolized from above in a manner that is, in principle, out of reach of the peoples of the globe. Globalization is not a unitary process or system. It is better seen as a set of intersecting processes that falter as much as they advance, which often have the quality of networks rather than structures, and which have limits set by counter-trends and movements within the global field. The politics of the 'global field' may, it is true, be the site of conflict as well as co-operation since major issues of global inequality and injustice remain unresolved. In this respect, global politics is no different from any other political struggle over social purposes and the allocation of resources between conflicting interests. Since it is not a system, however, I doubt whether an antisystemic challenge to globalization *per se* makes much analytical or political sense.

Understood in this way, globalization processes are not necessarily to be feared and can even be something to be enjoyed or in which to find fulfilment. It has been said of some schools of social enquiry that they function to talk people out of their happiness and into a more critical standpoint towards social life. A critical approach to global rhetoric and pieties about globalization as an unambiguous social good is certainly highly necessary. Identifying the winners and losers from processes of globalization is a major task of social science. Yet it may equally be said that certain social enquiries into globalization stand in need of less gloom and despair. What is required instead is a greater appreciation of the ways in which social groups in all parts of the world have been influenced by and borrowed from each other, thereby meeting a wider range of human needs.

Bibliography

Abu-Lughod, J. (1989) *Before European Hegemony, The World System, AD 1250–1350* (New York: Oxford University Press).

Abu-Lughod, J. (1993) 'Discontinuities and persistence: one world system or a succession of systems', in Frank, A.G. and Gills, B.K. (eds) *The World System: Five Hundred Years or Five Thousand?* (London: Routledge), pp. 278–91.

Ahmed, A.A. (1992) *Postmodernism and Islam* (London: Routledge).

Albrow, M. (1990) 'Introduction', in Albrow, M. and King, E. (eds) *Globalization, Knowledge and Society* (London: Sage), pp. 3–13.

Alexander, J. (1982–4) *Theoretical Logic in Sociology*, 4 vols (London: Routledge).

Alexander, J. (1988) 'Core solidarity, ethnic outgroup, and social differentiation', in *Action and its Environments* (New York: Stanford University Press), pp. 78–106.

Alston, P. (1992) 'Appraising the United Nations human rights regime', in Alston, P. (ed.) *The United Nations and Human Rights* (Oxford: Oxford University Press), pp. 1–21.

Alston, P. (1995) 'Reform of treaty-making processes: form over substance', in Alston, P. and Chiam, M. (eds) *Treaty-Making and Australia* (Sydney: Federation Press), pp. 1–28.

Anderson, B. (1983) *Imagined Communities* (London: Verso).

Anderson, B. (1994) 'Exodus', *Critical Inquiry*, **20**, Winter, pp. 313–27.

Anglade, C. and Fortin, C. (1990) 'Accumulation, adjustment and the autonomy of the State in Latin America', in Anglade, C. and Fortin, C. (eds) *The State and Capital Accumulation in Latin America*, 2 vols (Pittsburgh: University of Pittsburgh Press), pp. 211–340.

Appadurai, A. (1990) 'Disjuncture and difference in the global cultural economy', in Featherstone, M. (ed.) *Global Culture* (London: Sage), pp. 295–310.

Asante, M.K. (1991) 'Multiculturalism: an exchange', *American Scholar*, **60**, pp. 267–72.

Australian Council on Population and Ethnic Affairs (1982) *Multiculturalism for All Australians* (Canberra: AGPS).

Bailey, D., Harte, G. and Sugden, R. (1994) *Transnationals and Governments: Recent Policies in Japan, France, Germany, the United States and Japan* (London: Routledge).

Banton, M. (1994) 'Modelling ethnic and national relations', *Ethnic and Racial Studies*, **17**(1), pp. 1–19.

Barber, B. (1991) 'Jihad vs McWorld', *Atlantic*, **269**(3), pp. 53–63.

Barber, B. (1995) *Jihad vs McWorld* (New York: Ballantine Books).

Bartlett, C.A. and Ghoshal, S. (1992 [1989]) *Managing Across Borders: The Transnational Solution* (London: Random House).

205

206   *Globalization and the Nation-State*

Beck, U. (1992) *Risk Society: Towards a New Sociology of Modernity* (London: Sage).
Bercovitch, J. (1996) 'The United Nations and the mediation of international disputes', in Thukur, R. (ed.) *The United Nations at Fifty: Retrospect and Prospect* (Dunedin: University of Otago Press), pp. 73–88.
Bernal, M. (1987) *The Afro-Asiatic Roots of Classical Civilization* (New Brunswick: Rutgers University Press).
Billig, M. (1995) *Banal Nationalism* (London: Sage).
Blainey, G. (1966) *The Tyranny of Distance* (Melbourne: Sun Books).
Boddewyn, J., Soehl, R. and Picard, J. (1986) 'Standardization in international marketing', *Business Horizons*, Nov/Dec, pp. 69–75.
Bouras, G. (1986) *A Foreign Wife* (Fitzroy: McPhee, Gribble/Penguin).
Boyne, R. (1990) 'Culture and the world-system', in Featherstone, M. (ed.) *Global Culture: Nationalism, Globalization and Modernity* (London: Sage), pp. 57–62.
Braithwaite, J. (1993) 'Transnational regulation of the pharmaceutical industry', *Annals*, AAPSS, **525**, pp. 12–30.
Braithwaite, J. (1995) 'Sovereignty and globalisation of business regulation', in Alston, P. and Chiam, M. (eds) *Treaty-Making in Australia: Globalisation versus Sovereignty?* (Sydney: Federation Press), pp. 115–28.
Brandt, W. (1980) *North–South: A Programme for Survival: The Report of the Independent Commission on International Development Issues* (London: Pan).
Braudel, F. (1982) *Civilisation and Capitalism 15th–18th Century*, vol. 2, *The Wheels of Commerce* (London: Collins).
Braudel, F. (1988) *The Identity of France*, vol. 1, *History and Environment* (London: Collins).
Brenner, R. (1977) 'The origins of capitalist development: a critique of neo-Smithian Marxism', *New Left Review*, **104**, pp. 25–93.
Brett, E.A. (1985) *The World Economy Since the War: The Politics of Uneven Development* (Basingstoke: Macmillan).
Brubaker, R. (1992) *Citizenship and Nationhood in France and Germany* (Cambridge, MA: Harvard University Press).
Cameron, D. (1978) 'The expansion of the public economy: a comparative analysis', *American Political Science Review*, **72**(4), pp. 1243–61.
Campbell, A.J. and Verbeke, A. (1994) 'The globalization of service multinationals', *Long Range Planning (International Journal of Strategic Management)*, **27**(2), pp. 95–102.
Carnoy, M. (1993) 'Multinationals in a changing world economy: wither the nation-state?', in Carnoy, M., Castells, M. and Cohen, S.S. (eds) *The Global Economy in the Information Age* (University Park, PA: Pennsylvania State University Press), pp. 45–96.
Carnoy, M., Castells, M. and Cohen, S.S. (eds) (1993) *The Global Economy in the Information Age* (University Pack, PA: Pennsylvania State University Press).
Cassese, A. (1988) *Violence and the Law in the Modern Age* (Cambridge: Polity Press).
Cassese, A. (1992) 'The general assembly: historical perspective 1945–89', in Alston, P. (ed.) *The United Nations and Human Rights: A Critical Appraisal* (Oxford: Oxford University Press), pp. 25–54.
Castells, M. (1993) 'The information economy and the new international order', in Carnoy, M., Castells, M. and Cohen, S.S. (eds) *The Global Economy in the*

Information Age (University Park, PA: Pennsylvania State University Press), pp. 15–44.

Castles, S. and Miller, M. (1993) *The Age of Migration* (Basingstoke: Macmillan).

Chase-Dunn, C. (1989) *Global Formation: Structures of the World-economy* (Oxford: Blackwell).

Cohen, S.S. (1993) 'Geo-economics: lessons from America's mistakes', in Carnoy, M., Castells, M. and Cohen, S.S. (eds) *The New Global Economy in the Information Age* (University Park: Pennsylvania State University Press), pp. 97–148.

Connor, W. (1973) 'The politics of ethno-nationalism', *Journal of International Affairs*, **27**, pp. 1–21.

Connor, W. (1987) 'Ethno-nationalism', in Weiner, M. and Huntington, S. (eds) *Understanding Political Development* (Boston: Little, Brown), pp. 196–220.

Connor, W. (1994) *Ethno-Nationalism: The Quest for Understanding* (Princeton: Princeton University Press).

Corley, T.A.B. (1989) 'The nature of multi-nationals', in Teichova, A. *et al.* (eds), *Historical Studies in International Corporate Business* (Cambridge: Cambridge University Press), pp. 43–56.

Craig, R.B. (1989) 'Mexican narcotics traffic: binational security implications', in Mabry, D.J. (ed.) *The Latin American Narcotics Trade and US National Security* (New York: Greenwood Press), pp. 27–42.

Curtin, P.D. (1984) *Cross-cultural Trade in World History* (Cambridge: Cambridge University Press).

Dassbach, C.A. (1989) *Global Enterprises and the World Economy: Ford, General Motors, and IBM, the Emergence of the Transnational Enterprise* (New York: Garland Publishing).

Davis, M.C. (ed.) (1995) *Human Rights and Chinese Values* (Oxford: Oxford University Press).

Delanty, G. (1995) *Inventing Europe: Idea, Identity, Reality* (Basingstoke: Macmillan).

Donnelly, J. (1981) 'Recent trends in UN human rights activity: description and polemic', *International Organization*, **35**(4), pp. 633–56.

Dore, R. (1973) *British Factory, Japanese Factory* (London: Allen & Unwin).

Drahos, P. (1995) 'Global property in information: the story of TRIPS at the GATT', *Prometheus*, **13**(1), pp. 6–19.

Dror, D. (1984) 'Aspects of labour law and relations in selected export processing zones', *International Labour Review*, **123**, Nov/Dec, pp. 705–22.

Dunning, J.H. (1993) *The Globalization of Business* (London: Routledge).

Eisenstadt, S.N. (1992) 'The order-maintaining and order-transforming dimensions of culture', in Munch, R. and Smelser, N. (eds) *Theory of Culture* (Berkeley, CA: University of California Press), pp. 64–87.

Elvin, M. (1973) *The Pattern of the Chinese Past* (Stanford: Stanford University Press).

Enloe, C. (1990) *Bananas, Beaches, and Bases: Making Feminist Sense of International Politics* (Berkeley: University of California Press).

Fantasia, R. (1995) 'Fast food in France', *Theory and Society*, **24**, pp. 201–43.

Featherstone, M. (ed.) (1990) *Global Culture* (London: Sage).

Featherstone, M., Lash, S. and Robertson, R (1995) *Global Modernities* (London: Sage).

Fischer, M.M.J. (1992) 'Is Islam the odd-civilisation out?', *New Perspectives Quarterly*, Spring, pp. 54–9.

Flora, P. (ed.) (1987) *Growth to Limits: The Western Welfare States Since World War Two*, 4 vols (Berlin: de Gruyter).

Fortin, C. (1984) 'The failure of repressive monetarism: Chile 1973–83', *Third World Quarterly*, **6**(2), pp. 310–26.

Frank, A.G. (1990) 'A theoretical introduction to 5000 years of world-system history', *Review*, **13**(2), pp. 155–248.

Freemantle, B. (1986) *The Fix: Inside the World Drug Trade* (New York: Tom Doherty Associates).

Friedan, J. (1991) 'Invested interests: the politics of national economic policies in a world of global finance', *International Organisation*, **45**(4), pp. 425–51.

Friedman, J. (1994) *Cultural Identity and Global Process* (London: Sage).

Friedman, J. (1995) 'Global system, globalization and the parameters of modernity', in Featherstone, M., Lash, S. and Robertson, R. (eds) *Global Modernities* (London: Sage), pp. 69–90.

Friedmann, J. (1986) 'The world city hypothesis', *Development and Change*, **17**, pp. 69–83.

Frith, S. (ed.) (1989) *World Music, Politics and Social Change* (Manchester: Manchester University Press).

Frobel, F. *et al.* (1980) *The New International Division of Labour* (Cambridge: Cambridge University Press).

Fukuyama, F. (1992) 'Asia's soft-authoritarian alternative', *New Perspectives Quarterly*, Spring, pp. 60–1.

Gangjian Du and Song Gang (1995) 'Relating human rights to Chinese culture: the four paths of the Confucian analects and the four principles of a new theory of benevolence', in Davis, M.C. (ed.) *Human Rights and Chinese Values* (Oxford: Oxford University Press), pp. 33–56.

Garrett, G. and Mitchell, D. (1996) 'Globalization and the welfare state: income transfers in the industrial democracies, 1966–90', unpublished paper presented to the 1996 Annual Meeting of the American Political Science Association, San Francisco, USA.

Gellner, E. (1983) *Nations and Nationalism* (Oxford: Blackwell).

Gereffi, G. (1994) 'The organisation of buyer-driven global commodity chains', in Gereffi, G. and Korzeniewicz, M. (eds) *Commodity Chains and Global Capitalism* (Westport: Praeger), pp. 95–122.

Gereffi, G. (1996) 'Global commodity chains: new forms of coordination and control among nations and firms in international industries', *Competition and Change*, **1**, 4.

Gereffi, G. and Korzeniewicz, M. (eds) (1994) *Commodity Chains and Global Capitalism* (Westport: Praeger).

Gerlach, G. (1992) *Alliance Capitalism: The Strategic Organisation of Japanese Business* (Berkeley, CA: University of California Press).

Ghils, P. (1992) 'International civil society', *Social Science Journal*, **133**, pp. 417–31.

Giddens, A. (1981) *A Contemporary Critique of Historical Materialism*, vol. 1, *Power, Property, and the State* (Berkeley, CA: University of California Press).

Giddens, A. (1990) *The Consequences of Modernity* (Cambridge: Polity Press).

Gilpin, R. (1975) *US Power and the Multinational Corporation* (New York: Basic Books).

Gilroy, P. (1993) *The Black Atlantic: Modernity and Double Consciousness* (London: Verso).

Giroux, H. (1994) 'Consuming social change: the "United Colours of Benetton"', *Cultural Critique*, Winter, pp. 5–32.

Girvan, N. (1971) *Foreign Capital and Underdevelopment in Jamaica* (Jamaica: University of West Indies).

Glazer, N. (1983) *Ethnic Dilemmas 1964–1982* (Cambridge, MA: Harvard University Press).

Granovetter, M. (1985) 'Economic action and social structure', *American Journal of Sociology*, **91**, pp. 481–510.

Griggs, R. (1992) 'The meaning of "nation" and "state" in the Fourth World', Center for World Indigenous Studies, Occasional Paper #18 (abridged version at http://www.halcyon.com/FWDP/fouthw.html), pp. 1–4.

Griswold, W. (1992) 'The writing on the mud wall: Nigerian novels and the imaginary village', *American Sociological Review*, **57**, December, pp. 709–24.

Grunwald, J. and Flamm, K. (1985) *The Global Factory* (Washington, DC: Brookings).

Gupta, A. and Ferguson, J. (1992) 'Beyond "culture": space, identity and the politics of difference', *Current Anthropology*, **7**(1), pp. 6–23.

Haas, P.M., Keohane, R.O. and Levy, M.A. (eds) (1993) *Insitutions for the Earth: Sources of Environmental Protection* (Cambridge, MA: MIT Press).

Habermas, J. (1979) *Communication and the Evolution of Society* (London: Heinemann).

Hannerz, U. (1990) 'Cosmopolitans and locals in world culture', in Featherstone, M. (ed.) *Global Culture* (London: Sage), pp. 237–51.

Hannerz, U. (1992) *Cultural Complexity* (New York: Columbia University Press).

Harris, N. (1986) *The End of the Third World* (London: Penguin).

Harvey, D. (1989) *The Condition of Postmodernity* (Oxford: Blackwell).

Hawkins, F. (1989) *Critical Years in Immigration: Canada and Australia Compared* (Kingston: McGill-Queens Press).

Hebdige, D. (1987) *Cut n' Mix: Culture, Identity, and Caribbean Music* (London: Methuen).

Held, D. (1991) 'Democracy, the nation-state and the global system', in Held, D. (ed.) *Political Theory Today* (Oxford: Polity Press), pp. 197–235.

Held, D. (1995) *Democracy and the Global Order* (Cambridge: Polity Press).

Held, D. and McGrew, A.G. (1993) 'Globalization and the liberal democratic state', *Government and Opposition*, **28**(2), pp. 261–8.

Hirschman, A. (1970) *Exit, Voice and Loyalty* (Cambridge, MA: Harvard University Press).

Hirst, P. and Thompson, G. (1992) 'The problem of globalization: international economic relations, national economic management, and the formation of trading blocs', *Economy and Society*, **21**(4), pp. 357–96.

Hirst, P. and Thompson, G. (1996) *Globalization in Question* (Cambridge: Polity Press).

Hobsbawm, E. (1990) *Nations and Nationalism Since 1780* (London: Clarendon).

Hobsbawm, E. and Ranger, T. (eds) (1983) *The Invention of Tradition* (Cambridge: Cambridge University Press).

Hodgson, M. (1974 [1958–9]) *The Venture of Islam,* 3 vols (Chicago: University of Chicago Press).

Holm, H-H. and Sorensen, G. (1995) *Whose World Order: Uneven Globalization and the End of the Cold War* (Boulder: Westview Press).

Holton, R.J. (1985) *The Transition From Feudalism to Capitalism* (Basingstoke: Macmillan).

Holton, R.J. (1992) *Economy and Society* (London: Routledge).

Hourani, A. (1991) *Islam in European Thought* (Cambridge: Cambridge University Press).

Huntington, S. (1993) 'The clash of civilizations', *Foreign Affairs,* **72**(3), pp. 22–49.

Huntington, S. (1996) *The Clash of Civilizations and the Remaking of World Order* (New York: Simon & Schuster).

Hussain, A. (1990) *Western Conflict with Islam: Survey of the Anti-Islamic Tradition* (Leicester: Volcano Books).

Hutchinson, J. (1994) *Modern Nationalism* (London: Fontana).

Ionescu, G. (1993) 'The impact of the information revolution on parliamentary sovereignties', *Government and Opposition,* **28**(2), pp. 221–41.

Jackson, R.H. (1990) *Quasi-States: Sovereignty, International Relations and the Third World* (Cambridge: Cambridge University Press).

Johnson, C. (1962) *Peasant Nationalism and Communist Power* (Stanford: Stanford University Press).

Johnson, C. (1982) *MITI and the Japanese Miracle* (Stanford: Stanford University Press).

Kapstein, E. (1994) *Governing the Global Economy: International Finance and the State* (Cambridge, MA: Harvard University Press).

Keohane, R.O. (1984) *After Hegemony* (Princeton, NJ: Princeton University Press).

Keohane, R.O. (1995) 'Hobbes' dilemma and institutional change in world politics: sovereignty in international society', in Holm, H-H. and Sorensen, G. (eds) *Whose World Order? Uneven Globalisation and the End of the Cold War* (Boulder, CO: Westview Press), pp. 165–86.

Kern, S. (1983) *The Culture of Time and Space 1880–1918* (Cambridge, MA: Harvard University Press).

Kline, S. (1995) 'The play of the market: on the internationalization of children's culture', *Theory, Culture and Society,* **12**, pp. 103–29.

Kopal, Z. (1973) 'Foreward', in Bienkowska, B. (ed.) *The Scientific World of Copernicus* (Dordrecht: Reidel Publishing Co), pp. vii–xii.

Kotkin, J. (1993) *Tribes, How Race, Religion and Identity Determine Success in the New Global Economy* (New York: Random House).

Krasner, S. (1985) *Structural Conflict: The Third World Against Liberalism* (Berkeley, CA: University of California Press).

Lash, S. and Urry, J. (1987) *The End of Organised Capitalism* (Oxford: Polity Press).

Lee, R.W. (1989) 'The cocaine dilemma in South America', in Mabry, D.J. (ed.) *The Latin American Narcotics Trade and US National Security* (New York: Greenwood Press), pp. 59–74.

Leftwich, A. (1993) 'Governance, democracy, and development in the Third World', *Third World Quarterly,* **14**(3), pp. 605–24.

Lei, D. (1993) 'Offensive and defensive uses of alliances', *Long Range Planning (Journal of Strategic Management)*, **26**(4), pp. 32–41.

Lever-Tracy, C., Ip, D. and Tracy, N. (1996) *The Chinese Business Diaspora and Mainland China* (Basingstoke: Macmillan).

Levi-Strauss, C. (1955) *Tristes Tropiques* (Paris: Plon).

Levitt, T. (1983) 'The globalization of markets', *Harvard Business Review* May/June pp. 92–102.

Levy, M.A., Keohane, R.O. and Haas, P.M. (1993) 'Improving the effectiveness of international environmental institutions', in Haas, P.M., Keohane, R.O. and Levy, M.A. (eds) *Institutions for the Earth: Sources of Effective International Environmental Protection* (Cambridge, MA: MIT Press), pp. 397–426.

Lillrank, P. (1995) 'The transfer of management innovations from Japan', *Organization Studies*, **16**(6), pp. 971–89.

Loh, C. (1995) 'The Vienna process and the importance of universal standards in Asia' in Davis, M.C. (ed.) *Human Rights and Chinese Values* (Oxford: Oxford University Press), pp. 145–67.

McDonald, S. (1988) *Dancing on a Volcano: the Latin American Drug Trade* (New York: Praeger).

McGrew, A. (1992) 'Conceptualising global politics', in McGrew, A. and Lewis, P.G. (eds) *Global Politics* (Oxford: Polity Press), pp. 1–28.

McGrew, A. and Lewis, P.G. (eds) (1992) *Global Politics* (Oxford: Polity Press).

McNeill, W.H. (1964) *The Rise of The West: A History of the Human Community,* (Chicago: Chicago University Press).

McNeill, W.H. (1986) *Polyethnicity and National Unity in World History* (Toronto: University of Toronto Press).

McNeill, W.H. (1990) 'The *Rise of the West* after twenty-five years', *Journal of World History*, **1**, pp. 1–21.

Mann, M. (1986) *The Sources of Social Power*, vol. 1 (Cambridge: Cambridge University Press).

Mann, M. (1993) 'Nation-states in Europe and other continents: diversifying, developing not dying', *Daedulus*, Summer, pp. 115–40.

Manuel, G. (1974) *The Fourth World: An Indian Reality* (New York: Free Press).

Martinelli, A. (1982) 'The political and social impact of transnational corporations', in Makler, H., Martinelli, A. and Smelser, N. (eds) *The New International Economy* (London: Sage), pp. 79–116.

Marty, M and Appleby, R.S. (1991) *Fundamentalisms Observed*, vol. 1 (Chicago: Chicago University Press).

Marx, K. and Engels, F. (1962) 'Manifesto of the Communist Party', in Marx, K. and Engels, F., *Selected Works*, vol. 1 (Moscow: Foreign Languages Publishing House), pp. 34–65.

Mayer, A.E. (1990) 'The Shari'a: a methodology or a body of substantive rules?', in Heer, N. (ed.) *Islamic Law and Jurisprudence* (Seattle: University of Washington Press), pp. 177–98.

Mazlish, B. and Buultjens, R. (eds) (1993) *Conceptualising Global History* (Boulder, CO: Westview Press).

Mazrui, Ali A. (1990) *Cultural Images in World Politics* (London: Currey).

Mennell, S. (1990) 'The globalization of human society as a very long term process', in Featherstone, M. (ed.) *Global Culture* (London: Sage), pp. 359–72.

Mernissi, F. (1993) *Islam and Democracy* (London: Virago).

Mills, J. (1986) *Where Crime and Governments Embrace* (Garden City, NY: Doubleday).

Mitchell, J. (1992) 'The nature and government of the global economy', in McGrew, A.G. *et al.* (eds) *Global Politics* (Cambridge: Cambridge University Press), pp. 174–96.

Miyoshi, M. and Harootunian, H.A. (eds) (1989) *Postmodernism in Japan* (Durham: Duke University Press).

Modelski, G. (1978) 'The long cycle of global politics and the nation-state', *Comparative Studies in Society and History*, **20**, pp. 214–35.

Moore, W.E. (1966) 'Global sociology: the world as a singular system', *American Journal of Sociology*, **LXXI**(5), pp. 475–82.

Moran, T. (1974) *Multinational Corporations and the Politics of Dependency* (Princeton, NJ: Princeton University Press).

Mosley, P., Harrigan, J. and Toye, J. (1991) *Aid and Power: The World Bank and Policy-Based Lending*, 2 vols (London: Routledge).

Mosse, G. (1985) *Nationalism and Sexuality* (Madison, WI: University of Wisconsin Press).

Nagel, J. (1986) 'The political construction of ethnicity' in Olzak, S. and Nagel, J. (eds) *Competitive Ethnic Relations* (New York: Academic Press), pp. 93–112.

Nisbet, R. (1980) *History of the Idea of Progress* (New York: Basic Books).

Office of Multicultural Affairs (1989) *National Agenda for a Multicultural Australia* (Canberra: AGPS).

Ohmae, K. (1990) *The Borderless World: Power and Strategy in the International Economy* (London: Fontana).

Ohmae, K. (1996) *The End of the Nation State* (London: HarperCollins).

Oppenheim, L. (1905) *International Law*, vol. 1 (London: Longmans).

Opsahl, T. (1992) 'The Human Rights Committee', in Alston, P. (ed.) *The United Nations and Human Rights* (Oxford: Oxford University Press), pp. 369–443.

Parry, G. (1993) 'The interweaving of foreign and domestic policy', *Government and Opposition*, **28**(2), pp. 143–51.

Pateman, C. (1988) *The Sexual Contract* (Cambridge: Polity Press).

Paz, O. (1992) 'West turns east at the end of the century', *New Perspectives Quarterly*, Spring, pp. 5–9.

Pierson, C. (1991) *Beyond the Welfare State?* (Cambridge: Polity Press).

Pieterse, J.N. (1995) 'Globalization as hybridization', in Featherstone, M., Lash, S. and Robertson, R. (eds) *Global Modernities* (London: Sage), pp. 69–90.

Piore, M. and Sabel, C. (1984) *The Second Industrial Divide* (New York: Basic Books).

Polanyi, K. (1957) *The Great Transformation* (Boston: Beacon Press).

Pollard, S. (1965) *The Origins of Modern Management* (London: Edward Arnold) .

Porter, M. (1990) *The Competitive Advantage of Nations* (New York: Free Press).

Ravitch, D. (1990) 'Multiculturalism. E Pluribus Plures', *American Scholar*, **59**, pp. 337–54.

Ravitch, D. (1991) 'Multiculturalism: an exchange', *The American Scholar*, **60**, pp. 272–6.

Reich, S. (1989) 'Roads to follow: regulating direct foreign investment', *International Organisation*, **43**(4), pp. 543–84.

Rex, J. (1995) 'Multiculturalism in Europe and America', *Nations and Nationalism*, July, pp. 243–59.

Richmond, A. (1991) 'Immigration and multiculturalism in Canada and Australia', *International Journal of Canadian Studies*, **3**, pp. 87–110.

Richmond, A. (1993) 'Open and closed borders: is the New World Order creating a system of global apartheid?', *Refuge*, **13**(1), pp. 10–14.

Righter, R. (1995) *Utopia Lost: the United Nations and the World* (New York: Twentieth Century Fund Press).

Ritzer, G. (1993) *The McDonaldization of Society* (Thousand Oaks, CA: Pine Forge Press).

Roberts, M. (1992), '"World music" and the global cultural economy', *Diaspora*, **2**(2), pp. 229–42.

Robertson, R. (1992) *Globalization: Social Theory and Global Culture* (London: Sage).

Robertson, R. (1995) 'Glocalization: time-space and homogeneity–heterogeneity', in Featherstone, M., Lash, S. and Robertson, R. (eds) *Global Modernities* (London: Sage), pp. 25–44.

Robinson, F. (1979) 'Islam and Muslim separatism', in Taylor, D. and Yapp, M. (eds) *Political Identity in South Asia* (London: Curzon Press).

Rosenau, J.N. (1980) *The Study of Global Interdependence* (London: Francis Pinter).

Rosenau, J.N. (1996) 'The Adaptation of the United Nations to a turbulent world', in Thukur, R. (ed.) *The United Nations at Fifty: Retrospect and Prospect* (Dunedin: University of Otago Press), pp. 229–40.

Rowlands, I. (1995) *The Politics of Global Atmospheric Change* (Manchester: Manchester University Press).

Russell, R.B. and Muther, J. (1958) *A History of the United Nations Charter* (Washington: Brookings Institution).

Said, E.W. (1978) *Orientalism* (New York: Penguin).

Said, E.W. (1993) *Cultural Imperialism* (London: Chatto & Windus).

Sartori, G. (1989) 'Undercomprehension', *Government and Opposition*, **24**(4), pp. 391–400.

Sasaki, T. (1993) 'What the Japanese have learned from strategic alliances', *Long Range Planning (International Journal of Strategic Management)*, **26**(6), pp. 41–53.

Sassen, S. (1991) *The Global City, New York, London, Tokyo* (Princeton, NJ: Princeton University Press).

Sassen, S. (1994) *Cities in a World Economy* (Thousand Oaks, CA: Pine Forge Press).

Schama, S. (1991) 'Homelands', *Social Research*, **58**(1), pp. 11–30.

Schapiro, M.J. (1994) 'Images of planetary danger: Luciano Benetton's ecumenical fantasy', *Alternatives*, **19**, pp. 433–54.

Scharpf, F.W. (1991) *Crisis and Choice in European Social Democracy* (Ithaca, NY: Cornell University Press).

Schiller, H. (1976) *Communication and Cultural Domination* (New York: International Arts and Sciences).

Schlesinger, A. (1992) *The Disuniting of America* (New York: W.W. Norton).

Schmitter, P.C. (1996) 'Imagining the future of the euro-polity with the help of new concepts', in Marks, G., Scharpf, F.W., Schmitter, P.C. *et al.* (eds) *Governance in the European Union* (London: Sage), pp. 121–50.

Schneider, C. and Wallis, B. (eds) (1988) *Global Television* (Cambridge, MA: MIT Press).

Seade, J. (1995) 'The World Trade Organisation', *Global Economic Institutions Newsletter* (1), pp. 3–4.

Shibata, T. (1993) 'Sony's successful strategy for compact discs', *Long Range Planning (Journal of Strategic Management)*, **26**(4), 16–21.

Sklair, L. (1988) 'The costs of foreign investment: the case of Egyptian free zones', in Kedourie, E. and Haim, S. (eds) *Essays in the Economic History of the Middle East: Second Series* (London: Cass).

Sklair, L. (1989) *Assembly for Development: The Maquila Industry in Mexico and the US* (Boston: Unwin Hyman).

Sklair, L. (1991) *Sociology of the Global System* (New York: Harvester).

Skrbis, Z. (1994) Ethno-Nationalism, Immigration and Globalization with particular reference to Second Generation Croatians and Slovenians in Australia, unpublished PhD thesis, Flinders University of South Australia.

Smith, A.D. (1971) *Theories of Nationalism* (London: Duckworth).

Smith, A.D. (1986) *The Ethnic Origins of Nations* (Oxford: Blackwell).

Smith, A.D. (1990) 'Towards a global culture?', *Theory, Culture, and Society*, **7**, pp. 171–191.

Soysal, Y.N. (1994) *Limits of Citizenship* (Chicago: Chicago University Press).

Stam, R. (1992) 'Mobilising fictions; the Gulf War, the media, and the recruitment of the spectator', *Public Culture*, **4**(2), pp. 101–26.

Stephenson, C. (1989) 'Going to MacDonalds in Leiden: reflections on the concept of self and society in the Netherlands', *ETHOS, Journal of the Society of Psychological Anthropology*, **17**(2), pp. 241–62.

Sturmer, C. (1993) 'MTV's Europe', in Dowmunt, T. (ed.) *Channels of Resistance: Global Television and Local Empowerment* (London: BFI Publishing), pp. 50–66.

Suter, K. (1996) 'Reforming the United Nations', in Thukur, R. (ed.) *The United Nations at Fifty: Retrospect and Prospect* (Dunedin: University of Otago Press) pp. 241–62.

Swidler, A. (1986) 'Culture in action: symbols and strategies', *American Sociological Review*, **51**, pp. 273–86.

Sylvan, L. (1995) 'Global trade, influence and power', in Alston, P. and Chiam, M. (eds) *Treaty-Making in Australia: Globalisation versus Sovereignty?* (Sydney: Federation Press), pp. 107–14.

Tai, S.H.C. (1997) Advertising in Asia: localize or regionalize?, *International Journal of Advertising*, **16**, pp. 48–61.

Templeton, M. (1996) 'The achievements and shortcomings of the United Nations', in Thukur, R. (ed.) *The United Nations at Fifty: Retrospect and Prospect* (Dunedin: University of Otago Press), pp. 41–58.

Thernstrom, S. (ed.) (1980) *Harvard Encyclopaedia of American Ethnic Groups* (Cambridge, MA: Belknap Press).

Thompson, J.E. and Krasner, S. (1989) 'Global transactions and the consolidation of sovereignty', in Czempiel, E.O. and Rosenau, J.N. (eds) *Global Changes and Theoretical Challenges* (Lexington, MA: Lexington Books), pp. 195–219.

Thomson, J.E. (1995) 'State sovereignty in international relations: bridging the gap between theory and empirical research', *International Studies Quarterly*, pp. 213–33.

Tibi, B. (1988) *The Crisis of Modern Islam* (Salt Lake City: University of Utah Press).

Tibi, B. (1994) 'Islamic law/*Shari'a*, human rights, universal morality and international relations', *Human Rights Quarterly*, **16**(2), pp. 277–99.

Tilly, C. (1984) *Big Structures, Large Processes, Huge Comparisons* (New York: Russell Sage Foundation).

Toennies, F. (1955 [1887]) *Community and Association* (London: Routledge).

Toynbee, A. (1934–61) *A Study of History*, 12 vols (Oxford: Oxford University Press).

Tuckey, B. (1997) 'Discordant variations on a world car theme', *Business Review Weekly*, July 21.

UNCTAD, Programme on transnational corporations (1993) *World Investment Report: Trans-National Corporations and Integrated International Production* (New York: United Nations).

Varis, T. (1988) 'Trends in international television flow', in Schneider, C. and Wallis, B. (eds) *Global Television* (New York: Wedge Press).

Verne, J. (1873) *Le Tour du Monde en Quatre-vingts Jours* (Paris: Hetzel).

Vines, D. (1995) 'Reforming the international monetary system – lessons from the Mexican experience', *Global Economic Institutions Newsletter*, (1), pp. 7–12.

Vines, D. (1996) 'Global economic institutions. A historical overview and a modest reform agenda', unpublished paper, Australian National University, April 1996.

Wallerstein, I. (1974) *The Modern World System: Capitalist Agriculture and the Origins of the European World-Economy in the Sixteenth Century* (New York: Academic Press).

Wallerstein, I. (1979) *The Capitalist World Economy* (Cambridge: Cambridge University Press).

Wallerstein, I. (1984) *The Politics of the World-Economy* (Cambridge: Cambridge University Press).

Wallerstein, I. (1990) 'Culture as the ideological battleground of the modern world system', in Featherstone, M. (ed.) *Global Culture* (London: Sage), pp. 31–56.

Wallerstein, I. (1991) *Geopolitics and Geoculture* (Cambridge: Cambridge University Press).

Warner, M. (1994) 'Japanese culture, western management: Taylorism and human resources in Japan', *Organization Studies*, **15**(4), pp. 509–33.

Waters, M. (1995) *Globalization* (London: Routledge).

Weber, E. (1976) *Peasants into Frenchmen: The Modernisation of Rural France 1870–1914* (Stanford: Stanford University Press).

Weissbrodt, D. (1988) 'Human rights: an historical perspective', in Davies, P. (ed.) *Human Rights* (London: Routledge), pp. 1–20.

Wete, F.N. (1988) 'The new world information order and the US press', in Schneider, C. and Wallis, B. (eds) *Global Television* (Cambridge, MA: MIT Press), pp. 137–46.

Wight, M. (1992) *International Theory. The Three Traditions* (New York: Holmes & Meier).

Wilkinson, D. (1987) 'Central civilization', *Comparative Civilizations Review*, Fall, pp. 31–59.

Wilkinson, D. (1993) 'Civilizations, cores, world economies, and Oikumenes', in Frank, A.G. and Gills, B.K. (eds) *The World System: Five Hundred Years or Five Thousand?* (London: Routledge), pp. 221–46.

Williams, G.A. (1994) *The Search for Arthur* (London: BBC Books).
Williams, R. (1993) 'Technical change: political options and imperatives', *Government and Opposition*, **28**(2), pp. 152–69.
Wolf, E. (1982) *Europe and the People Without History* (Berkeley, CA: University of California Press).
Worsley, P. (1980) 'One world or three? A critique of the world system theory of Immanuel Wallerstein', *Socialist Register*, pp. 298–338.
Worsley, P. (1990) 'Models of the modern world-system', in Featherstone, M. (ed.) *Global Culture: Nationalism, Globalization and Modernity* (London: Sage), pp. 83–96.
Yapp, M. (1979) 'Language, religion and political identity', in Taylor, D. and Yapp, M. (eds) *Political Identity in South Asia* (Atlantic Highlands: Curzon Press), pp. 1–34.
Yapp, M. (1992) 'Europe in the Turkish mirror', *Past and Present*, **37**, pp. 134–55.
Young, I.M. (1989) 'Polity and cultural difference: a critique of the ideal of universal citizenship', *Ethics*, **99**, pp. 250–74.

Index